NICHOLSON'S

IN LON

Symbols used in the guide
Average cost of a meal for one without wine:

£	Under £5	£££	Under £15
££	Under £10	£££+	Over £15

Key map showing the 31 separate areas covered

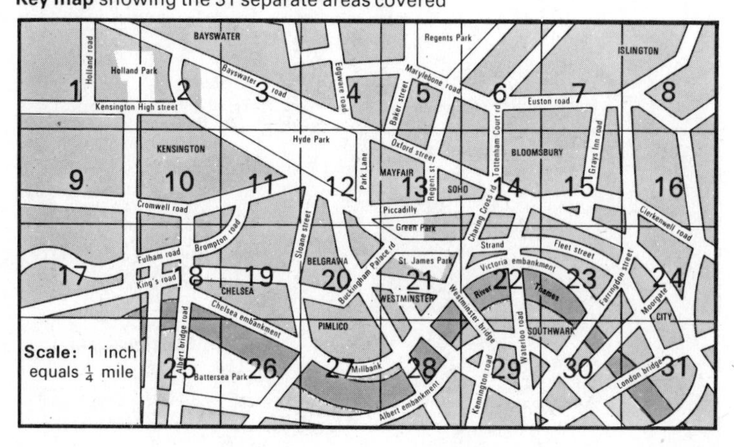

First published 1983
Reprinted 1985

Text by **Judy Allen**
Photographs by **Tony Ashton**
Additional photographs by Anne Nicholson

Robert Nicholson Publications Limited
17-21 Conway Street
London W1P 6JD

London Underground map by kind permission of London Regional Transport

Set in Univers by Rowland Phototypesetting Ltd
Bury St Edmonds, Suffolk

Printed and bound in Great Britain by
Chorley & Pickersgill Ltd, Leeds

ISBN 0 905522 69 9

Map 1 HAMMERSMITH AND OLYMPIA

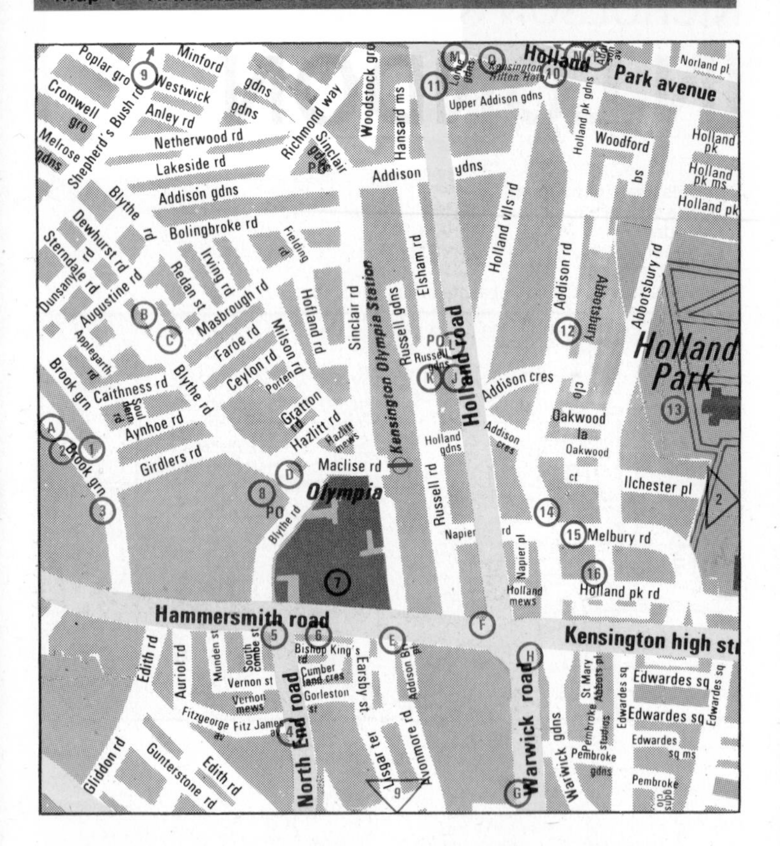

By far the largest building is the vast exhibition hall, Olympia. It stands on the site of the most famous of the many market gardens which once covered Hammersmith – The Vineyard – producer of some of the first trees planted in Regent's Park. Its famous shows, which recur reliably with the seasons, are a strong tourist attraction.

The streets around are principally residential with the grandest and most attractive of their houses around the perimeters of Holland Park. At the beginning of the 19thC this area, and especially Melbury Road and Holland Park Road, attracted the successful artists and architects of the day, whose houses still stand. The feeling of the period can best be evoked by a visit to the enchanting Leighton House, once the home of the painter and sculptor, now a small and wholly accessible museum of Victorian high art.

Brook Green, with the Roman Catholic church of Holy Trinity at one end and a cosy 'local' pub towards the other, remains a village within the larger Hammersmith. From the time of the Reformation it has remained predominantly Catholic. Its convent, off the map to the west, is said to have been too ill-endowed to draw the attention of Henry VIII and the area has traditionally been so free of religious persecution that it is sometimes called 'Pope's Corner'.

South of Hammersmith Road lie the small-scale working-class terraces and busy shops of Fulham whose lively, scruffy appeal makes an intriguing contrast with the cool elegance north of Kensington High Street.

PLACES OF INTEREST

1 Brook Green
W6. The brook runs under the narrow green, once wasteland belonging to Fulham Manor, which became a public park in the 18thC with tennis courts added later. A 1930s plan to site the new Hammersmith Town Hall here was vigorously opposed by residents and the green was happily preserved.

St Paul's School for Girls

2 St Paul's School for Girls
Brook Grn W6. Gerald Horsley designed the amply proportioned red brick building which went up in 1904–7 to accommodate this younger sister of the famous boys' school which Dean Colet founded in 1509. Gustav Holst was once Director of Music here.

3 Holy Trinity and St Joseph's Almshouses
Brook Grn W6. The Catholic church, in decorated English style, and the adjoining grey and scholarly-looking almshouses, were designed by Wardell in 1851. The colourful interior has a rood screen by Pugin, lovely stained glass, some by Meyer of Munich, and an unusual font with a high Gothic canopy.

Holy Trinity and St Joseph's Almshouses

4 Olympia Cycles
28 North End Pde, North End Rd W14. 01-602 4499. Will rent you a cycle for sightseeing, by the day, week or month. Also sells and repairs all makes.

5 Carnival Stores
95 Hammersmith Rd W14. 01-603 7824. A theatrical costumier, specialising in animal outfits which can be hired for the run of a panto or the night of a party. Camels and cows especially well-represented. *Closed Sat afternoon & Sun.*

6 Barnum's Carnival Novelties
67 Hammersmith Rd W14. 01-602 1211. A cornucopia of plastic creepy-crawlies, paper hats, monster masks and the equipment for expressing intemperate joy – hooters, bleepers, rattles and streamers.

7 Olympia
Hammersmith Rd W14. 01-603 3344. Gargantuan exhibition hall, opened in 1866 but refaced and extended by Joseph Emberton in 1936. Its Empire Hall now houses the Ukay Furnishing Centre. The rest is for the regular and popular shows and exhibitions: the Fine Arts and Antiques Fair in early June; the Festival for Mind, Body and Spirit in late June; the Cat Club Show in early December and, most spectacular of all, the International Show Jumping at the end of December. Bars and snack bars inside. *Charge for entry.*

Olympia

8 Old Post Office Building
Blythe Rd W14. A massive and imposing construction of brick, with portland stone facings, whose twin cupolas overlook every other building in the area. Purpose-built in 1901–3 for the Post Office Savings Bank, it serves as storage space for some of London's major museums, now the Bank has moved to Glasgow.

9 Bush Theatre
Bush Hotel, Shepherd's Bush Grn W12. 01-743 3388. At the top of Shepherd's Bush Road, a few hundred yards off the map, is this small pub theatre with curtainless stage and raked seating. It was specifically established to attract the non-theatre-going public and often tries out new productions in an informal and friendly atmosphere. *Closed Mon.*

10 Royal Crescent
W11. Rather grand early Victorian terrace, four storeys high and white, with little turrets.

Royal Crescent

The nearby Norland Gardens and Norland Square have more large, dignified terraces, principally in Bath stone.

11 St John the Baptist Church
Holland Rd W14. A rather fancy piece of neo-Gothic by James Brooks, 1889, with a very detailed rood screen and some rich stained glass.

12 8 Addison Road
W14. Dazzling great house designed by Halsey Ricardo, in 1906–7, faced with brilliant blue and green glazed tiles, some by William de Morgan.

8 Addison Road

13 Holland Park
W14. 55 acres of woodland and formal garden, once the private park of the badly war-damaged Holland House. In enclosed woodland, British birds mingle with exotic species, such as Muscovy ducks, Polish bantams, distinguished by feathers on their feet, and two small emus from South America. Alas, flamingos and demoiselle cranes were mugged by a fox one night in 1982 and survivors were taken away to a safe place. Peacocks strut among the rose arbours and cloistered walkways, and there is an open-air theatre on the terrace in summer. Exhibitions held in the Orangery. See map 2.

14 St Barnabas
Addison Rd W14. A cosy-looking rectangular church with corner turrets, designed by Vulliamy in 1828, with good stained glass and an unusual chancel arch added by T. Johnson in 1861.

Melbury Road

15 Melbury Road
W14. Many of the artists who gravitated to the area lived here, and the varied and whimsical architecture is worth a look. Sir John Belcher built No 2 for the sculptor Thornycroft, Norman Shaw built No 8 for the painter Marcus Stone, William Burges built the typically medieval No 9 for himself, and Holman-Hunt lived in No 18.

16 Leighton House
12 Holland Pk Rd W14. 01-602 3316. Designed by Aitchison in 1865, in collaboration with Lord Leighton, as the latter's home and studio. Now an intimate museum of high Victorian art, including Leighton's own paintings. The exquisite Arab Hall on the ground floor is lined with 15thC eastern tiles, acquired with the help of the explorer Sir Richard Burton. Light filters through Damascus lattice to a tinkling central, sunken fountain. Mind you don't fall in.
Music recitals, poetry readings and lectures are held in the barrel-vaulted studio above.
Open 11.00–17.00 Mon–Sat. Free.
Note that the Theatre Museum has gone into hibernation – leaving a commemorative sapling in the attractive garden.

EATING AND DRINKING

A Queen's Head *Pub*
Brook Grn W6. 01-603 3174. A 300-year-old wayside inn with wood panelling, leather upholstery and a pretty beer garden at the back. Dick Turpin is said to have hidden here many times. Goes in for food in a big way, in the steak restaurant with its Mon to Fri lunches and its Wed to Sat dinners, and in the bar with its permanent home-cooked buffet. £.

Queen's Head Pub

B **Jonathan's** *Restaurant*
71 Blythe Rd W14. 01-602 2758. Darkly woody bar leads down to a basement restaurant, fragrant with fresh flowers and usually alight with candles and flambées. Hot Avocado Jonathan is a meal in itself but you could go on to noisette d'agneau or duck with honey and apple and end with crêpe suzette or chocolate fudge gateau. *Closed Sat lunch & Sun evening.* ££.

C **Old Parr's Head** *Pub*
120 Blythe Rd W14. 01-603 2281. Here is a calm, if foodless, atmosphere in which to take a jar of traditional ale among settled and regular customers.

D **Phroggs Music** *Wine Bar*
26 Blythe Rd W14. 01-603 4224. Frog images abound on walls and bar, and frogs' legs are served with sparkling white house wine. Downstairs, among the mirrors, eat a hamburger or a full French meal. A guitarist sometimes plays gentle music. £.

E **Hand and Flower** *Pub*
1 Hammersmith Rd W14. 01-602 1000. Great big restaurant and pub which has flowered in the hands of the same family for more than 50 years. Hearty English roasts and pies served daily. Courage Director's Bitter adds extra punch. £.

F **Royal Kensington** *Hotel*
380 Kensington High St W14. 01-603 3333. The *Coffee Shop* is open daily for breakfast, snacks or the odd steak, £. *The Flaming Ox Restaurant* has a continental à la carte menu – mostly English, French or Italian. ££.

G **Radnor Arms** *Pub*
247 Warwick Rd W14. It's only small but the cellars are stocked with real ale – try IPA, Bass, Ruddles, Godson's Black Horse, Everard or Huntsman. Lunchtime snacks. £.

H **Renato's** *Restaurant*
200 Warwick Rd W14. 01-603 7995. Large and Italian with pale wood panelling. The food is reliable and reasonable and the manager cruises continually among the tables to check on your welfare. £.

J **Mama San Chinese** *Restaurant*
11 Russell Gdns W14. 01-602 0312. Cool and tiled with bamboo screens, a neat cocktail bar and dishes from Canton and Peking. Try scallop mousse with prawn and ginger sauce, steamed bass with pickled Chinese cabbage and, in season, the speciality pheasant with plum sauce. *Closed Sat lunch.* ££.

K **Oliver's** *Café*
10 Russell Gdns W14. 01-603 7645. Sit at a round table, with a brown checked cloth, for a plateful of lasagne or a full meal. Mixed Mediterranean cuisine with a crème-de-menthe-crunch dessert that brings tears of joy to the eyes. Unlicensed but there's an off-licence on the corner. ££.

L **Franco Ovest** *Restaurant*
3 Russell Gdns W14. 01-602 1242. Simple, white-painted and Italian, with fish a speciality – fresh crab, salmon, sea bass and mussels. Good choice of Italian wines and friendly service. *Closed Sat lunch & all Sun.* ££.

M **Duke of Clarence** *Pub*
203 Holland Pk Av W11. 01-603 5431. Built in 1939 on a 400-year-old tavern site, with a medieval-style interior and a Victorian bar. Beautiful flagged courtyard with imitation gas lamps and its own garden bar. Regular barbecues in summer. £.

N **Kleftiko** *Restaurant*
186 Holland Pk Av W11. 01-603 0807. Simple and jolly with true Greek food and wine at encouragingly low prices. Even if you order Meze – six selected courses of authentic Greek dishes – you won't break the bank. *Closed Sun.* £.

Holland Park

O **Kensington Hilton** *Hotel*
179 Holland Pk Av W11. 01-603 3355. Head for the *Crescent Lounge* for sandwiches, snacks, drinks and afternoon tea, £; for the mock-*Tudor Grill* for breakfast, lunch or dinner from the international menu, ££; or for the mock-*Tudor Pub* for a weekday buffet lunch. Or break out and try the *Hiroko*, the genuine Japanese restaurant where smiling waiters guide you through the highly specialised menu. £££.

P **Chez Moi** *Restaurant*
3 Addison Av W11. 01-603 8267. 'Olde-worlde' French decor with silk walls and shining mirrors. Famous for their lamb and thoughtfully-fried brains. For something a little different try sautéed kidneys in pernod and pear sauce followed by home-made cranberry ice cream. *Closed Sat lunch & all Sun.* £££.

Morning Coffee and Afternoon Tea

Royal Kensington Hotel; 380 Kensington High St W14. 01-603 3333. Tea, coffee, cakes.
Oliver's Café; 10 Russell Gdns W14. 01-603 7645. Tea and home-made mousse.
Kensington Hilton; 179 Holland Pk Av W11. 01-603 3355. Coffee, traditional tea.

Map 2 HOLLAND PARK, NOTTING HILL AND KENSINGTON

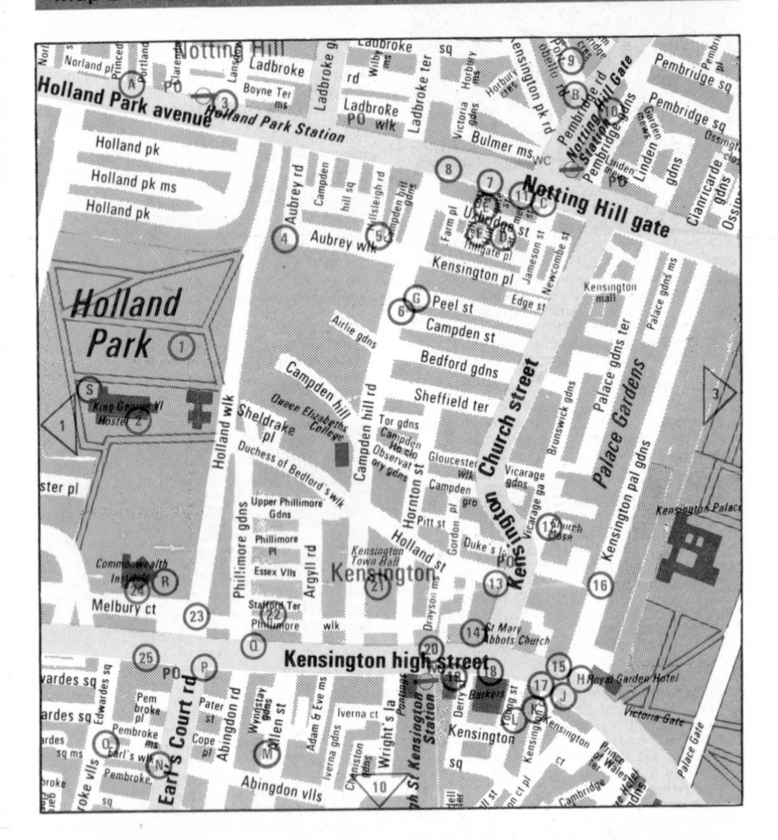

The compelling, heavily-wooded Holland Park was the last of the great parks to admit the public. It retains a private, mysterious air, reinforced by the presence of the war-shattered remnants of the once lovely house. Built in 1605, its heyday was the late 18thC when Henry Fox, Baron Holland, began the lavish entertaining for which it became famous and which attracted the great politicians, writers and philosophers of the time. Now a modern youth hostel extends from the surviving east wing, but the new partnership is softened by the ancient rose and Dutch gardens

To the north is Notting Hill, 18thC site of the great Hippodrome Race Track which encircled its summit. In the more recent past the Notting Hill Gate area has been associated with smouldering racial problems, but its lighter side is the three-day summer carnival and the year-round fascination of Portobello Road market.

Despite modern building, Kensington today is still characterised by elegant 18thC and 19thC houses, some in extensive gardens, and by exquisite squares; Kensington Square is one of the oldest in London, Edwardes Square one of the most graceful. The High Street is rivalled only by Oxford Street for its shops and Kensington Church Street is rich in select antique emporia. Campden Hill Road, once a fashionable spa with medicinal springs, has several fine houses and the shades of illustrious residents – Swift, Gray and Galsworthy. In fact the whole area is haunted by names of renown, among them Leigh Hunt and G. K. Chesterton in Edwardes Square, Lord Macaulay in Holland Walk and Thackeray, who wrote Vanity Fair *in Young Street.*

PLACES OF INTEREST

1 Holland Park
W8. Once the private park of Holland House, a Jacobean mansion which was the seat of the Whig Foxes – Lords Holland from the 18thC. Largely destroyed by bombing in 1941, the remaining wing of the house is a youth hostel; the old Orangery and Ice House hold changing exhibitions of paintings and ceramics from March to November. This area, with its attendant Dutch and rose gardens, is floodlit every night. The northern part is 28 acres of verdant woodland where tree creepers, owls and green woodpeckers live among 3,000 species of trees and plants. *Area around house closed 24.00. Rest of park closed dusk.*

2 Court Theatre
Holland Pk W8. From Tuesday to Saturday during July you can enjoy opera and ballet in the courtyard of Holland House. The melancholy splendour of the surroundings is a perfect setting for such romantic entertainment. Advance booking unnecessary.

3 Peter Eaton
80 Holland Pk Av W11. 01-727 5211. A treasure trove of antiquarian and second-hand out-of-print books, presided over by knowledgeable staff.

4 Aubrey House
Aubrey Rd W8. The last of Holland Park's smaller country houses still to survive as a private residence. Built in 1698, on the site of a dried-up medicinal spring. The classical frontage and cupola were added in the 18thC. Spacious grounds remain.

St George's Church

5 St George's Church
Aubrey Walk W8. Built by E. Bassett Keeling in 1864, in what has been called his 'aggressive continental Gothic style'. Inside the unusual coloured bricks have been whitewashed and the distinctive cast iron pillars encased in stone columns, but the somewhat threatening exterior and clumsy cloistered porch are unchanged.

6 Albert's of Kensington
110 Campden Hill Rd W8. 01-221 4216. Reassuring proof that people still collect cigarette cards; nostalgia-inducing stock may be browsed through on weekdays, 11.00 to 17.00. *Closed Tue & Sat afternoons.*

7 Coronet Cinema
103 Notting Hill Gate W11. 01-727 6705. Once a theatre with Ellen Terry, Sarah Bernhardt and Mrs Patrick Campbell on its stage. The exterior is an 1890s version of Italian Renaissance architecture by W. G. R. Sprague, designer of the Ambassadors, Wyndhams and other West End theatres. The interior, only slightly changed, is in opulent Louis XVI style.

8 Quality Delicatessen
133a Notting Hill Gate W11. 01-229 3689. Here, the best brie in town is brought to maturity by genial Mr Salik, who has presided over this quality delicatessen for the past 30 years. Central European cold and cooked meats, delicious black olives, freshly ground coffee and an array of finely flavoured cheeses are temptingly laid out on the long, marble counter. *Closed Sun.*

9 Portobello Road Market
W11. The famous welter of glorious junk lies heaped enticingly on stall after stall every Saturday, half a mile north from Notting Hill Gate along this long thin road. During the week the permanent antique shops – with their old lace, pub mirrors, silver, china and floral chamber pots – come into their own. Abundant fruit and veg too.

10 Gate Theatre Club
Prince Albert, 11 Pembridge Rd W11. 01-229 0706. Fringe theatre, in a room above a pub, which specialises in trying out plays by new writers. Informal and relaxed but with a proper stage and lighting facilities.

11 Gate Cinema
Notting Hill Gate W11. 01-727 5750. Adventurous, specialising in quality art films, often foreign in origin. There are late night shows throughout the week.

12 Church Close
Kensington Church St W8. Don't be fooled by the barley-sugar chimneys, lattice windows, weathered red brick and secretive courtyard – this Tudor-style block of shops and flats only went up in 1927. However, it is pretty.

Church Close

13 Strangeways
3 Holland St W8. 01-937 3251. Off-beat, glossy little gift shop dedicated to satisfying peculiar cravings for quilted model aeroplanes, sawn-in-half-lady book-ends or china ashtrays in the form of cupped hands.

St Mary Abbots Church

14 St Mary Abbots Church
Kensington Church St W8. In the 12thC, this land belonged to the Abbey of Abingdon, hence the unusual name. The present cool and dignified church was rebuilt on the old site in 1869–72 by Sir Gilbert Scott, one of the principal interpreters of 14thC Gothic. You may hear the clock chime but you won't see it – it was considered that the design would be spoiled if a hole was left to show its face.

15 Antique Hypermarket
26–40 Kensington High St W8. 01-937 7696. Easy to spot by the patient caryatids supporting the entrance. Inside, individual dealers show off alluring displays of small furniture, books both beautifully bound and badly battered, coins and silver.

16 Kensington Palace Gardens
W8. Grand Italianate mansions, laid out by Pennethorne in 1843 and commonly known as 'millionaires row'. Crown property, except for the several embassies, each automatically a part of its own country. The road is private and security is understandably tight. The porters won't let you pass with a camera.

17 Kensington Market
Kensington High St W8. Has something of the flavour of an eastern bazaar with clumps of Indian cotton dresses and glittery-threaded scarves hanging above displays of jewellery and antiques. The stallholders don't just sell, they will buy and barter too, which makes for a lively atmosphere.

18 Barkers
Kensington High St W8. 01-937 5432. Large and traditional department store, on five floors, wherein to furnish the house and person in style. Grew from a small draper's opened in 1870 by the enterprising John Barker. It has two cafeterias, an ice-cream-and-waffle bar, and a coffee shop where you can buy a cupful to drink or a bagful to take home.

19 Garden Club
99 Kensington High St W8. Exclusive club on the site of what was once Derry and Toms famous roof garden. In summer the public are allowed up to see the flamingoes and golden pheasants wandering among the full-sized trees and exotically planted flower beds. No access to the club, but with claret at around £70 a bottle that may be no bad thing.

20 Tree House
237 Kensington High St W8. 01-937 7497. Enchanting toy shop with presents at all prices.

21 New Town Hall and Library
Phillimore Walk W8. The library, by E. Vincent Harris in what he calls 'modern English Renaissance style', opened in 1960, and the more austere Town Hall, by Sir Basil Spence, in 1977. The buildings aroused the ire of local residents, who were appalled at the cost and unimpressed by the pseudo-antiquity of the library design.

Town Hall, by Sir Basil Spence

22 Linley Sambourne House
18 Stafford Ter W8. An unspoiled Victorian house. Linley Sambourne, who lived here from 1879–1910, was Punch's chief political cartoonist and the decor and furnishings remain unchanged since he sat at the drawing board in his study. They include the works of some more famous contemporaries – Kate Greenaway, Walter Crane and Tenniel. Administered by The Victorian Society, 1 Priory Gardens W4. 01-994 1019. *Open by appt Mar–Oct. Charge.*

23 Dog Lavatories
Holland Pk W8. There are two of these rarities at the park entrance, conspicuously labelled but little patronised – only 10% of visiting dogs use them, so the park survey tells us.

24 Commonwealth Institute
230 Kensington High St W8. 01-603 4535. Modern building like a great glass tent. Colourful displays and costumes from the 47 Commonwealth states. Sit in a wild west saddle (Canadian gallery), try the tropical climate simulator (Malaysian gallery), and see the transparent cow making milk (New Zealand gallery). Films, live music and dance in the theatre (Box Office 01-602 3660). Bar, coffee shop and restaurant. *Free. Charge for theatre.*

25 Church of Our Lady of Victories
Kensington High St W8. Tucked between The Tree House toy shop and Banham's Burglary Prevention is this severe little 20thC rebuild of the 19thC bomb-damaged church.

EATING AND DRINKING

A **Tootsies** *Restaurant*
120 Holland Pk Av W11. 01-229 8567. Despite the coy name this is a most pleasant hamburger joint, with a wine bar ambiance. Also serves breakfasts, though not before noon. £.

B **Sun in Splendour** *Pub*
7 Portobello Rd W11. 01-727 5444. Village-type pub at the quiet beginning of Portobello Road. Good atmosphere and food and handy for the market. £.

C **Hoop (Finch's)** *Pub*
83 Notting Hill Gate W11. 01-727 5324. Prominently placed beside Notting Hill Gate tube. Large and welcoming with hot and cold snacks daily in the pub and upstairs in the wine bar. Part of a chain owned by wine merchants, so the quality and variety of wines are better than in most pubs. £.

D **Geales Fish** *Restaurant*
2–4 Farmer St W8. 01-727 7969. Simple, informal restaurant. The tapestry upholstery and wooden tables seem more suited to a tea room than a fish and chip place, but fish in all the popular varieties and real chips, are what it so cheerfully serves, with champagne if you wish, and perfect pickled onions. *Closed Sun & Mon.* £.

E **Uxbridge Arms** *Pub*
13 Uxbridge St W8. 01-727 7326. In harmony with this little enclave of small-scale peaceful roads behind Notting Hill Gate – low-beamed, pretty and gently convivial. Good food weekday lunchtimes. £.

F **Costas Grill** *Restaurant*
14 Hillgate St W8. 01-229 3794. Good Greek food – try lamb-on-the-spit followed by honey cakes. In summer, sit out at a table under the jasmine. *Closed Sun.* £.

G **Windsor Castle** *Pub*
114 Campden Hill Rd W8. 01-727 8491. Built in 1835, before intervening buildings blocked the distant view of the castle. Three lovely old bars with beamed ceilings and open fires, and a large walled garden. £.

H **Royal Garden Hotel** *Restaurants*
Kensington High St W8. 01-937 8000. Dine by candlelight in *The Royal Roof Restaurant* with its staggering views, French menu, cabaret and dance floor, *closed Sun.* £££+. On the ground floor try breakfast, tea or a snack in *The Garden Café*, £, or a set-price meal in *The Bulldog Chophouse*, with unlimited wine and particularly good roast beef. *Closed Sat lunch.* ££.

J **Alcove** *Restaurant*
17 Kensington High St W8. 01-937 1443. One of Wheeler's Fish Restaurants with their typically genial clublike atmosphere and bustling service. Shellfish in general, oysters in season, white fish in sauce and fruit or cheese to follow. *Closed Sun.* ££.

K **Ark** *Restaurant*
35 Kensington High St W8. 01-937 4292. The entrance is just around the corner in Kensington Court. Good, French provincial food eaten in booths. A bar in the basement. *Closed Sun.* ££.

L **Thackerays** *Wine Bar and Bistro*
9 Young St W8. 01-937 9403. On the street where he lived, hence the name. Amiably phoney olde-worlde decor, and live music from a duo most evenings. Straightforward food with a French bias – anything from a snack to a full meal. *Closed Sun lunch.* £.

M **Britannia** *Pub*
1 Allen St W8. 01-937 1864. This one is so polished and pretty it looks as though it should be on someone's mantlepiece. The ale is real, the flowers are fresh, the food (weekdays only) is home-cooked and the patio has a fragrant old honeysuckle plant. £.

N **Hansom Cab** *Pub*
84 Earls Ct Rd W8. 01-937 5364. The genuine old hansom is suspended from the ceiling in the Cab Bar, and the theme is carried on throughout with carriage lamps, red plush seating and old photographs of cabs in action. Food on weekdays. £.

O **Scarsdale** *Pub*
23a Edwardes Sq W8. 01-937 1811. Set at one corner of an enchanting square, with gas lamps glowing a permanent welcome and plane trees shading the wide terrace. Inside there's an open fire, antique clocks, stuffed animals and very good bar lunches. £.

P **Witchity's** *Restaurant*
253 Kensington High St W8. 01-937 2654. Open virtually all the time, in the style of a continental café, for breakfast, afternoon tea, steaks, hamburgers or a full dinner. The downstairs disco opens at 21.30. *Closed 08.00–10.00.* £ or ££.

Q **Yangtze** *Restaurant*
222 Kensington High St W8. 01-937 1030. Comfortable, airy, inexpensive and offering both Cantonese and Pekingese cooking. Be prepared to wait a little if you order something special – Peking duck, perhaps, or crab fried with ginger. £.

R **Commonwealth Institute** *Restaurants*
Kensington High St W8. 01-602 3252. *Flags Restaurant*, to the side of the main entrance, serves lunch and afternoon tea (££); the *Theatre Foyer Bar* has real ale on tap and pub food; the *Coffee Shop* sandwiches, pastries and coffee. *Closed evenings & Sun.* £.

S **Belvedere** *Restaurant*
Holland Pk W8. 01-602 1865. Behind the old Orangery and most speedily reached by the Abbotsbury Road entrance to the park. The food is rather ordinary but the setting has a magical quality, especially in summer. ££.

Morning Coffee and Afternoon Tea
Barkers; Andronica's Coffee Shop or, for tea, The Rendezvous, lower ground floor.
Commonwealth Institute; Flags Restaurant or The Coffee Shop. *Not Sun.*
Dino's Restaurant and Café; 16 Kensington Church St. 01-937 3896. Coffee, tea and pastries, or snacks.
Notting Hill Restaurant and Coffee House; 215 Kensington Church St. 01-229 9359. Tea, coffee and snacks. *Closed evenings.*
Royal Garden Hotel; Garden Café. Excellent coffee, formal tea.
Witchity's; 253 Kensington High St W8. 01-937 2654. Set afternoon tea.

Map 3 KENSINGTON GARDENS AND PADDINGTON

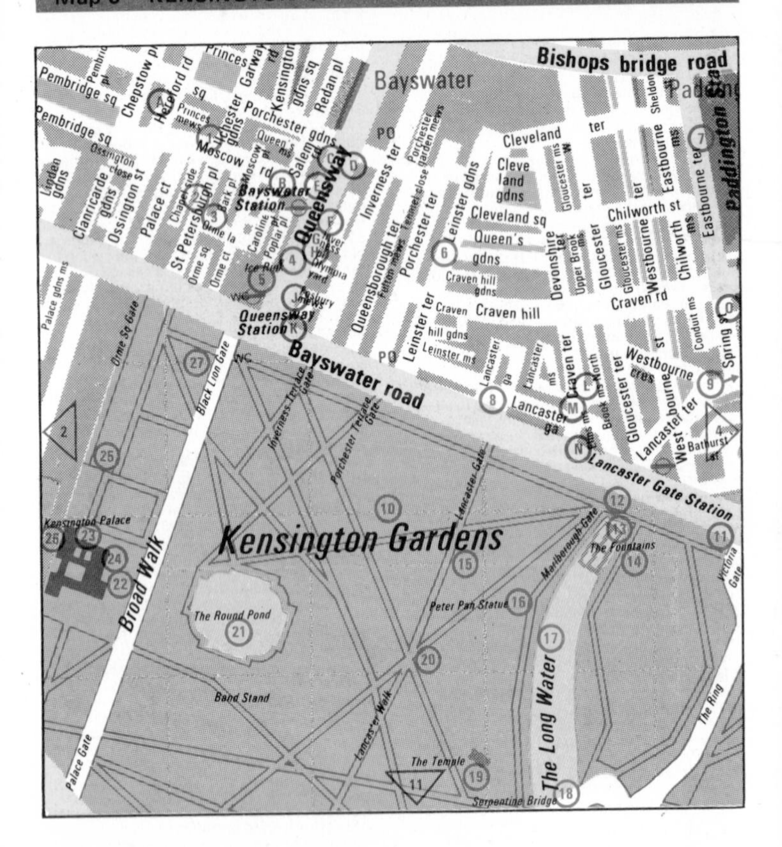

The 275 green acres of Kensington Gardens fill half the map, screened from the busy Bayswater Road by tall trees and thick shrubbery. This land, together with the adjoining Hyde Park, once belonged to the Abbey of Westminster. On his historically famed falling out with the church Henry VIII acquired it for a royal hunting ground, which it remained until the reign of James I when it was opened to the public. Hyde Park still has the flavour of common land but Kensington Gardens has been elegantly civilised with formal lakes, statuary and tended flower beds.

The transformation began when William III bought Nottingham House and commissioned Christopher Wren to enlarge it into Kensington Palace. The gardens were later extended by Queen Anne. But it was George II's Queen, Caroline, who enlarged the Gardens to their present size, was responsible for their landscaping and the creation of the Long Water and the Round Pond, and gave the scene the gently formal air it still has today.

To the north, residential Paddington, an isolated village drawn into London by the suburban development of the 19thC, was laid out by S. P. Cockerell in a scheme of tree-lined avenues, squares and crescents. The opening of the Great Western Railway in 1838, with its terminus at Paddington, pushed the development further and small hotels established themselves nearby to cater for travellers. Many of the high stuccoed buildings are now divided into apartments and bed sitters but the plethora of shops and restaurants dismisses any dormitory torpor. Queensway, especially, has a constant hum of cosmopolitan activity.

PLACES OF INTEREST

1 **St Sophia's Cathedral**
Moscow Rd W2. Oldrid Scott, son of that famous exponent of Victorian Gothic, Sir George Gilbert Scott, designed this red brick Byzantine Cathedral of the Greek Orthodox Church in 1877. Lovely mosaic work inside is by Boris Anrep.

St Sophia's Cathedral

2 **St Matthew's Church**
St Petersburgh Pl W2. Large, high-spired, dominating building, its stone now furry with London grime, by J. Johnson, 1880.

3 **New West End Synagogue**
St Petersburgh Pl W2. The twin cupolas of the large, imposing, red brick synagogue give a somewhat Moorish cast to this late 1870s version of early Gothic by Audesley and Joseph.

4 **Queensway**
W2. Busy, cosmopolitan street that rarely sleeps. The shops flourish cheap clothes, clouds of sparkly Greek and Indian scarves, and newspapers in various tongues and many scripts. Whatever language you're hungry in, you'll find food to take home, or to eat at table in one of the small and crowded restaurants. Slightly tatty but very alive.

5 **Queen's Ice Skating Club**
17 Queensway W2. 01-229 0172. Glamorous, rather disco-like atmosphere in which to show off your fancy footwork. There's a bar for Dutch courage and tuition for beginners. *Membership fee & skate hire fee. Open daily until 22.00. Until 22.30 Sat.*

6 **23–24 Leinster Gardens**
W2. Two tall lime trees give discreet cover to this odd-looking pair, seemingly identical to the rest of the terrace but for blank windows and handleless doors. They are no more than façades, hiding London's first underground, the Metropolitan Line, which emerges from the earth immediately behind them.

7 **Paddington Station**
W2. Railway cathedral engineering at its best, by Isambard Kingdom Brunel; the Gothic ornament by Wyatt and Owen Jones and the adjoining Renaissance-Baroque hotel – in its heyday the most splendid in all England – by the younger Hardwick. The mainline station for the west.

8 **Earl of Meath's Memorial**
Lancaster Gate W2. The stone column with the worn-away child crouched on the top was fashioned by Herman Cawthra in 1934 to commemorate Reginald Brabazon, 12th Earl of Meath, who fought in the Boer and First World Wars.

9 **St James' Church**
Sussex Gardens W2. Tall, cool, flinty-faced building, originally by Goldicutt and Gutch in 1841–3, but rebuilt in 1881 by George Edmund Street, architect of the Law Courts in the Strand, all of whose work embodied the principles of the late Victorian Arts and Crafts Movement.

10 **Kensington Gardens**
W2. Originally laid out as the private gardens of Kensington Palace, this lovely spread of tree-lined walks, man-made lakes and luxuriant flower beds has long been a children's paradise. Once they were escorted by uniformed nannies, now by au pairs, parents or teachers. They may account for the fact that this is the most endearingly fey of London's parks, with its Elfin Oak, Pets' Cemetery and statue of Peter Pan.

11 **Pets' Cemetery**
Peer through the railings into the back garden of Victoria Lodge to see the cluster of diminutive headstones. The Duke of Cambridge started it in 1880 for his Duchess's much-loved, defunct dog. Now completely full.

12 **Queen Anne's Bower**
An elegant free-standing alcove by William Kent, with wood panelling and a long bench seat, rather like a right royal bus shelter.

13 **Pumping Station**
The neat classical structure, standing like a headboard at the top of the Long Water, is no longer in use, but look through the arches at the side to surprise the old Westbourne River, one of the Thames' hidden tributaries, on its way to feed the man-made lakes.

14 **Fountains**
W. Calder Marshall's statue of Edward Jenner, he who introduced vaccination, broods over the attractive arrangement of formal ponds, each with fountain and attendant ducks, separated from the Long Water by a stone balustrade ornamented with flower-filled urns.

Fountains in Kensington Gardens

15 **Speke's Monument**
To remind us of the great African explorer, J. H. Speke, discoverer of the source of the Nile – a stern granite obelisk.

16 Peter Pan's Statue
J. M. Barrie's famous celebration of arrested development blows his horn and attracts all manner of nymphs and rabbits to clamber up his pedestal. Sir George Frampton's statue is burnished as high as young fingers can reach to stroke it – which puts cynical adults in their place.

Peter Pan's Statue

17 Long Water
A graceful artificial lake formed in the 1730s, together with the adjoining Serpentine, on the instructions of George II's Queen, Caroline. Fed by the Westbourne and murmurous with ornamental ducks, geese, swans, and indignant-looking crested grebes.

Long Water and Serpentine Bridge

18 Serpentine Bridge
The plain bridge, with its satisfyingly smooth arches, divides the Long Water from the Serpentine. By the brothers George and John Rennie, 1826.

19 Temple
A cosy, domed summerhouse designed by Kent for Queen Caroline when the gardens were first laid out. Unfortunately attracts graffiti devotees.

20 Physical Energy
The bronze of a sinewy naked man, astride an impatient charger, who appears to be planning an assault on the Albert Memorial to the south, is Physical Energy by G. F. Watts, set up here in 1906.

21 Round Pond
For well over a hundred years children, adults and even the poet Shelley, have sailed model boats across the 7 acres of duck-filled water, while others fly increasingly complicated kites from the flat land around its brim.

22 Queen Victoria's Statue
The dignified white marble figure, showing the Queen at the time of her accession to the throne, is doubly royal – it was the work of her fourth daughter, Princess Louise.

Queen Victoria

23 Kensington Palace
01-937 9561. A modest and approachable palace with a more domestic air than most, despite its long and continuing royal connections. Queen Victoria and Queen Mary were born here, this is where Victoria received the news of her accession, and Princess Margaret, the Prince and Princess of Wales, the Duke and Duchess of Gloucester and Princess Michael of Kent still have apartments in the private wings. Bought in 1689 by William III, both house and gardens are rich in examples of the work of the great who refurbished them – William Kent, Christopher Wren, Grinling Gibbons, Nicholas Hawksmoor. Also paintings from the Royal Collection, busts, furniture and ornaments. *Closed 17.00 & Sun morn.*

24 Dutch Garden
Sunken, secret and peaceful, enclosed by pleached limes, with a central pond sprouting fountains and year-round flowers and foliage.

25 Orangery
A pleasingly proportioned sun-trap, built for Queen Anne in 1704, its light, airy interior full of plants and statuary. Lovely setting for occasional concerts of chamber music.

26 William III's Statue
The statue of William, who bought Nottingham House and transformed it into Kensington Palace, stands at its south wall. It is by Baucke, the pedestal by Sir Aston Webb, and was set up in 1907, a gift to Edward VII from the German Emperor, William II.

27 Elfin Oak
An aged stump from Richmond Park, carved by Ivor Innes in the 30s into a tiny world of clambering, peeping gnomes, winged fairies, small animals and birds. Iron railings protect it from destruction by loving hands.

Physical Energy

Kensington Palace

EATING AND DRINKING

A **Chez Franco** *Restaurant*
3 Hereford Rd W2. 01-229 5079. Small and neat with photographs of some famous regular customers around the walls. The menu is principally Italian with some international dishes as well. Most welcoming. *Closed Sat lunch & all Sun.* ££.

B **King's Head** *Pub*
33 Moscow Rd W2. 01-229 4233. Quietly traditional with a very good chess team, Truman's Best on draught and casseroles and quiches at lunchtime. In the evening they'll do you a sandwich – 'toasted, roasted or incinerated'. £.

C **Le Bistingo** *Restaurant*
117 Queensway W2. 01-727 0743. Provincial French cooking at very reasonable prices in a cosy restaurant, one of a chain, with dishes of the day chalked up on a blackboard. £.

D **Prince Alfred** *Pub*
112 Queensway W2. 01-229 1474. A crowded, cosmopolitan tourists favourite with home-cooked lunches, Director's bitter and cheery background music. £.

E **Pizza Hut** *Restaurant*
103 Queensway W2. 01-727 0855. One of a chain of jaunty, cheap, eating places with sub-Tyrolean decor, fresh-cooked pizzas, salads and good ice cream. £.

F **La Brasserie** *Restaurant*
68 Queensway W2. 01-221 6529. Small, bright, French-Italian place specialising in superior pasta dishes and lots of sea food. Good choice of French wines. ££.

G **Maharajah** *Restaurant*
50 Queensway W2. 01-727 1135. Authentic Indian cooking with a real attention to detail and presentation. Eat as mildly or as spicily as you wish – helpful waiters will guide you if necessary. ££.

H **New Lee Ho Fook** *Restaurant*
48 Queensway W2. 01-229 8624. Go up the steps and into the smart, plant-crowded interior for some tasty Chinese dishes – sea bass with ginger and spring onions or with chilli, peppers and black bean sauce – delectable crab – spicy spare ribs – and banana or pineapple fritters to round it all off. ££.

J **Mandarin Kitchen** *Restaurant*
14 Queensway W2. 01-727 9468. Cantonese cooking with the emphasis on fish. Try a dish of hors d'oeuvres including fried squid, oysters and a special pancake, followed by particularly good and large lobster. The set meals come cheaper. £ or ££.

K **Le Mignon** *Restaurant*
2 Queensway W2. 01-229 0093. Lively Hungarian restaurant with a gypsy orchestra for extra jollity in the evenings. Hungarian home-cooking includes paprika chicken, spicy goulash and beef lasco – cooked with peppers, tomatoes and onions. Afterwards, fresh fruit and gateaux trundle towards you on a trolley. *Closed Mon.* ££.

L **Mitre** *Pub*
24 Craven Ter W2. 01-262 5240. Victorian pub with two bars and a haunted cellar which has recently been turned into Moriarty's Wine Bar. The pub does shepherd's-pie-type meals at every session; the wine bar does pâté-and-stilton-type meals in the evenings. £.

M **Taormina** *Restaurant*
19 Craven Ter W2. 01-262 2090. Instantly recognisable by the two large cartwheels, one in each window. Behind them, authentic Italian food with plenty of veal dishes and a particularly nice squid. £.

N **Swan** *Tavern*
55 Bayswater Rd W2. 01-262 5204. Hundred-year-old pub with a large paved forecourt, illuminated from dusk on, which looks across Bayswater Road to the trees of Kensington Gardens. Popular, with much-used juke box and a uniformed chef to carve the cold joints. £.

O **Gyngleboy** *Wine Bar*
27 Spring St W2. 01-723 3351. One of the chain of Davy's Wine Bars, its plain wood floors, aged casks and convivial masculine atmosphere bringing a taste of the City to Paddington. Great selection of wines; food limited but very good. *Closed 21.00 & weekends.* £.

Paddington Station

Morning Coffee and Afternoon Tea

Strikes; Lancaster Gate W2. 01-262 5090. Various branches in the area. This one part of the Charles Dickens Hotel. Tea, coffee, cake, pie – also burger-type meals.

Royal Lancaster Hotel; Lancaster Ter W2. 01-262 6737. Coffee by the cup, formal tea, in the first floor lounge.

Maison Pechon; 127 Queensway W2. 01-229 0746. Excellent patisserie. Also serves good lunches. *Closed Sun.*

Map 4 PADDINGTON AND MARYLEBONE

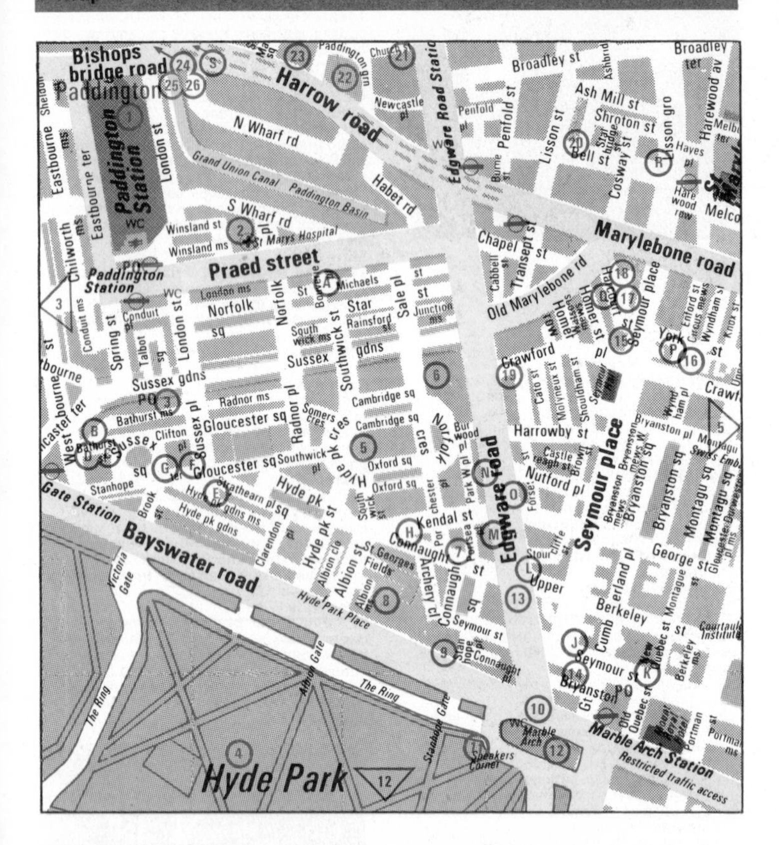

This busy residential and shopping area is sliced down the centre and across the bottom by Edgware and Bayswater Roads, each following the line of old straight Roman routes through London. In 1827 the area dominated by these roads grew fashionable as S. P. Cockerell's scheme of tree-lined avenues, squares and terraces grew into being. It was known as Tyburnia after the River Tyburn which once wound its way from Hampstead to the Thames at Westminster. It has long been culverted but has left its mark on the landscape, lending gentle curves to the streets along its banks and giving its name not just to the hideous gallows but to altogether pleasanter places; St Marylebone, for example, originally St Mary's Church By The Bourne, or stream. But all is not 19thC. Some squares east of the Edgware Road are 18thC and there is earlier building to its west; a pleasant area for a gentle stroll with sudden pockets of added interest – the mews and restaurants at the confluence of Sussex Place and Gloucester Square and the delightful small shops of Connaught Street.

To the south lie the soothing green expanses of Hyde Park, once one of Henry VIII's many hearty hunting grounds, now 340 acres of parkland where people may ride, swim, fish, walk or just sit.

To the north the Grand Union Canal, which links London with the Midlands, leads off the map to that part of its route known as Little Venice, where the long boats lilt on the water, the handsome Victorian houses and plane trees reflect in it, and a welcoming pub or two offers sustenance on its banks.

PLACES OF INTEREST

1 Paddington Station
W2. Railway cathedral engineering at its best, by Isambard Kingdom Brunel; the Gothic ornament by Wyatt and Owen Jones and the adjoining Renaissance-Baroque hotel – in its heyday the most splendid in all England – by the younger Hardwick. The main line station for the west.

2 St Mary's Hospital
Praed St W2. 01-262 1280. A complex of buildings, the oldest, by Hopper and Wyatt, of 1843–51, the late-Victorian Baroque Clarence Wing by Sir W. Emerson and the newer neo-Georgian Medical School by Sir Edwin Cooper, 1933. Bears a plaque commemorating the accidental discovery of penicillin by Alexander Fleming, who realised the potential of a passing mould spore in a small lab overlooking Praed Street.

St Mary's Hospital

3 St James' Church
Sussex Gardens W2. Tall, cool, flinty-faced building, originally by Goldicutt and Gutch in 1841–3, but rebuilt in 1881 by George Edmund Street, architect of the Law Courts in the Strand, all of whose work embodied the principles of the late Victorian Arts and Crafts movement.

4 Hyde Park
W2. Once a private hunting ground favoured by Henry VIII, now a public expanse of grass and trees spreading south to the Serpentine and that famous ride for London horses, Rotten Row. *See Map 12.*

5 St John the Evangelist Church
Hyde Park Cres W2. In the fashionable Hyde Park Estate, once known as Tyburnia because of the proximity of the Tyburn river. Begun as the Connaught Chapel and finished in perpendicular style by Fowler in 1831. Modern cross and altar candlesticks and a 1930s monumental brass.

6 Water Gardens
Off Cambridge Sq W2. The beautiful formal gardens with lakes, fountains, willows, waterlilies and ducks form the centre of an unusual late 60s housing scheme by Philip Hicks – all on top of an underground car park.

7 Connaught Street
W2. Attractive little 19thC street with several intriguing and appealing small shops; Rye Tiles with its lovely pottery at No 12; Hosain's Rare Book Shop, specialising in Africa, Asia and the Islamic World at No 25; and Joan Price's Face Place, where you can experiment with cosmetics, at No 31; as well as shops for clothes and antiques, an excellent coffee specialist, a creamy patisserie and John Gow's old-fashioned open-fronted wet fish shop at No 55.

8 St George's Fields
W2. The housing estate stands on the former burial ground of St George's Church, Hanover Square. It was from here in 1768 that Laurence Sterne's body was stolen for medical research – and returned with some embarrassment by the Professor of Anatomy at Cambridge, a friend of Sterne's who recognised the corpse. It now lies in Coxwold in Yorkshire.

9 Tyburn Convent
Bayswater Rd W2. More properly, The Shrine of the Sacred Heart and Tyburn Martyrs, an order of Roman Catholic nuns originally founded in Montmartre – the Mount of Martyrs – who pray still for the souls of those who died for their faith on the massive triangular gallows that once dominated the area.

10 Tyburn Tree
W2. There is nothing to see now but a brass plaque in the road near Marble Arch but this was the site of the notorious gallows, so substantial it could dispatch 24 heretics, highwaymen and thieves at one go. In its day it stood beside the river Tyburn which has itself vanished and now flows underground, beneath the park.

11 Speaker's Corner
Hyde Pk W2. Every Sunday, unknown orators express strong and often strange views on life, death and politics. At least half the wit and insight comes from the hecklers.

12 Marble Arch
W2. The imposing arch with finely-wrought gates is a famous landmark – and a kind of failure. It was designed by Nash in 1828, as a gateway to Buckingham Palace; declared too narrow and moved here in 1851 as an entrance to Hyde Park; then left stranded when road-widening in the early 1900s pushed back the park boundaries.

13 Edgware Road
W2. A wide and noisy thoroughfare that follows the straight line of the old Roman Watling Street. A good hunting ground for cheap hi fi's, videos and other electronic specialities, with one or two surprisingly smart clothes shops at its southern end and, right at the foot, the huge Odeon Cinema, 01-723 2011, showing premieres and 'U' certificate block-busters.

14 Church of the Annunciation
Bryanston St W1. By Sir Walter Tapper, 1913, plain outside but dignified within. Don't miss the carved wooden screen, pulpit and stations of the cross by M. Beule of Ghent.

15 Jimcar Reproductions
155 Seymour Pl W1. 01-402 9714. Strange little shop with its extraordinary stock tumbling out into the street – weathervanes, aged china dolls, ships' wheels, china dogs and among them some modern and ugly china dishes and ornaments. *Closed Sun.*

16 St Mary's Church
Wyndham Pl W1. Large imposing church by Sir Robert Smirke, 1823, with a semi-circular

portico, a round tower with stone cupola and a galleried interior.

17 Chess Centre
3 Harcourt St W2. 01-402 5393. Tiny shop full of chess sets, traditional and modern, wooden, metallic, stone – even a full set of hand-painted politicians. *Closed Sat afternoon & Sun.*

18 Swedish Church
Harcourt St W1. Built in 1910 by Wigglesworth, its wide façade with diminutive bell-cote based on a design by A. H. Hägg, the Swedish architect.

19 Paddington and Friends
22 Crawford Pl W1. 01-262 1866. Small but lavishly stocked shop. A mecca for the young (and not-so-young) fans of Michael Bond's world-famous Paddington Bear. Here you can buy bears and books and benefactions – both large and small. *Closed lunchtime & Sun.*

20 Bell Street Bikes
73 Bell St W2. 01-724 0456. New and second hand bikes to buy, but also to hire by the day, week or month, and what better way of seeing an area. Don't hurry out of Bell Street, it has a cheerful working class appeal, some intriguing junk shops and a couple of floor-to-ceiling stacked second-hand bookshops.

21 Church Street Market
W2. A wonderful – in the literal sense of the word – place to spend a Saturday morning among the stalls-ful of junk and oddments, clothes, chamberpots, prints, lamps old and new, fruit, vegetables, candy and multiple bric-a-brac.

Church Street Market

22 Paddington Green
W2. The traditional song connects it with 'Pretty Little Polly Perkins' but it is the tragedienne Sarah Siddons who presides over it now. Her weatherworn statue by Leon Joseph Chavalliaud is based on Sir Joshua Reynolds' painting of her as The Tragic Muse, her mortal remains lie under the recreation ground behind the church.

23 St Mary's Church
Paddington Grn W2. The green retains its village-like soul despite the roar of the modern road (which was probably already inevitable in 1829 when the first omnibus service left here for the Bank of England). The church of 1788–91, by J. Plaw, is small and attractive with a curving, columnar interior and some interesting monuments.

St Mary's, Paddington Green

Off the Map

24 Little Venice
W2. Just off the map, north-west of Paddington Green, you will find the section of Regent's Canal, with its brightly painted houseboats, its large Victorian houses and the plane trees reflected in the green water, christened 'Little Venice' by Browning. Peaceful towpath, pleasant pubs and a somewhat 'arty' fraternity.

Little Venice

25 Jason's Trip
Blomfield Rd W2. 01-286 3428. From Little Venice you can take a 1½ hour return trip in a traditional narrow boat along the canal through Regent's Park and the zoo to Camden Lock. *Charge.*

26 Zoo Waterbus
Delamere Ter W2. 01-286 6101. Go to the zoo on a British Waterways boat. Visit to the zoo itself optional. *Charge.*

EATING AND DRINKING

A Sir Alexander Fleming *Pub*
Corner St Michael's St and Bouverie Pl W2. Pretty, almost dainty pub with hanging baskets and food always available. £.

B Archery *Tavern*
4 Bathurst St W2. 01-723 9230. Decor commemorates the 19thC revival of the sport in Bayswater. Real ale and snacks. £.

C Père Michel *Restaurant*
11 Bathurst St W2. 01-723 5431. Simple but pretty French restaurant with Lautrec prints on the walls. Snails, of course. Then try forcemeat of pike blended with cream and

lobster sauce or beef in green peppercorn sauce, followed by a rich little 'pot de chocolat'. *Closed Sat lunch & all Sun.* ££.

D Deodar *Restaurant*
12a Bathurst St W2. 01-262 5603. Small, cheap, gentle and Indian with a menu which pleads 'The essence of culinary art is time – we ask your kind indulgence'. Grant it and you will enjoy excellent results. £.

E Victoria *Tavern*
10a Strathearn Pl W2. 01-262 7474. The etched glass doors lead to some genuine Victoriana, warmed by coal fires in winter. Outside tables face the trees of Gloucester Square. Plentiful snacks except at weekends. £.

F Ruby's *Wine Bar*
28 Sussex Pl W2. 01-262 4654. A ruby red bistro-like place with a reliable wine list and a long menu of nicely presented, home-made dishes – pâtés, prawns and soups; quiches, pies, boeuf bourgignon, salads; cheeses and gooseberry crumble. £.

G Le Mange Tout *Restaurant*
Sussex Pl W2. 01-723 1199. Prints, plants and the judicious use of mirrors make the two small rooms light and spacious. Try ragout de poissons – mixed fish and shellfish casserole – or beef tartare. Pricey unless you stick to the set meal. £££.

H Great Mughal *Restaurant*
50 Connaught St, Hyde Pk Sq W2. 01-258 3615. Comfortable elegance in this large Indian restaurant – which even sells picture postcards of itself. Watch the Tandoori oven in operation as you await your perfectly cooked, graciously served meal. ££.

J Indira *Restaurant*
62 Seymour St W2. 01-402 6733. Friendly and pretty, the authenticity of the Indian cuisine vouched for by the many Indian regulars. Take away service, too. ££.

K Shirreffs *Wine Bar*
25 New Quebec St W1. 01-723 0095. Civilised and charming. Enjoy anything from a single glass from the range of about 140 wines to a full bottle and a full meal; grills, risottos, New York pastrami with green figs and bread, crème caramel cheered up with apricots – all prepared on the premises. *Closed weekends.* ££.

L La Loggia *Restaurant*
68 Edgware Rd W2. 01-723 0554. Large and Italian with much decorative greenery and a few French dishes. Try frogs legs or gaspacho to start with – then breast of chicken in artichoke and cheese sauce – and finish off with traditional Italian puddings. ££.

M Lotus House *Restaurant*
61–69 Edgware Rd W2. 01-262 4341. Make an evening of it here, with reliable Cantonese cookery and dancing nightly until 01.00. ££.

N Bali *Restaurant*
101 Edgware Rd W2. 01-723 3303. Bamboo furnishings, palms, temple statues and waitresses in sarongs set the scene for Malaysian dishes on the ground floor or a 14 course Indonesian banquet in the basement. Large portions and good value set menus. ££.

O Al Amir *Restaurant*
114 Edgware Rd W2. 01-262 6636. Lebanese specialities here, amid fresh flowers and courteous service. To start with, fatayer – pastry stuffed with spinach and served with lemon or, for the thoughtful, brain salad. Next, a variety of charcoal grills. At last, syrupy crêpes or othmalieh – a delicious pastry filled with cream. £££.

P Raw Deal *Restaurant*
65 York St W1. 01-262 4841. Earnestly wholesome and endearing small bistro offering home-made vegetarian dishes. Lovely salads, savoury pancakes, trifles. Unlicensed but they don't frown if you bring a bottle. *Closed 22.00 & all Sun.* £.

Q Jörgens *Wine Bar*
22 Harcourt St W1. 01-402 5925. German wine bar and bistro with a good range of the better-known German wines and very reasonably priced casseroles, frankfurters or bratwurst with fresh salads or hot vegetables. On Tue and Fri evening a classical violinist plays gentle music. *Closed Sun.* £.

R Seashell Fish Bar *Restaurant*
35 Lisson Grove NW1. 01-723 8703. Reputedly one of the best fish and chip shops in London – and the reputation is deserved. Pretty decor, up to 14 kinds of fish, all bought fresh, excellent chips and trimmings and (very important, this) no overwhelming smell of frying. *Closed Sun & Mon.* £.

S Warwick Castle *Pub*
6 Warwick Pl W9. 01-286 6868. Wood-panelled Regency pub in Little Venice decorated with prints of the old canal system. A few self-consciously arty types among the clientele. Simple snacks. £.

Marble Arch

Morning Coffee and Afternoon Tea
Great Western Royal Hotel; Paddington Stn W2. 01-723 8064. In the mock-Austrian decor of Oscar's Viking Coffee House. Snacks, too, or 'roasts' in the Brunel Restaurant and Grill.
Paddington Station; Snack Bar.
Brasserie de Champs Elysées; Corner Edgware Rd and Birwood Pl. Afternoon tea inside or at a pavement table.
Wyndham's Tea Rooms; 37a Crawford St W1. 01-258 0376. *Closed 16.00 Sat and Sun.*
Cumberland Hotel; Marble Arch W1. 01-262 1234. The Coffee Shop does both, and light meals.

Map 5 MARYLEBONE AND REGENT'S PARK

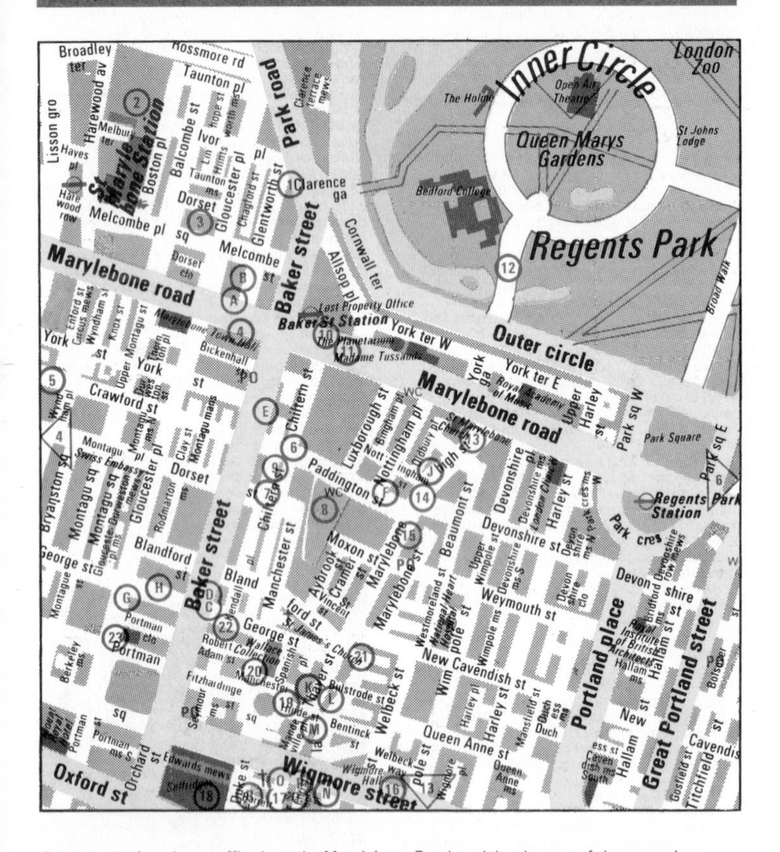

Between the ferocious traffic along the Marylebone Road, and the clamour of shoppers along Oxford Street to the south, lies lovely Marylebone, living and functioning proof that a village atmosphere can survive not only the crassness of developers but also the affectionate mauling of the annual influx of tourists. The small-scale High Street, still winding gently beside the Tyburn River although that Thames tributary has long since gone underground, does have some luxury shops, but it also has grocery stores to cater to the needs of residents – albeit well-heeled ones.

The village became part of the West End during the 18thC with the creation of Cavendish Square to the south (1717), Portman Square (1764), Portland Place by the Adam brothers (1775), and Manchester Square (1776). The reconstruction was completed early in the 19thC when the Prince Regent commissioned John Nash to develop old Marylebone Park into the present roughly circular Park with its lakes, trees and ornamental shrubs, its bandstand and theatre and the beautiful stretch of Regent's Canal that carries boats through the Zoological Gardens – all protected by elegant Regency terraces.

Within this compact, appealing area the famous names beckon the diligent sight-seer in all directions. Here is music at the Wigmore Hall, splendid paintings, porcelain and furniture in the Wallace Collection, the exclusive medicine of Harley Street, the shade of Elizabeth Barrett in Wimpole Street, the Planetarium and Madame Tussaud's to boggle the mind and chill the marrow, and of course Baker Street where the fictitious Sherlock Holmes and the dim Dr Watson resided.

PLACES OF INTEREST

1 **St Cyprian's Church**
Glentworth St NW1. By Ninian Comper in 1901–3 and the most complete surviving example of his work. Dull exterior leads into a 20thC celebration of medieval architecture, glowing with gilding.

2 **Marylebone Station**
Boston Pl NW1. 01-387 7070. Opened in 1899, the last of the mainline terminals to be built. Small in scale, with the look of a country station, its suburban lines lead to Amersham, High Wycombe, Banbury and Aylesbury.

Marylebone Station

3 **Dorset Square**
NW1. This verdant square was the original site of Thomas Lord's Marylebone Cricket Club (the MCC), founded in 1787 and Britain's premier cricket club – now at St John's Wood.

4 **Marylebone Town Hall and Library**
Marylebone Rd NW1. Sir Edwin Cooper built the massive, columned structure, with its tall landmark of a tower and its guardian lions wearing expressions of pained surprise, in 1914. He added the matching but noticeably low-key library extension in 1939.

5 **Crawford Street Market**
43 Crawford St W1. A series of stalls sell small antiques in an arcade through No 43. There is a board outside to aid navigation. *Closed weekends.*

6 **Chiltern Street**
W1. After the high blocks and high commerce of Baker Street try a peaceful stroll along something on a smaller scale with its boutiques, its modest, cheerful eating places – and, too, the Nicholas Treadwell Gallery of modern and frequently outrageous paintings and sculptures at No 36 and Howarth, the manufacturers of wind instruments, at No 31.

7 **All Flutes Plus**
5 Dorset St W1. 01-935 3339. The shop looks small but it has the widest range of flutes in Europe, and in the workshops which spread beneath the pavement craftsmen are designing and making more daily. They even make miniature silver jewellery in the form of flutes. Friendly, welcoming and informative. Closed *14.30 on Sat & all Sun.*

8 **Paddington Street Park**
NW1. The old churchyard and gardens have been landscaped into two nice little parks (the one south of the road is the sunniest) the perfect place to enjoy sandwiches bought at

Barcaglia's street-sweeper

one of the shops along Paddington Street. The statue of the weary little street-sweeper by Donato Barcaglia, should remind you to dispose of your wrappers correctly.

9 **Seen Gallery**
39 Paddington St W1. 01-486 4292. Original paintings and drawings, mostly by young British artists, on the ground floor. Downstairs – limited editions of lovely prints. Friendly and informal. *Closed Sun.*

10 **London Planetarium**
Marylebone Rd NW1. 01-486 1121. The beginner's guide to the universe – stars, planets, galaxies are represented hourly on the domed ceiling, with full commentary. First show of the day about 12.15. If you wish to be dazzled yet further there are laser concerts most evenings – for information on these ring 01-935 3726. *Charge.*

11 **Madame Tussaud's**
Marylebone Rd NW1. 01-935 6861. Tableaux of waxen images of the famous and notorious, both life-size and unsettlingly life-like. The Chamber of Horrors, a magnet to the ghoulish, includes the original moulds made by Madame herself of the heads severed by the guillotine during the French Revolution. And, yes, the guillotine is genuine, too. *Charge.*

12 **Regent's Park**
NW1. Originally part of Henry VIII's royal hunting grounds, the park took on its present handsome form when the Prince Regent appointed John Nash to connect it by way of Regent Street to the now demolished Carlton House. The design of 1812–26 was never completed but the 470 acres of lawns and lakes were encircled by elegant Regency terraces and imposing gateways. Here you will find the Grand Union Canal – called Regent's Canal at this point – the zoo, a boating lake with 30 species of birds, the exotic onion-domed mosque and, in the Inner Circle, Queen Mary's lovely rose gardens with their bandstand and the open air theatre (01-486 2431) where, in good weather, you can watch performances, primarily of Shakespearean plays, from May to August.

13 **St Marylebone Parish Church**
Marylebone Rd NW1. The village church that gave the area its name has been rebuilt ever since 1400. Thomas Hardwick designed the latest version in 1813 and Nash added the portico to tone with his York Gate into

Regent's Park

Regent's Park. High, airy, golden and blue inside. Scene of the secret wedding of Browning and Elizabeth Barrett.

14 Marylebone High Street
NW1. A walk down its length is recommended to anyone who wants to savour Marylebone. Despite the march of progress all around, it still feels like a village, or at most market town, street – good dress shops, luxury galleries, antique bookshops, jewellers and expensive flower and cake shops mingle with the usual food shops, dry cleaners and tobacconists.

15 David Shilling's Hats
36 Marylebone High St W1. 01-487 3179. This is the man whose highly eccentric designs are modelled annually by his mother at Royal Ascot. He will make you a simple hat in a few hours – a special-occasion extravaganza takes a little longer.

16 Wigmore Hall
Wigmore St W1. 01-935 2141. By tradition, international musicians make their London debut in its intimate atmosphere with the excellent accoustics. Also welcomes the lesser known and more unusual – such as a medieval band and verse reading by well-known actors.

17 St Christopher's Place
W1. Bijou pedestrianised shopping street, made even prettier with frondy shrubs in tubs and vividly flowering window boxes. Here you can buy clothes, shoes and jewellery, or eat outside at Plexi's bistro and watch others spending their money.

18 Selfridge's
400 Oxford St W1. 01-629 1234. One of the most exciting of the large department stores with lavish food halls and glamorous displays of clothes, toys, furniture, household goods, perfumery, clothes and so on. *Closed Sun.*

Selfridge's

19 Methodist Church
Hinde St W1. Has not stood up well to London grime but remains dingily impressive. It was built by Weir in 1881–7 with a two-storied portico after St Paul's Cathedral, but lacking the latter's panache.

20 Wallace Collection
Hertford House, Manchester Sq W1. 01-935 0687. This dignified town house, with its discreetly landscaped garden, contains an outstandingly rich private collection of art treasures amassed by two Marquesses of Hertford and Sir Richard Wallace and bequeathed to the nation by Lady Wallace in 1897. The French 17thC and 18thC are especially well represented. There are also Rembrandts, Titians, Rubens, Canalettos, Bonnington oil and water colours and Sèvres porcelain. *Closed 17.00 & Sun morning. Free.*

St James', Spanish Place

21 St James' Church
Spanish Place W1. Cathedral-like Roman Catholic church in Early English style by George Goldie, 1885–90, the arrangement of London grime on its white Kentish ragstone exterior giving it a curiously shaded effect. Dignified interior with pillars and full gallery rising to a lovely vaulted ceiling.

22 Arenski
29–31 George St W1. 01-486 0678. Where to buy extravagantly flamboyant antique furniture and ornaments – carved ladies raising lamps, inlaid tables and cabinets, gilt-encrusted urns holding massive arrangements of dried flowers and huge sea-shells. *Closed 17.00 & all weekend.*

23 RIBA Heinz Gallery
21 Portman Sq W1. 01-580 5533. Gallery owned by the Royal Institute of British Architects which mounts changing (though *not* continuous) exhibitions of architectural interest – drawings, photographs, models. *Open 11.00–17.00 Mon–Fri, 10.00–13.00 Sat. Closed Sun. Free.*

EATING AND DRINKING

A Boos *Wine Shop and Bar*
1 Glentworth St NW1. 01-935 3827. Tiny, wood-panelled and discreet. Take wine only, to test what you might care to buy in bulk, or try the pâté and cheese to help absorb the alcohol. *Closed 20.00 & all weekend.* £.

B Viceroy of India *Restaurant*
3 Glentworth St NW1. 01-486 3401. Wood and marble elegance with fountains among the plants in foyer and dining area and courteous

service. Delicately spiced dishes. Try tandoori mehi – fish slices marinated in spices or choose one of the two reasonably priced set meals – the Maharajah, or the cheaper Maharani! ££.

C **Reubens** *Deli and Restaurant*
20a Baker St W1. 01-935 5945. Kosher Jewish restaurant with a snack bar next to the delicatessen and a full restaurant above. Salt beef is unwaveringly popular. To start with, gefilte fisch or chicken soup with kreplech or kneidlech and to finish, lockshen pudding. Drink lemon tea or Israeli wine. *Closed Fri 15.00, Sat, Jewish hols.* £ or ££.

D **Ikaros** *Restaurant*
36 Baker St W1. 01-935 7821. Small, and authentically Greek, the tables that spill on to the unpromising pavement packed with cheery diners. Most reasonably priced, especially if two share a full meze – a selection of specialities. *Closed Sun.* £.

E **Flanagan's Fish Parlour** *Restaurant*
100 Baker St W1. 01-935 0287. Blithely phoney Victorian dining rooms – with stalls and sawdust and cockney songs, breezy service and spirited pianist. How about pea and ham soup, whitebait, game pie with mash and carrots, tripe and onions, fish and chips, lobster Lillie Langtry and the inimitable spotted dick for afters. ££.

F **Baker and Oven** *Pub and Restaurant*
10 Paddington St W1. 01-935 5072. Outwardly colourful (orange and green) corner pub with a cosy basement restaurant serving traditional roasts and pies from the original 100-year-old baker's ovens. *Closed Sun.* ££.

G **Worcester Arms** *Pub*
89 George St W1. 01-935 6050. Red and yellow free house. The decor is mock-Regency but the ales are real – always three on the go plus a guest beer of the month. Faithful following of regulars. £.

H **Mikado** *Restaurant*
110 George St W1. 01-935 8320. Pretty, pale wood, rather secretive frontage in a long modern block. Simple tiled sushi bar on street level, restaurant downstairs for other Japanese specialities – tempura, beef or chicken teryaki, bean curd dishes. *Closed Sat lunch & all Sun.* £££+.

J **Prince Regent** *Pub and Restaurant*
71 Marylebone High St W1. 01-935 2018. Amply impressive Regency, with 'Prinny's' bust outside among the hanging baskets, mighty torch-bearing blackamoor statues on the bar, period caricatures and letters from Mrs Fitzherbert on display. Partitioned-off restaurant for French and English dishes. *Restaurant closed Sat eve & all Sun.* ££.

K **Genevieve** *Restaurant and Wine Bar*
13 Thayer St W1. 01-486 2244. Comfortable and congenial with tables on the forecourt in good weather, a long and predominantly French wine list and reliable cuisine bourgeoise – coq au vin and other old friends. *Closed Sat lunch & all Sun.* ££.

L **Hellenic** *Restaurant*
30 Thayer St W1. 01-935 1257. Spirited Greek place with jaunty service and good farmhouse cooking – fish kebabs, moussaka and, to follow, loukomades. *Closed Sun.* ££.

M **Angel** *Pub*
37 Thayer St W1. 01-486 7763. Samuel Smith Old Brewery bitter from Yorkshire can be enjoyed here in a highly decorative Victorian pub. Plentiful food. £.

Cock and Lion Pub

N **Cock and Lion** *Pub*
62 Wigmore St W1. 01-935 8727. Sophisticated, cheery, wood-panelled, with sporting prints and a pleasant restaurant offering charcoal grills and steaks for lunch. *Closed Sun.* ££.

O **Pontefract Castle** *Pub*
Wigmore St W1. 01-486 3551. Exuberant free house with several real ales, 20 malt whiskies, a flourish of flowery painting outside and antiques, sea chests, pictures from Pears Annual and Victorian porn inside. The *Twisted Root Wine Bar* has candlelight and sometimes a pianist. Food, too. £.

P **Masako** *Restaurant*
6 St Christopher's Pl W1. 01-935 1579. Authentically Japanese, the main restaurant with a miniature Noh stage, the side rooms with floor seating. Try the set Sukiyaki or tempura meals with Sake or Japanese beer. *Closed Sun.* £££.

Q **Plexi's** *Restaurant*
1c St Christopher's Pl W1. 01-935 1047. Café-style bistro with plentiful seating in the traffic-free street with its luxury small shops. Varied menu, but try the chicken speciality – covered in cheese, cream and mushroom sauce and served on rice. *Closed Sun.* £.

R **Coconut Grove** *Restaurant*
3–5 Barrett St W1. 01-486 5269. The glamour of old Hollywood is brought up to date in this huge mirrored silvery extravaganza at the end of St Christopher's Place. *Polo Bar* serves anaesthetising cocktails and the restaurant banquet-style food with gargantuan desserts. Glittery clientele. £££.

Morning Coffee and Afternoon Tea

Selfridges; Oxford St W1. Two coffee shops. *Closed 17.30 & all Sun.*
Bonne Bouche; 2 Thayer St W1. 01-935 3502. Lovely patisserie. Coffee, tea, cream cakes. *Closed 18.00 & all Sun.*
Maison Sagne; 105 Marylebone High St W1. 01-935 6240. Traditional tea shop. *Closed Sun.*
Sherlock Holmes Hotel; Baker St W1. 01-486 6161. On the street where he is supposed to have lived. Coffee and tea in Moriarti's (*sic*) Restaurant – also Italian meals – or a drink in the Holmesian Dr Watson's Bar.
Regent's Park; Cafés.

Map 6 EUSTON AND FITZROVIA

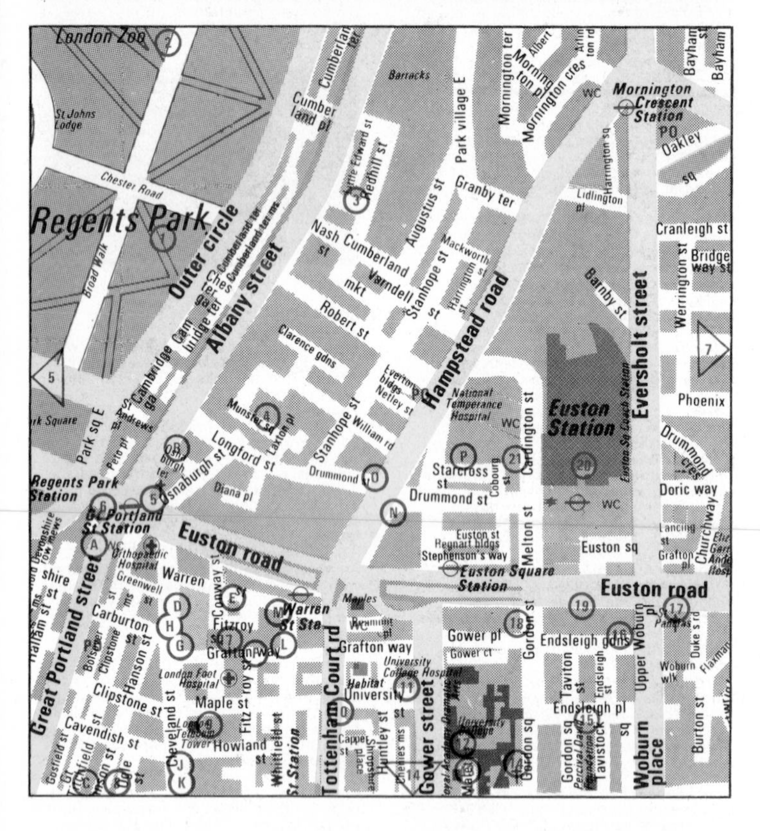

The modest area north of Euston Road and east of the Prince Regent's gracefully designed Park, was put on the map in 1837 when the original Euston Station was built to serve the London and Midland Railway. It was the first terminus to be built in a capital city, and had such high Victorian grandeur it was sometimes called the eighth wonder of the world. But it was demolished and rebuilt in the late 60s in such a plain and ordinary style that it was almost as if a light had gone out.

Yet although this area keeps its centre to itself for quiet residential purposes, and the tourist attractions remain very much at its edges, a tour around it gives a surprisingly good idea of the immense variety London as a whole has to offer – variety of architecture, scale and entertainment.

A circular perambulation touches on Regent's Park with its tended lawns and flowers, its trees, zoo, open-air theatre and elegant Nash architecture; the simple streets approaching the 19thC extension of Nash's vision at Mornington Crescent; the stark practicalities of the station; the terraced garden squares of North Bloomsbury, laid out by Cubitt in the first half of the 19thC; the Dickensian Duke's Road and Woburn Walk with their 18thC shop fronts; through the rich complex around University College with its theatre and two small, exquisite museums; to Tottenham Court Road, its architecture a drab mixture of Victorian and modern but some of its shops quite excellent; and on to the Adam architecture in Fitzroy Square, whilst the Post Office Tower, now the London Telecom Tower, looms above everything with its red and watchful eye. Television's newest Channel, 4, took up residence in nearby Charlotte Street late in 1982.

PLACES OF INTEREST

Cumberland Terrace

1 **Regent's Park**
NW1. Originally part of Henry VIII's royal hunting grounds, the park took on its present handsome form when the Prince Regent appointed John Nash to connect it by way of Regent Street to the now demolished Carlton House. The design of 1812–16 was never completed but the 470 acres of lawns and lakes were encircled by elegant Regency terraces and imposing gateways. Here you will find the Grand Union Canal – called Regent's Canal at this point – the zoo, a boating lake with 30 species of birds, the exotic onion-domed mosque and, in the Inner Circle, Queen Mary's lovely rose gardens with their bandstand and the open air theatre (01-486 2431) where, in good weather, you can watch performances, primarily of Shakespearean plays, from May to August.

Park Crescent

2 **London Zoo (The Zoological Gardens)**
Regent's Pk NW1. 01-722 3333. First laid out by Decimus Burton in 1827 with imaginative new animal houses added in recent years, on the lines of a redevelopment planned by Sir Hugh Casson, of which the most famous is probably still the pointed shrugging structure that is Lord Snowdon's aviary. One of the largest collections of creatures in the world saunters in the enclosures, swims or shambles in the Marine and Tropical Aquarium, or obligingly reverses its nocturnal habits in the eerie light of the Moonlight Hall. *Closed dusk. Charge.*

Snowdon's Aviary

3 **Christ Church**
Albany St NW1. Large with a plain exterior in yellow brick and galleried interior, by Pennethorne, 1838, with a few Butterfield alterations in 1867. Rossetti was responsible for the south window, showing the Sermon on the Mount, and the first man to hold the office of Vicar was the Rev. William Dodsworth.

4 **St Mary Magdalene Church**
Munster Sq NW1. Mid 19thC Gothic church by Carpenter, restored in the 1960s and very much part of the local community. The 'Double M Club' in the crypt (membership readily available) is run by a non-profit-making trust and offers a lunch club, parties, music and a bar against a vivid backdrop of illuminated stained glass windows.

5 **Holy Trinity Church**
Albany St NW1. Sir John Soane's early 19thC church is, like several of its contemporaries, no longer used as such, but has undergone a more fitting transmogrification than most – it is now the HQ of the SPCK – The Society for the Propagation of Christian Knowledge.

6 **John F Kennedy Memorial**
1 Park Cres NW1. The bust by Jacques Lipchitz, which stares stoicly out from the gardens of the International Students' Hostel, was bought by public contribution and unveiled in 1965 by Edward and Robert Kennedy.

7 **Fitzroy Square**
W1. The south and east sides of the attractive square are by Robert Adam, 1790–4. The large bronze in the central gardens is by Naomi Blake, 1977, and is enigmatically entitled View II. Both Virginia Woolf and George Bernard Shaw lived at No 29, though not at the same time.

8 **St Charles Church**
Ogle St W1. Small and welcoming on its corner, with its door usually standing open, is the Roman Catholic church designed by Nicholl in 1862. Inside, the reredos is by Bentley.

9 **London Telecom Tower**
Maple St W1. 198 metres, including mast, of telecommunications gadgetry, familiar as the Post Office Tower until 1982, constantly transmitting radio, television and telephone signals around the country and, via a

London Telecom Tower

Goonhilly Down/satellite link-up, the world. Visible for miles but a misleading landmark since it gives the illusion of moving through the landscape.

10 Tottenham Court Road
W1. Furniture and household shops (including the 50,000 sq ft of Maples at No 145, 01-387 7000) and camera shops, but most of all electronics, hi-fis, videos and their relations can be priced, compared and cross-checked within the confines of one road.

11 University College Hospital
Gower St WC1. 01-387 9300. This gabled and spired general hospital was designed in 1897–1906 by Alfred Waterhouse – perhaps more famous for the Natural History Museum and the splendid red cliffs of the Prudential Assurance buildings in Holborn.

12 University College
Gower St WC1. 01-734 3667. Mostly designed by William Wilkins in the early 19thC and incorporated with the University of London in 1907, it contains the Slade School of Art and is said to be haunted by one of its founders, the philosopher Jeremy Bentham, whose dignified skeleton, clad in his own clothes, may be visited by prior arrangement.

13 University of London
Malet St WC1. Originally an examining body which only became a teaching university at the turn of the century, its colleges are scattered around London. The admin buildings are here, including Senate House, whose distinguished library is open to visiting scholars. This was the first university to admit women on the same terms as men.

14 Christ the King Church
Gordon Sq WC1. 01-387 0670. The university church, built by Raphael Brandon in 1853. The west front and tower are unfinished but this does not diminish its cathedral-like dignity or the fine interior.

15 Percival David Foundation of Chinese Art
53 Gordon Sq WC1. 01-387 3909. In 1950 Sir Percival David gave a fine library and a priceless collection of Sung, Yuan, Ming and Ch'ing Dynasty Chinese ceramics to the University of London. They are housed here not solely for serious students but for anyone wanting to enjoy the cool serenity of their presence. *Opening times vary. Check.*

16 Jewish Museum
Woburn House, Upper Woburn Pl WC1. 01-387 3081. Jewish life and worship are illustrated here by a comprehensive collection of ritual objects and antiquities and two audio-visual programmes. The most famous single item is the elaborate 17thC ark from Italy. *Open Mon–Thur 12.30–15.00; Sun 10.30–12.45. Free.*

17 St Pancras New Church
Upper Woburn Pl WC1. Designed by W. and W. H. Inwood in 1819, avowedly on the lines of the Ionic temple of the Erechtheum on the Acropolis at Athens, and then restored in the early 1950s. Flat ceiling and galleried interior, columns and caryatids outside. Sometimes offers lunchtime music.

18 Bloomsbury Theatre
Gordon St NW1. 01-387 9629. An alternative theatre, on the touring circuit, putting on professional productions – drama, dance and mime. As it belongs to the University of London it can also offer twice-yearly student productions.

19 Wellcome Library of the History of Medicine
183 Euston Rd NW1. 01-387 4477. The Wellcome Institute's library has more than 400,000 items – early and modern books and manuscripts – on all aspects of medical history and related matters, all available for browsing. *Closed weekends. Free.* Their Museum of Medical Science, in the same building, is open only to the medical and allied professions but they have two major exhibitions on the subject at the Science Museum in Exhibition Road. *See Map 11.*

20 Euston Station
Euston Rd NW1. 01-387 7070. Modern structure, set back from the road behind lawns and a large forecourt, which dispatches trains north to Birmingham and Manchester, Liverpool, Glasgow and Inverness. The original station was by Robert Stephenson, he whose statue stands in the forecourt. The triumphal Doric entrance arch by Philip Hardwick was demolished, to cries of anguish, in the late 1960s.

21 B R Collector's Corner
Old NCL Garage, Cardington St NW1. 01-387 9400 Ext 2537. If driven by an urge to possess an obsolete British Railways name plate, a hand lamp, signal, station clock or railman's hat, this is the place. A little hard to find but the enthusiasts manage. *Closed 17.00; 16.30 on Sat, all Sun & occasional lunchtimes.*

University College

EATING AND DRINKING

A **Albany** *Pub*
240 Gt Portland St W1. 01-387 8690. Real ales and very good lunches in this traditional pub with its imposing red and black frontage. Every evening in the Dive Bar the younger element gathers to hear a live group play jazz-funk. £.

B **White House Hotel** *Restaurant*
Albany St NW1. 01-387 1200. Modern but restful with still-lifes and the glow of candleflames at night. Menus change with the seasons – dressed crab claws, pike quenelles with champagne sauce, carré d'agneau saladaise in summer – game and mignon de boeuf Sarah Bernhardt in winter. Own patisserie; good wine list. *Closed Sat lunch & all Sun.* £££.

White House Hotel

C **Crown and Sceptre** *Pub*
86 Gt Titchfield St W1. 01-636 7940. Large and heartily Victorian with lunchtime food, a Tue night guitarist and a jovial atmosphere. £.

D **Aunties** *Restaurant*
126 Cleveland St W1. 01-387 3226. Small and comfortable. You may also eat outside, admittedly on the pavement, but in a plant-sheltered arbour. Victoria pie is beef in guinness and garlic sauce; the traditional steak and kidney steamed suet pudding is recommended; the vegetables are fresh; the trifles and syllabubs creamy. *Closed Sat lunch & all Sun.* ££.

E **Smuggler's Tavern** *Pub*
28 Warren St W1. 01-387 3564. Has a vaguely Victorian look with its ships' figureheads and murky lighting. Seats outside or seats in booths for privacy. Good snacks. £.

F **Grafton Arms** *Pub*
72 Grafton Way W1. 01-387 7923. Smart little one-bar pub with real ale, food and outdoor seating for clement weather. Intimate wine bar tucked away upstairs. £.

G **Averof** *Restaurant*
86 Cleveland St W1. 01-387 2375. Simple and motherly Greek kebab house – small, popular, cheap and good. *Closed Sun.* £.

H **Four Lanterns** *Restaurant*
96 Cleveland St W1. 01-387 0704. Serves exceptionally good kebabs and moussaka. Varied selection of wines and retsina. Dance to taped music in the evenings. *Closed Sat lunch & all Sun.* £.

Fitzroy Square

J **Trattoria La Torre** *Restaurant*
55 Cleveland St W1. 01-636 7974. Small, friendly restaurant with varied menu, including tasty veal dishes. *Closed Sun.* £.

K **Cuisine Sri Lanka** *Restaurant*
57 Cleveland St W1. 01-636 9098. Experience the subtle and unusual flavours of Sri Lankan cooking in this friendly, family-run restaurant. *Closed Sun.* £.

L **Agra**
135–37 Whitfield St W1. 01-387 4828. Very popular and crowded restaurant. Don't expect a table to yourself; the friendly atmosphere makes up for any inconvenience. The waiters, although rushed, try to be as helpful as possible. Specialises in tandoori rather than curry dishes. £.

M **Diwan-I-Am** *Restaurant*
161 Whitfield St W1. 01-387 0293. Plain dining room, with some princely high-backed chairs. Try the thali – a selection of small side dishes: mutton moghlai, bhoona gosht, and the specialities – tandoori chicken and prawn bhoona. £.

N **Drummonds** *Bar Brasserie*
137 Drummond St NW1. 01-387 3799. Informally classy New York-style bar with what it calls a 'neo-classic romantic decor'. Charming, friendly and deservedly popular. Cocktails a speciality, wines and beers good, quiches, pies, chilli, salads, passion cake and bread and butter pudding all delicious. *Closed Sun.* £.

O **Shah** *Restaurant*
124 Drummond St NW1. 01-387 1480. Small and cheap Indian restaurant where you can sample more than eleven different chicken curries. Specialises in lavish Mogul dishes, which can only be cooked for groups. £.

P **Exmouth Arms** *Pub*
1 Starcross St NW1. Drink Director's Bitter in a generously redecorated pub which stands on one of the last streets in the area to retain its original cobbles. £.

Morning Coffee and Afternoon Tea
Euston Station; Snack Bar.
White House Hotel; Albany St NW1. 01-387 1200.

Map 7 KING'S CROSS AND ST. PANCRAS

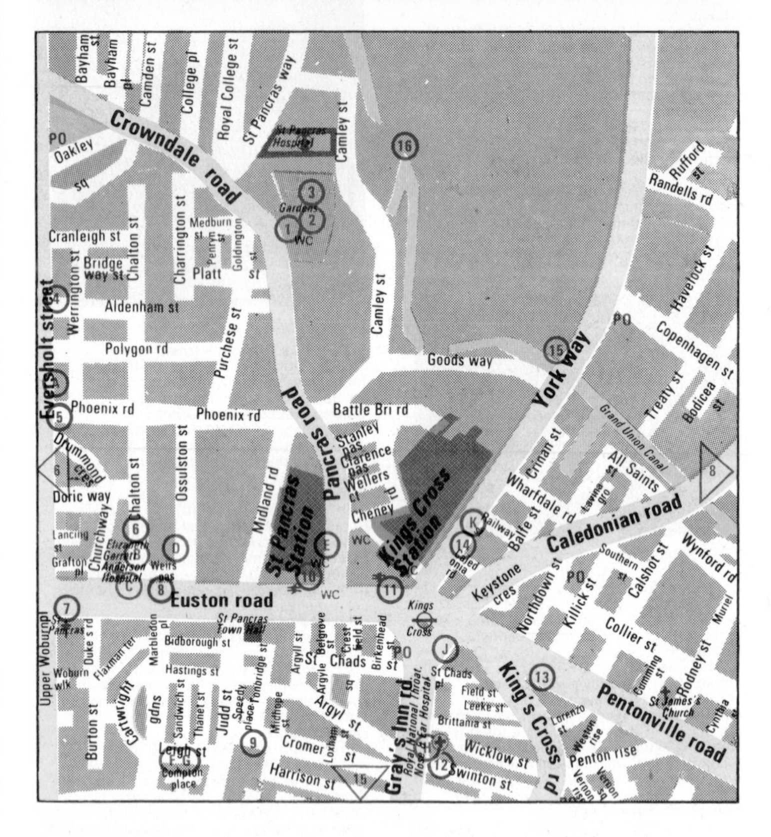

The two prominent rail termini sit at the map's centre like twin castles commanding their land; King's Cross discreet and modern-looking despite its primarily 19thC structure – St Pancras a Gothic exuberance of towers, turrets and iron and glass tunnel-vaulting which becomes wholly magical in the evening sun. To the north spread tracks, goods yards and warehouses bordered by that curious mixture of new building, dereliction and small hotels which seems to surround most important stations.

To the south and east the broad major roads – Euston, Pentonville, Caledonian and York Way – are daily attacked by relentless traffic, its noise and fumes forming part of the grimy, restless character of the place and cutting the top two thirds of the map off from the gentler lands of Bloomsbury to the south.

Although this does not seem very promising territory for the average tourist, he who perseveres will have a few pleasant surprises. As well as road and rail another, gentler, form of transport is here – the Grand Union Canal winds down through the midst of goods yards, its surroundings grim but its towpath rimmed with wild flowers, brightly painted narrow boats navigating a serene course down its length. Old St Pancras Church, its large churchyard a blend of monuments, roses and benches, lends dignity; Chalton Street's tiny market and the Shaw Theatre lend vitality; and the extraordinary washing poles in the estates around Brideway Street with their carved demons, blackbirds and galleons lend eccentricity to this Victorian stronghold of the railways.

PLACES OF INTEREST

1 **St Pancras Old Church**
Pancras Rd NW1. 01-387 8818. On the third oldest Christian site in Europe stands this small, country-style church, with its 4thC foundations and Saxon altar stone. Mostly rebuilt in Norman style in 1848 by Roumieu and Gough. Open for services on Wed and Sun.

St Pancras Old Churchyard

2 **St Pancras Old Churchyard**
Pancras Way NW1. The large churchyard has been made into a public garden, very tree-shaded, with the heavy table tombs still ponderously in place but the slab tombstones stacked with odd precision around an ash tree whose roots have grown protectively around them.

3 **Sir John Soane's Mausoleum**
St Pancras Old Churchyard, Pancras Way NW1. Remarkable tomb designed by the

Sir John Soane's Mausoleum

St Pancras Old Church

sometimes wayward but brilliant architect of, among many important buildings, the Bank of England, to protect the remains of his wife who died in 1815. In 1837 he was placed beside her.

4 **St Aloysius Old Church**
Aldenham St NW1. Imposing Roman Catholic church designed by Leroux in 1816 with Tuscan detailing in the pilasters and reredos. Atmospheric interior.

5 **St Aloysius New Church**
Phoenix St NW1. Modern plain brick building opened in the 1960s with an interior like a tastefully furnished cinema. Yet it already has the feeling of a living church – and don't miss the tiny but fascinating local history exhibition behind the font.

6 **Chalton Street Market**
NW1. Cheery general market – lots of cheap clothes, some with known labels. Open on Fridays only, from 08.30 until the traders pack up for tea.

7 **St Pancras New Church**
Upper Woburn Pl WC1. Designed by W. and W. H. Inwood in 1819, avowedly on the lines of the Ionic temple of the Erechtheum on the Acropolis at Athens, and then restored in the early 1950s. Flat ceiling and galleried interior, columns and caryatids outside. Sometimes offers lunchtime music.

8 **Shaw Theatre**
100 Euston Rd NW1. 01-388 1394. Used by the National Youth Theatre to put on varied, sometimes unusual, productions.

Shaw Theatre

9 **Church of the Holy Cross**
Cromer St WC1. A plain exterior by Peacock in 1887. Unexpected, low, flying buttresses inside.

St Pancras Station (and right)

10 St Pancras Station
Euston Rd NW1. 01-387 7070. In the midst of the grimy practicalities of this railway landscape, the fairytale turrets of Sir George Gilbert Scott's Gothic extravaganza bring a rare and happy excitement to the skyline. The vast pinnacled frontage, with its 300 ft clock tower, once a grand hotel but now offices, cannot be missed – but don't omit to admire W. H. Barlow's train shed of 1868, an impressive feat of engineering with its glass and iron tunnel vault spanning 243 ft without supporting pillars. The trains, by the way, go to the Midlands.

11 King's Cross Station
Euston Rd NW1. 01-278 2477. Wholly modern-looking, although only the concourse is new, the rest was built by Cubitt in 1851. The name comes from a monument to George IV which was here until 1845, the tower clock comes from the original Crystal Palace in Hyde Park, the trains go to Leeds, York, Newcastle and Edinburgh.

King's Cross Station

12 Pindar of Wakefield
328 Gray's Inn Rd WC1. 01-837 7269. A public house with the usual facilities – and much more. On Thur to Sat evening inclusive it is *the* place for Old Time Music Hall. Excellent shows, packed with participating regulars, and basket meals served while you watch (though you don't have to eat). Book on 01-722 5395.

13 Scala Cinema
275–277 Pentonville Rd N1. 01-278 8052. Much beloved of movie-buffs for its ever-changing repertory of double bills which includes everything from Hollywood greats to art films, from trash through horror to old classics. Licensed café inside. It's a club, but membership is cheap and immediate.

14 Model Railways
14 York Way NW1. 01-837 5551. Beautifully made scale models of British, American and Continental engines and rolling stock. Also some more ordinary train sets and their accoutrements – including packs of miniature plastic sheep and railway workers. *Closed Sun.*

15 Canal Walk
NW1. Steps down by the York Way bridge bring you to the towpath of the Grand Union Canal. The surroundings are dominated by the railway but the banks grow buddleia, wild sweet peas and many of the prettier weeds. Once on the track you are committed to walking as far as Royal College Street, just off the map to the north. In an hour you can take a leisurely stroll as far as Regent's Park, *see Maps 5 and 6.*

St Pancras Lock

16 St Pancras Lock
NW1. Traditional and pretty lockkeeper's cottage, with hanging baskets and tiny garden. Good place to get a close look at the painted narrow boats – mostly pleasure boats these days – as they wait for the water level to change.

EATING AND DRINKING

A Mogador *Restaurant*
108 Eversholt St NW1. 01-387 4935. Large, light, motherly sort of grill restaurant with huge windows on to the street and simple but satisfying grilled or Italian dishes. *Closed 19.00; 15.00 Sat & all Sun.* £.

B Victoria *Pub*
37 Chalton St NW1. A genuine local, off the tourist beat, but full and lively. The market traders come in on Friday, a pianist plays on Saturday night. £.

C Rising Sun *Pub*
120 Euston Rd NW1. 01-387 2419. Now a one-bar pub, with serried ranks of tables at which to eat substantial snacks. Wonderful yellowing photographs of boxing champs and film stars hang frame to frame on the walls. Lots of glass and mahogany, too. £.

D Eliza Doolittle *Pub*
5 Ossulton St NW1. 01-387 0836. Inoffensive reproduction Victoriana, its theme taken from the Shaw Theatre next door, with glass shaded lights, booths and modern wood panelling. Very crowded at lunchtime with office workers in search of good snacks. One of the few places where you can eat Humble Pie and enjoy it. £.

Eliza Doolittle Pub

E Shires *Pub*
St Pancras Station NW1. Unusually appealing station bar, comfortable and tastefully decorated, with 7 real ales and excellent value hot and cold meals. *Closed Sun.* £.

F Klompen *Wine Bar*
15 Leigh St WC1. 01-387 0040. Small and pretty with an attractive back garden with tables and a full-sized telephone box should you want to call a friend. Will welcome you for a cup of coffee, a snack or a full meal. Nicely presented crêpes, trout, salads and delectable 'Ice Cream Klompen' which is chocolate with advocaat and whipped cream. £.

Klompen Wine Bar

G Knights *Restaurant*
19 Leigh St WC1. 01-380 0522. Simple, jolly steak and hamburger place specialising in burgers with a difference, encased in a savoury golden batter of bubble and squeak. Eat here (bringing your own wine) or take away. £.

H Pindar of Wakefield *Pub*
328 Gray's Inn Rd WC1. 01-837 7269. Snacks downstairs or basket meals from Thur to Sat evening while you watch Old Time Music Hall. *See entry 12.* £.

J Monte Grappa *Restaurant*
337 Gray's Inn Rd WC1. 01-837 6370. A reassuringly nourishing find in a rather desolate area. Leave the traffic noise behind and settle in to typical London-Italian decor, with friendly waiters and several imaginative dishes on a traditional menu. Often full of movie enthusiasts en route for the Scala. ££.

K Goan *Restaurant*
16 York Way NW1. 01-837 7517. This small and friendly family concern is one of London's rare Goan restaurants. Try their famous stuffed mackerel – filled with Goan spices and served with green salad, or mutton sakuti – lamb in spices and coconut. Exotically lovely puddings are made from coconut, mango juice or guavas and their halva, from a family recipe, is delicious. £.

Morning Coffee and Afternoon Tea
New Ambassadors Hotel; Upper Woburn Pl WC1. 01-387 1456. Tea and sandwiches in the lounge.
King's Cross Station; Snack Bar.
St Pancras Station; Snack Bar.
Mogador Restaurant; 108 Eversholt St NW1. 01-387 4935.
Klompen Wine Bar; 15 Leigh St WC1. 01-387 0040.

Map 8 PENTONVILLE AND ISLINGTON

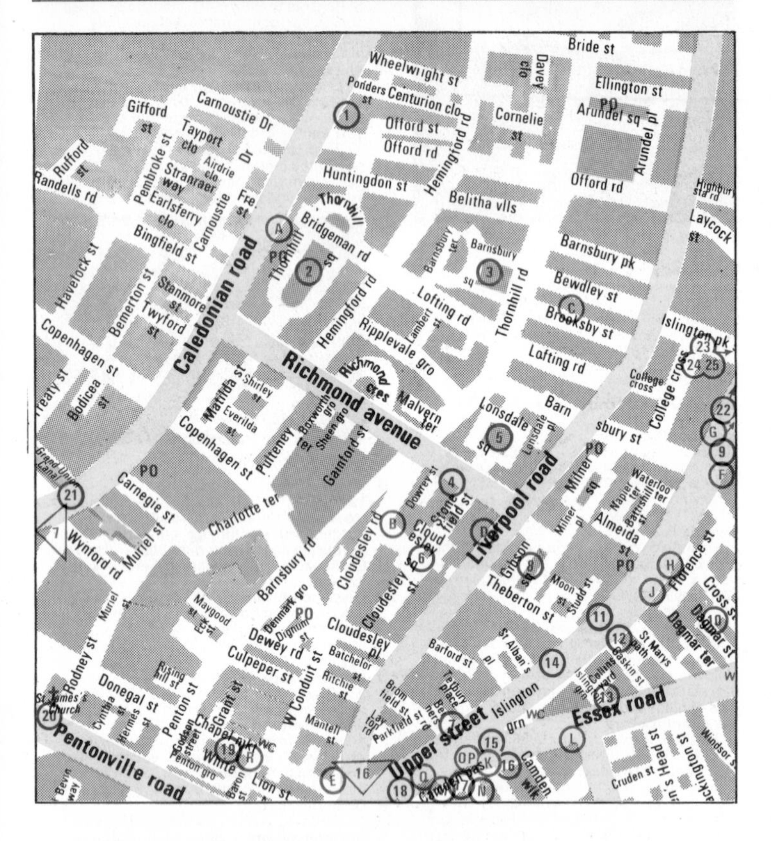

For the visitor, the most immediately rewarding part of this area is the south-east corner. For anyone excited by antiques there is a prime experience waiting along Camden Passage and the King's Head produces consistently good plays at lunchtime and in the evening. But north of this is a pleasant hinterland of terraces and green-centred squares.

The squares are Islington's most notable architectural feature, most of them late 18th or very early 19thC, most very well preserved and each with such individual character that a wander around them is endlessly fascinating. One of them, Barnsbury, is the centre of a development of the same name, laid out in 1820 by Thomas Cubitt, the principal architect of Belgravia and Bloomsbury. In fact in the late 19thC, Islington was regarded as a second Bloomsbury and to an extent still is. It certainly has its down-at-heel aspects but even those houses which are visibly decaying are doing so with a dusty gentility which is most appealing.

Islington has stood on various rungs of the social ladder. Until the great Marylebone/Euston Road was built in 1756 it was the setting for the country houses of the nobility. The new road turned it into a suburb, beginning around the Green and spreading rapidly. A drastic drop in population between the wars sent it into a decline and then in the 60s it was designated up-and-coming and its run-down houses subjected to what came to be called gentrification, by incoming intellectuals. Its present flavour, a blend of working class and radical intellectual, of seedy streets and elegant squares, is lively and richly repays exploration.

PLACES OF INTEREST

1 **Caledonian Road and Barnsbury Station**
N1. From the elevated platform of the station there is a panoramic view of north London and particularly of the sober structure of Pentonville Prison, designed in 1840 by the first Surveyor General of Prisons, Major Jebb, along the lines of the Eastern Penitentiary in Philadelphia.

2 **Thornhill Square**
N1. Charming early 19thC square around a lovely tree-shaded public garden with swings, roses and a miniature wooded hill. The peaceful church of St Andrew, which drowses just north of it, was designed by Newman and Johnson and was built in 1854.

3 **Barnsbury Square**
N1. Traditionally believed to have been the site of a Roman camp – the stone sign of the 20th legion was dug up here in 1842. The whole Barnsbury area, including its square, was laid out in the 1820s by Thomas Cubitt, the master builder of so much of 19thC residential London.

Richmond Avenue

4 **Richmond Avenue**
N1. Nos 46–72 are ordinary, plain terraced houses of the 1840s – with a difference. Beside each front door crouches a rather crude sphinx. It seems the builder was carried away by the British victories on the Nile at the beginning of the decade.

5 **Lonsdale Square**
N1. A perfectly preserved Gothic square, all vertical lines – even to the quatrefoils instead of fanlights above the doors – laid out by Richard Cromwell Carpenter in 1838.

6 **Holy Trinity Church**
Cloudesley Sq N1. If the picturesque outline seems vaguely familiar it is because Sir Charles Barry modelled it on King's College Chapel, Cambridge. Built in 1826 and recently taken over by a Pentecostal sect, its name has been changed to The Celestial Church of Christ and the pews have been removed. Vivid stained glass.

7 **Royal Agricultural Hall**
Liverpool Rd N1. A masterpiece of Victorian engineering with twin towers and massive pavilion ironwork. The Smithfield Club exhibited their cattle here, and in 1884 it saw Charles Cruft's first dog show – to which Queen Victoria submitted three entries. Exhibitions and shows continued until the

Royal Agricultural Hall

Second World War. Now derelict but due to be refurbished – perhaps for use as a warehouse.

8 **Gibson Square**
N1. Laid out by Thomas Cubitt in the 1820s, with formal central gardens, and named after the Cobdenite statesman Thomas Milner Gibson who owned this and other land in the area.

9 **Islington Town Hall**
Upper St N1. 01-226 1234. Neat little neo-classical structure by E. C. P. Morison – erected in 1925.

10 **Little Angel Marionette Theatre**
14 Dagmar Passage, off Cross St N1. 01-226 1787. London's only permanent puppet theatre which presents an excellent variety of weekend shows (with extra ones during school holidays) by the resident company and visiting puppeteers. Essential to book.

11 **King's Head**
115 Upper St N1. 01-226 1916. Large, tatty pub where live music plays nightly from 22.00. The room at the back holds one of London's most respected pub theatres – eat a meal and stay at the table for the performance, or book a chair only. Experimental and established plays, lunch-time and evening. Not for the claustrophobic.

12 **St Mary's Church**
Upper St N1. 01-226 3400. The church was almost destroyed in the war and most of it is the result of 1956 restoration. All that remains of Launcelot Dowbiggins building of 1751–4 is the strikingly baroque steeple.

13 **Collins Music Hall**
Islington Grn N1. A blue plaque marks the reputedly haunted building which ran as a music hall from 1862 to 1958, when it burnt out and was taken over by Anderson's, the timber merchant next door. The list of the famous who played here seems endless and includes Lily Langtry, Nellie Wallace, Harry Lauder, George Robey, Tommy Trinder and Norman Wisdom.

14 **Screen on the Green**
Islington Grn N1. 01-226 3520. Small, arty and friendly cinema showing non-general release films. Late shows and pre-show snacks every weekend.

15 **Sir Hugh Myddleton's Statue**
Islington Grn N1. The rather worn figure outside the Ladies Lavatory was unveiled by Mr Gladstone in 1860 in honour of the

goldsmith who brought fresh water to north London by creating the New River. Springs at Chadwell and Amwell are fed to New River head near Sadler's Wells and thence to the man-made river bed – once 40 miles long, it now ends at Stoke Newington Water Works after 27.

16 Le Gourmet
349 Upper St N1. Delicatessen and patisserie with small but creditable selection of foods and wine, a comfortable counter at which to enjoy coffee, cake or cold snacks in situ, and an excitable manager to add extra zest.

17 Camden Passage
N1. This is what puts Islington on the tourist map – a narrow paved street lined with antique shops, both general and specialist, with unexpected arcades opening off it filled with yet more treasures. There is an open antique market here on Wed morning and Sat, and second-hand-book stalls on Thur and Fri.

Camden Passage

18 The Mall Antiques
359 Upper St N1. 01-359 0825. A covered complex of small antique emporia at one end of the famous Camden Passage. Try the ground floor for glass, china, books, dolls, pictures and bric-a-brac. Downstairs, bow-fronted shop windows reveal furniture, more paintings and larger antiques. *Closed Sun.*

19 Chapel Market
Chapel Mkt N1. Busy general market for fruit and veg, with the addition of a few knick-knacks on Sat. First received its trading charter in the 18thC.

20 St James' Church
Pentonville Rd N1. In the churchyard lies Joey Grimaldi, that most celebrated of clowns, whose memoirs were edited by Charles Dickens. The pretty church is by Aaron Hurst, 1787, who used artificial Coade stone in the façade.

21 Regent's Canal and Islington Tunnel
Caledonian Rd N1. The London stretch of the Grand Union Canal, which links the capital with the Midlands, collects this name as it passes through Regent's Park. Here it sports a brief verdant towpath, with benches, before vanishing into 970 yards of early 19thC tunnel, to emerge on the other side of Islington, on Map 16. In the other direction, it is possible to walk its banks as far as Camden Lock with its market and flourishing restaurants.

Off the Map
It's worth leaving the map briefly for the sake of four places:

22 Canonbury Square
N1. Turn right off Upper Street, opposite Islington Park Street, and follow Canonbury Lane into the square, one of London's most beautiful. The gracious terraces were built by Henry Leroux and first occupied in 1826. The actor-manager Samuel Phelps lived at No 8 and George Daniel at No 18.

23 Tower Theatre
Canonbury Pl N1. 01-226 5111. Leave Canonbury Square by the NE corner to find an active repertory company presenting good modern plays and classics in a 16thC building with a romantic history of an elopement, a father's wrath and the intervention of Queen Elizabeth I. Guided tours for parties after the Sat evening performance.

24 Union Chapel
Compton Ter N1. Continue north along Upper Street and you will come upon James Cubitt's hearty Victorian building of 1876. A small case over the door by the altar holds a fragment of the rock first stepped on by the Pilgrim Fathers – given to a past minister on a lecture tour of America.

New River

25 New River
Willow Bridge Rd N1. An idyllic stretch of Sir Hugh Myddleton's New River; narrow, sheltered by massive lilacs and delicate weeping willows, and scattered with mallards and white nursery-rhyme ducks. To find it, leave Canonbury Square by Canonbury Road going south, turn left up Alwyne Road and go through the unprepossessing gate in Willow Bridge Road.

EATING AND DRINKING

A Prince of Wales *Pub*
342 Caledonian Rd N1. 01-607 0997. Early Victorian pub that burnt down in 1980, but has been restored in its own likeness. Lunchtime snacks and live rock-pop groups from Fri to Sun. £.

B Crown *Pub*
116 Cloudesley Rd N1. 01-837 7107. Pretty

Crown Pub

polished-wood-and-brass pub with tree shaded forecourt, real ales, and home-cooking – beef in beer pie, chicken with tarragon, tandoori chicken. Easy listening live jazz on Sun evening, except in summer when the doors are open and the neighbours hear more than they want to. £.

C Rising Sun *Pub*
55 Brooksby St N1. 01-607 2844. Enthusiastically restored Victorian pub with small rear beer garden. Original 18thC prints of London line the walls, genuine Britannia tables stand about and old musical instruments cling to the ceiling. Lunchtime snacks. £.

D Due Franco *Restaurant*
207 Liverpool Rd N1. 01-607 4112. Much patronised by the locals drawn by its reliable menu. (Italian with a few nods towards France) and amiable atmosphere. Try medallion of beef, veal in cream and white wine with lemon and mushrooms, lamb with rosemary, oranges in Grand Marnier. *Closed Sun.* ££.

E Pied Bull *Pub*
1 Liverpool Rd N1. 01-837 3218. Once Sir Walter Raleigh's house and reputedly one of the first buildings in England to have its walls stained with tobacco smoke. The haunted kitchen is out of bounds but there's a snug, a public bar and a lounge bar complete with stage where rock bands play 7 nights a week. No food.

F Hope and Anchor *Pub*
207 Upper Street N1. 01-359 4510. The cellar pulsates nightly with good live rock, attracting everyone from young punks to elderly hippies. The juke box in the beery, cheery bar, its walls covered in pop pictures, plays a huge selection of little-known singles.

G Julius *Restaurant*
39 Upper St N1. 01-226 4380. Watch through the glass wall of the kitchen as your meal is cooked especially for you. Principally Austrian food with exceptional cakes. Very reasonable set lunch. *Closed Sun.* ££.

H Roxy Diner *Restaurant*
297 Upper St N1. 01-359 3914. Burgers, steaks and club sandwiches in a small room, plain but with plants. Traditional Sunday lunch attracts the local families. £.

J Sultan's Delight *Restaurant*
301 Upper St N1. 01-226 8346. Pretty Turkish restaurant specialising in kebabs, plenty of lamb, sticky puddings steeped in honey. Take-away, too. *Closed Sun lunch.* £.

K Uppers *Bistro*
349 Upper St N1. 01-226 5650. Under the same management as the delicatessen next door with the same rich gateaux for dessert. Good soup, trout with almonds, steak in wine, fresh vegetables. Friendly and relaxed – rather dainty portions. *Closed Sun.* ££.

L Mr Bumble *Restaurant*
Islington Grn N1. 01-354 1952. Young family place with good home-cooked English meals. Customers return again and again for the steak and kidney pud and game pie, and the treacle tart brings a smile to the stiffest of upper lips. On Wed and Sat (market days) home-made pies are sold on a stall outside. *Closed Sun night, all Mon.* ££.

M Frederick's *Restaurant*
Camden Passage N1. 01-359 2888. Large and smart with an intimate dining room, a conservatory with oil paintings, a garden room with indoor trees, and finally a pretty patio. Wherever you sit you may eat deep fried mushrooms, carré d'agneau, breast of duckling with wild mushrooms followed by one of the pastry chef's triumphs. *Closed Sun.* £££.

N Carrier's *Restaurant*
2 Camden Passage N1. 01-226 5353. The well-known cookery writer conceived this one with as much attention to decor as food. Sit in the pink room, the mirror room or the lush, ivy-covered Gothic greenhouse at the back. Imaginative menu with the emphasis on rich sauces. Attentive service, excellent claret, luxurious ambiance. *Closed Sun.* £££.

O Trattoria Aqualino *Restaurant*
31 Camden Passage N1. 01-226 5454. Simple Italian-run restaurant offering good, satisfying meals at prices that won't make your hair stand on end. Lots of pasta, pizza and spare ribs. Related to the more expensive Portofino next door. *Closed Sun.* £.

P Portofino *Restaurant*
39 Camden Passage N1. 01-226 0884. Large, sophisticated and friendly, made dim by plant clogged windows. Don't miss the hors d'oeuvre trolley, succulent with seafood. Lots of veal dishes, calves liver with sage and butter, lobster in summer, and fresh fruit to follow. *Closed Sun.* ££.

Q Grapes *Wine Bar and Restaurant*
359 Upper St N1. 01-359 4960. On the light and airy top floor of an old tram shed, above The Mall Antiques, with skylights, bead curtains and French-style food – vichyssoise, frogs' legs, fresh salmon, medallions of pork, crême brulée and a well-filled cheeseboard. Set lunch on Sun. ££.

R Manzes *Restaurant*
Chapel Mkt N1. 01-837 4981. For something completely different try this family-owned pie and mash shop. Definitely a long running enterprise – it's kept going for 80 years. *Closed by 14.00 & all Sun & Mon.* £.

Morning Coffee and Afternoon Tea
Le Gourmet; 349 Upper St N1. 01-226 6798. Beverages and luxurious gateaux.

Map 9 WEST KENSINGTON AND EARL'S COURT

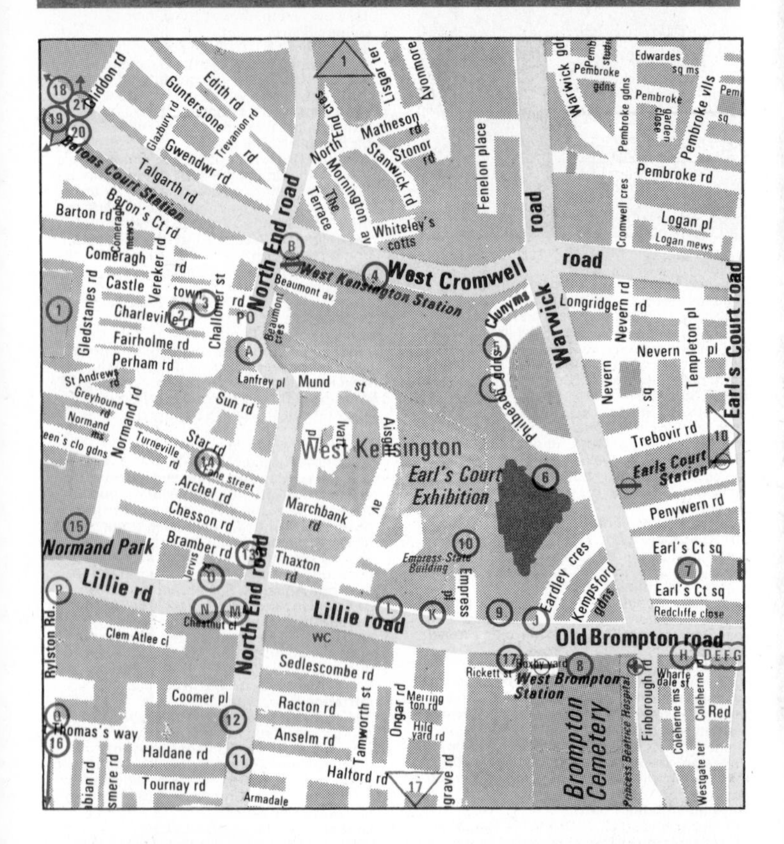

For the visitor, the focal point is undoubtedly the great Earl's Court Exhibition Hall itself, backing on to one of the major junctions of the London Underground system, and world-famous for its huge and various shows and trade fairs.

The surrounding architecture north of Lillie Road is mainly late 19thC residential. In fact much of this area serves as a dormitory for more commercially active parts of London, with several streets of imposing purpose-built apartments to the west and a number of boarding houses and small hotels, especially around Warwick Road. These impinge on Earl's Court Road, often called Kangaroo Valley because of the numbers of Australians and New Zealanders who form part of its floating population.

The area south of Lillie Road is properly Fulham. Here, despite the towering and windswept modern estates facing Normand Park, you can still see working class terraces, with their reassuringly human scale, unexpected little rows of cottages and quiet streets lined with blossom trees. Here family life bustles on, sustained by cheap food from the stalls of the vigorous North End Road market and by a pint in one of the large, plain 'locals', where the company matters more than the decor.

Just off the map to the west lies Hammersmith Broadway, a mini-West End outside London. It is surrounded by opportunities to watch live theatre, often with well-known actors, to listen to music or see an exhibition of modern painting. It is well worth a detour.

PLACES OF INTEREST

1 **Queen's Club**
Palliser Rd W14. 01-385 3421. Try a preview of the stars of 'Wimbledon Fortnight', most of whom play here in the Stella Artois Lawn Tennis Championships two weeks before the more famous event. In winter the club holds the National Raquets and Real Tennis (as played by Henry VIII) Championships. Booking not usually necessary.

Queen's Club

2 **Westken Wholefoods**
6 Charleville Rd W14. 01-385 0956. It's worth visiting this tiny shop where, as well as lentils, dried fruit and herbal remedies you can buy wholesome quiches, pizzas and vegetable burgers. Normand Park is nearby if you want to sit down to eat them. *Closed Sun.*

Bharatiya Vidya Bhavan

3 **Bharatiya Vidya Bhavan**
Old Church Bldg, Castletown Rd W14. 01-381 3086. The Bhavan is well-established in India as a Vedic cultural centre, concerned with all aspects of spiritual and intellectual life. The first overseas branch was opened in 1972 and this centre inaugurated in 1978 by James Callaghan, then Prime Minister. There are lectures, concerts, study circles and classes in yoga, meditation, music, dance and language. Visitors welcome. Membership necessary for full involvement. *Closed 20.00 & Sun.*

4 **West Cromwell Road**
Stand on the bridge between North End Road and Warwick Road and look south towards the Exhibition. You'll see the great complex of underground railway tracks, laid out before you like a model trainset. The church to the left is St Cuthbert with St Matthias.

Underground railway tracks

5 **St Cuthbert with St Matthias**
Philbeach Gdns W14. Very large late 19thC church by Gough which Pevsner cites as a 'memorial to the art of W. Bainbridge Reynolds, one of the best Arts and Crafts men.' His are the pulpit, lectern, clock and stained glass windows of saints Sebastian and Oswald.

6 **Earl's Court Exhibition Hall**
Warwick Rd SW5. 01-385 1200. The heart of the matter. This 19-acre Exhibition Hall (by C. Howard Crane, 1937) regularly fills its mighty space with shows which attract visitors from all over the world. In January there's the largest boat show in Europe. In February the Crufts judges pick the Top Dog. In March the Ideal Home Exhibition breeds discontent among the owners of ordinary homes. In July the walls reverberate with the brass bands and cannonfire of the Royal Tournament, possibly the most popular spectacle of them all. In August there's the Motor Cycle Show and in October, in odd-numbered years, the Motor Show. The year ends with the agricultural machinery and puzzled livestock of the Smithfield Show in December. In between are the trade shows, open only to those involved with them. Bars and buffets inside. *Charge for entry.*

7 **Earl's Court Square**
SW5. With its grass and shrubs and tall elegant plane trees, this is a private haven of peace after the roar and fumes of Warwick Road.

Brompton Cemetery

8 Brompton Cemetery
SW5. The mid-19thC saw the founding of the first London cemeteries, to take the increasing pressure off the choked churchyards and control the threat of cholera. This one was opened in 1839 and is huge. A walk around its several acres of partly overgrown memorials, a few with freshly cut flowers, is like entering another world, an ornate city of the dead with Baroque, neo-Gothic and even Egyptian-inspired designs on all sides. Wander through and you'll come out the other side, on Fulham Rd on Map 17.

9 Earl's Court Market
Lillie Rd SW6. Flourishing Sunday morning market, particularly good for clothes and bales of cloth. Don't miss the incongruous sight of the more affluent customers rolling up by taxi.

10 Empress State Building
Lillie Rd SW6. A triangular tower of 26 cream and turquoise storeys, visible from most points of this map. It was built in 1962 by Stone, Toms & Partners and contains some of the offices of the Ministry of Defence.

11 North End Road Market
SW6. The southern end of the road is lined with stalls selling food, cheap clothes, china, lampshades and plants. A market for 'real' people, not dealers. *Closed Sun & Thurs afternoon.*

12 T. Crowther
282 North End Rd SW6. 01-385 1375. Here are Georgian fireplaces, chimney pieces and wall panelling, on sale in a large Georgian house. Also beautiful furniture and ornate garden figures and ornaments in lead, stone, bronze and marble. *Closed Sat & Sun.*

13 Second-Hand City
Chesson Rd SW6. 01-385 7711. An ex-Methodist church stacked from crypt to crown with a vast mixture of good and awful furniture for every room in the house. *Closed Sun.*

14 Company D'Arts
1a Fane St W14. 01-385 6302. Unusual small firm of picture framers and fine art restorers, sympathetic to any job, however small or odd. Also sells prints, and the works of local artists. *Closed Sun.*

15 Normand Park
SW6. A relatively modern park, formed on a Second World War bombsite and taking its name from Normand House, which sheltered the nuns of St Catherine's Convent until enemy action demolished it. On summer afternoons, the soothing game of bowls is played on the green to the east side.

16 St Thomas of Canterbury
Rylston Rd SW6. For those interested in church architecture it is worth the walk off the map down Rylston Road, which runs off Lillie Road to the south, opposite the park. The Roman Catholic church at the end is one of London's few complete churches by Pugin (best known for his work on the Houses of Parliament). Joseph Hansom, who designed the 'Patent Safety Cab', is buried here.

17 Gregory Bottley
8–12 Rickett St SW6. 01-381 5522. One of the world's largest collections of fossils, minerals, and meteorites, together with essential geology equipment and some rough, uncut stones and jewels at reasonable prices. *Closed Sat & Sun.*

Royal Tournament, Earl's Court

Off the Map
Each map must stop somewhere but there is no need to be limited by its confines if exciting things lie just outside. Leave this one by Talgarth Road, going west, or travel one stop on the underground from Baron's Court to Hammersmith. Here you'll find:

18 Lyric Theatre, Hammersmith
King St W6. 01-741 2311. A large modern building with a full-sized theatre on the second and third floors and a small studio theatre on the first floor, where the huge foyer incorporates a bar and a wholesome snack area.

19 Riverside Studios
Crisp Rd W6. 01-748 3354. The old BBC studios have been converted into what Irving Wardle in *The Times* called 'a powerhouse of the arts'. Plays, music, films, children's events, regular art exhibitions, a bookshop and a licensed restaurant and café.

20 Odeon, Hammersmith
Queen Caroline St W6. 01-748 4081. A cinema which still occasionally shows films but is best-known for its wildly popular live rock shows. See the music press for details.

21 Hammersmith Palais
242 Shepherd's Bush Rd W6. 01-748 2812. Where Shepherd's Bush Rd reaches Hammersmith Broadway stands the birthplace of the 'Palais Glide'. Its heyday was the 30s, when top bands played beside the

large and glossy floor. Sequinned dresses are still seen, though nowadays groups and discos alternate with the big bands. *Closed Mon & Tue. Charge.*

EATING AND DRINKING

A **Strikes** *Restaurant*
100 North End Rd W14. 01-385 8544. One of a chain with good hamburgers, salads and cheesecake-type puds. Commemorates the strikes of the 30s – some branches have large photos of the bread queues on the walls. Purple paint, lush plants, and black glossy chairs and button-backed seats, as if the furniture had been made out of half-chewed Pontefract cakes. £.

Three Kings Pub

B **Three Kings** *Pub*
171 North End Rd W14. 01-603 6071. This was once the Nashville Rooms, known for its visiting bands and hard-wearing dance floor; now a new management has turned it into a temple of real ale, with 28 handpumps to serve it. Freshly-cooked food, but not on Sun evening. £.

C **Philbeach** *Hotel*
30 Philbeach Gdns SW5. 01-373 4544. Try the *Garden Restaurant* with its view of calming greenery and English and French menu. The friendly management is from Thailand. ££.

D **Tiger Lee Chinese Seafood** *Restaurant*
251 Old Brompton Rd SW5. 01-370 2323. A good fish restaurant with live fish in tanks on show. Try the shark's fin soup, fish stuffed with seafood, or delicately flavoured lobster. *Closed at lunchtime.* £££.

E **L'Artiste Affamé** *Restaurant*
243 Old Brompton Rd SW5. 01-373 1659. Good, simple, provincial French food in plain surroundings with appealing antiques scattered about – the sweet trolley is an old wine press and one table is inside half a carousel. The speciality is crespaline – a crêpe with spinach, nuts and cheese inside. The home-made mousse is good, too. *Closed Sat lunch & all Sun.* ££.

F **Toddies African** *Restaurant*
241 Old Brompton Rd SW5. 01-373 8217. An all night place which serves English and African food from 18.30 through to 07.00, and stays open for lunch on Sun. Menu includes lots of fish dishes as well as groundnut stew with cassava bread. ££.

G **Adams Barbecue** *Restaurant*
239 Old Brompton Rd SW5. 01-373 3502. Bright red corner premises, specialising in barbecued meats, but there's also a chunky chilli con carne and good American ice cream. Wine Bar Lounge (literally a lounge, with sofas) on the first floor, serves the same food as below. *Closed lunchtime, except Sun.* ££.

H **Coleherne** *Pub*
261 Old Brompton Rd SW5. 01-373 5881. A place for drinkers who don't bother with the irrelevancy of food. Faintly shabby, crowded, and very much a male gay stronghold. Women are rare but there's no hostility towards them.

J **Tournament** *Pub*
344 Old Brompton Rd SW5. 01-370 2449. Modern pub next to the Exhibition, decked out in mock-Tudor and called after the ever-popular Royal Tournament. The public bar has pool, darts and video juke box. The saloon is more sedate, with just a fruit machine to disturb the peace. Hot and cold food – always. £.

K **Valencia Spanish** *Restaurant*
Lillie Rd SW6. 01-385 0039. To one side of the wide tarmac'd forecourt of London Transport's Lillie Bridge Depot is a most unexpected sight – a single storey bright little restaurant that looks as though it's dropped out of a clear blue sky. Spanish food and Flamenco music are the attractions. *Closed lunchtimes & Sun.* ££.

L **Prince of Wales** *Pub*
Lillie Rd SW6. 01-385 7441. Two bars offering hot home-cooked food every day. On Sat and Sun evening a country and western soloist entertains.

M **Fulham Volunteer** *Pub*
North End Rd SW6. 01-385 3847. Nice, big and ordinary, handy for the market and with a few snacks on the go. £.

N **Netta's** *Restaurant and Café*
95–97 Lillie Rd SW6. 01-385 6706. Basic working men's café serving egg and chips and teas all day, with meat and two veg at lunchtime. Convenient for the market. £.

O **Bitter Lemons** *Restaurant*
Lillie Rd SW6. 01-381 1069. Friendly green and yellow place serving reliable Greek food at low prices. Very crowded at weekends. *Closed Sun lunch.* £.

P **Normand Arms** *Pub*
197 Lillie Rd SW6. 01-385 8639. Modern family pub, making a vague pretence at being a Norman castle on the outside. Pianist at weekends and food during the week. £.

Q **Clem Attlee** *Pub*
Rylston Rd SW6. 01-385 6833. Normand Park Estate is rather politically minded, each high block named after a Labour party politician. The theme is carried on in this smart house, with framed cartoons of Attlee covering the walls. No food, but handpumped real ale.

Morning Coffee and Afternoon Tea
Netta's Restaurant and Café; 95–97 Lillie Rd SW6. 01-385 6706. A cup of either any time – no formal tea.
West Centre Hotel; 47 Lillie Rd SW6. 01-385 1255. Tea, coffee or snacks. No set tea.

Map 10 EARL'S COURT AND SOUTH KENSINGTON

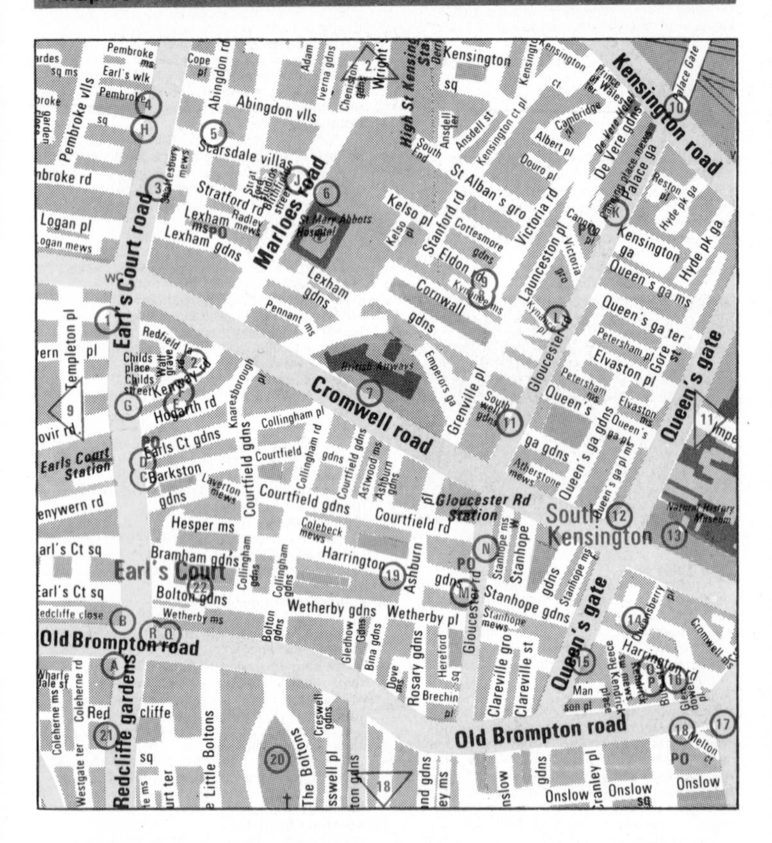

An area of strong contrasts. It is possible to be deafened by the relentless traffic along the wide Cromwell and Old Brompton roads, and seconds later to stand in serene peace in an early 19thC square with formal yet luxuriant vegetation to soothe the eye and high, heavy terraced buildings to cut down the sound of cars and trucks. Or to enjoy the bustle around the shops, restaurants and pubs of Gloucester Road and moments later walk along the cobbles of Kynance Mews and take the secretive steps up to Victoria Road with its detached Victorian villas and 18thC cottages.

The western boundary of Earl's Court Road has been called Kangaroo Valley because of the numbers of Australians and New Zealanders who live near or on it, and certainly the whole Earl's Court area is by tradition bed-sitter land, where laundrettes and cheap take-away restaurants provide substitutes for home comforts. It is also extremely cosmopolitan, with top-quality foreign restaurants interspersed with the instant curry and chips establishments.

The architecture is mostly late Victorian, with some genuinely 'good' addresses to the north east and south, especially around The Boltons and Queen's Gate, which has some lovely Norman Shaw houses. Of the major roads which strike across it, Earl's Court and Gloucester are good for pubs and restaurants, Cromwell has the large hotels, and this stretch of Old Brompton is in a residential mood, with most of its restaurants and antique shops towards the edges of the map. Immediately east of Queen's Gate lies the whole South Kensington Museum complex soaring into Victorian Gothic, see Map 11.

PLACES OF INTEREST

1 **Antique and Modern Furniture**
160 Earl's Ct Rd SW5. 01-373 2935. Elegant displays of small furniture, more antique than modern, with some fine china. Ring the bell to get in. *Closed Thur afternoon & Sun.*

2 **Wallgrave Rd**
W8. The centre of a small complex of neat, prettily-painted two-storey terraced houses in narrow leafy roads, a pocket-sized haven from the hectic Earl's Court Road.

3 **St Philip's Church**
Earl's Ct Rd SW5. A very welcoming church with a freshly-painted pillared interior, a lovely beamed ceiling and some 16thC Flemish stained glass in the adjoining Parish Room. Often has public recitals of choral or organ music.

4 **Rassells**
80 Earl's Ct Rd W8. 01-937 0481. A particularly luxuriant garden shop with all sorts of intriguing terracotta tubs, troughs and hanging bowls as well as plants, shrubs and a small rear garden, its glasshouse shaded by fruit trees. *Closed Sun.*

5 **Aquinas Lock**
87 Abingdon Rd W8. 01-937 4118. An unexpected find in a residential road, its large stock of pewter gleaming discreetly on its shelves. Here are mugs, platters, candle sticks, coffee sets and unusual jewellery, both 18thC and modern.

6 **St Mary Abbots Hospital**
Marloes Rd W8. 01-937 8181. Typical mid-19thC institutional architecture, in Jacobean-cum-Gothic style, softened by plentiful trees. Built as a workhouse and infirmary, it now cares principally for geriatric and psychiatric patients.

7 **British Airways Building**
SW7. For so long a travellers landmark, the former West London Air Terminal, with its spreading car park, is now used for British Airways offices, shops and an extensive Sainsbury's supermarket. British Airways fly the transit flag from the Piccadilly line these days, with its direct underground link with the airport.

8 **Kynance Mews**
SW7. One of the prettiest of the several mid-19thC mews in the area, with wisteria draped walls and brightly blooming window boxes. Towards the western end narrow steps lead up through foliage to Victoria Road and Christ Church, in its neat garden.

Kynance Mews

9 **Christ Church**
Victoria Rd W8. Plain Gothic church built in 1851 by Benjamin Ferrey, close friend of A. W. Pugin and author of *Recollections . . .*, which discusses the work and personality of the famous initiator of the Victorian Gothic revival.

Christ Church

10 **Palace Gate**
W8. The gate itself leads, by way of The Broad Walk, into the formal and elegant Kensington Gardens, with Kensington Palace at its western boundary. Immediately to the right the Flower Walk has become an established bird sanctuary with nuthatches, woodpeckers and tree creepers among its residents.

11 **St Stephen's Church**
Gloucester Rd SW7. Beautifully proportioned church of the 1860s by Peacock, with a glowing interior and lavish golden reredos by Bodley and Garner. Don't miss the strikingly canopied font or the touching memorial to T. S. Eliot in the south transept.

St Stephen's Church

12 **Baden-Powell House**
Queen's Gate SW7. 01-584 7030. The H.Q. of the Scout movement, with a permanent exhibition on its founding and history and on the life of Baden-Powell, the founder himself. *Free.*

13 **Natural History Museum**
Cromwell Rd SW7. 01-589 5323. This cathedral like twin-towered building, by Alfred Waterhouse in 1873–80, houses the national collections of zoology, entomology,

mineralogy, palaeontology and botany. Permanently awash with children come to see the dinosaurs, whales, crystals, meteorites, dazzling butterflies and exhibition on the biology of man. Don't miss the lovely Romanesque interior itself, best viewed from the second floor balcony. *Closed Sun morn. Free.* See Map 11 for South Ken Museums.

14 College of Psychic Studies
16 Queensberry Pl SW7. 01-589 3292. Behind a simple Victorian stuccoed frontage the 100-year-old college organises classes and workshops on every aspect of the psychic scene. Public lectures on Tue evening cover UFOs, reincarnation, biofeedback, healing, mediumship and astrology. You're welcome to call – they're probably expecting you. *Charge.*

15 St Augustine's Church
Queen's Gate SW7. One of the most impressive of William Butterfield's surviving London churches, in high Victorian Gothic, with pointed towers and towering bellcote, 1865–71. The colourful interior, painted white in the 20s, has now been restored. The baroque gold reredos and the Stations of the Cross were added by Martin Travers after the 20s whitewashing.

16 Bute Street
SW7. A neat little 'gourmet's row' of small-scale shops which include two patisseries with mouth-watering window displays, two excellent delicatessens, a well-stocked wet fish shop, two butchers and a high-quality greengrocer's.

17 Mitsukiku
15 Old Brompton Rd SW7. 01-589 1725. Japanese paper lampshades, silky embroidered kimonos, foods, dishes, novelties – and genuine saki together with the tiny carafes and bowls from which it is properly imbibed.

18 Christies of South Kensington
85 Old Brompton Rd SW7. 01-581 2231. The famous auctioneers who hold between 15 and 20 sales each week, covering all possible areas of antique and antiquarian objects, as well as jewellery, wines and furs. More plebeian and approachable than its posh St James's ancestor. Viewing daily. *Closed Sat.*

19 Society of Genealogists
37 Harrington Gdns SW7. 01-373 7054. If consumed with a need to unearth your ancestry, the society will organise the quest for a fee. Also for a fee you may use the library with its almost overwhelmingly large collection of copies of parish registers. *Closed Sun & Mon.*

20 St Mary the Boltons
The Boltons SW10. Pretty church in the tree-shaded centre of the fashionable Boltons. Originally by Godwin in 1850, its unusual angel-encircled spire was added later, and the whole much-restored after bomb damage. Excellent choir and active Music Society, responsible for public recitals.

21 St Luke's Church
Redcliffe Sq SW5. A classic Victorian church and one of the best surviving examples of the work of Godwin, principal architect of the aesthetic movement. Built in 1874, to grand proportions, and encircled by plane trees whose marbled bark blends beautifully with its mellowed stone.

The Boltons

22 Bramham Gardens
SW5. Part of the flavour of the area comes from its squares of imposing Victorian mansion blocks, each surrounding a private central garden. This is one of the most mysterious and appealing of these exclusive mini-parks, secretively hedged, with high trees and glimpses through the gates of exotic shrubs and perfect turf.

EATING AND DRINKING

A Adams Barbecue *Restaurant*
239 Old Brompton Rd SW5. 01-373 3502. Bright red corner premises, specialising in barbecued meats, but there's also a chunky chilli con carne and good American ice cream. Wine Bar Lounge (literally a lounge, with sofas) serves the same food. *Closed lunchtime, except Sun.* £.

B The Boltons *Pub*
216 Old Brompton Rd SW5. 01-373 8244. One of the more stately of London's gay pubs with three large bars, an open fire and walls lined with stags and lions heads and old photographs. Daily snacks. £.

C Dragon Palace *Restaurant*
Earl's Ct Rd SW5. 01-370 1461. Ornate little room with gold lights and a dragon frieze wherein to eat most reasonably. For something unusual try eel ball and garlic, stewed oysters with ginger and spring onion or stewed squid with chilli. £.

D Courtfield *Pub*
187 Earl's Ct Rd SW5. 01-370 2626. Very smart and restrained with four real ales, one keg bitter and full meals cooked to order by an unseen chef. £.

E Crystal Palace *Restaurant*
10 Hogarth Pl SW5. 01-373 0754. Simple black and white decor, attentive service and exceptional Pekingese and Szechuan dishes; sesame prawns with pigeon eggs; spicy Bang Bang Chicken; Szechuan duck; sweet red bean pancakes. Reliable 'leave-it-to-us' Feast. ££.

F La Primula *Restaurant*
12 Kenway Rd SW5. 01-370 3898. Classy and Italian with a delectable Chef's Special –

Scampi al Cantoccio – which is scampi, tomatoes, pimentoes, smoked salmon and brandy cooked in a paper bag. Cakes, pies, and profiteroles from the trolley, or go to town on a creamy zabaglione. ££.

G Sri Lanka *Restaurant*
19 Child's St SW5. 01-373 4116. Expertly prepared Sri Lankan, Malaysian and Indian dishes in a pretty setting (though it's a shame about the wallpaper). Tandoori chicken, murgh massalam or pittu fish biryani, with delicately flavoured curd honey for afters. ££.

H Hansom Cab *Pub*
84 Earl's Ct Rd W8. 01-937 5364. The genuine Hansom is suspended from the ceiling in the Cab Bar and the theme is carried on throughout with carriage lights, red plush seating and old pictures of cabs in action. Lunchtime food. £.

Typical architecture in Gledhow Gardens

J Sailing Junk *Restaurant*
59 Marloes Rd W8. 01-937 2589. If in the mood for a romantic Chinese feast, float through the 10-course Dragon Festival Dinner in an old sailing junk, while candles flicker to the soft Mandarin music. ££.

K Ma Barker *Café*
Gloucester Rd SW7. A jaunty mix of scarlet and white furniture, dim lights, huge mirrors and fuzzy photographs of old film stars. Call in for breakfast, coffee or a snack enlivened by a glass of wine. £.

L Scandies *Wine Bar*
4 Kynance Pl SW7. 01-589 3659. Intimate and very friendly with live classical guitar music at weekends, good house wine and the usual food with interesting additions – Greek chicken pie, for example. Often full but there's more room downstairs. £.

M Texas Lone Star *Restaurant*
Gloucester Rd SW7. 01-370 5625. Spicy Texan and Mexican food – tacos, nachos, burgers, chilli, barbecued chicken. Very jolly with self-conscious 'frontier decor' of rough wood and heaps of bristly straw. £.

N Stanhope *Pub*
97 Gloucester Rd SW7. 01-373 4192. Large and smart with morning coffee as well as the usual alcoholic beverages. Different groups play jazz nightly in the upstairs bar – trad, rock jazz or blues. Good snacks. £.

O Mardi Gras *Restaurant*
29 Harrington Rd SW7. 01-584 0600. Informal continental café with parasoled tables outside in summer and a mixed menu – pasta, kebabs, salads, liver and bacon, veal, or English breakfast. *Closed Sun.* £.

P Bangkok *Restaurant*
9 Bute St SW7. 01-584 8529. A simple setting for delicately presented and spicy Thai food. Start with sate, spiced beef with peanut sauce and cucumber salad. Later try beef with oyster sauce or chicken with ginger and mushroom. *Closed Sun.* £.

British Airways building

Q Malaysian Kitchen *Restaurant*
234 Old Brompton Rd SW5. 01-370 2421. Simple but sophisticated with authentic South East Asian cooking – wan tun soup, five spices chicken, Indonesian chilli king prawns. Open with a Malaysian Paradise cocktail; end with Chin Chow – grass jelly. *Closed lunch & Sun.* ££.

R Company Piano Bar and *Restaurant*
242 Old Brompton Rd SW5. 01-373 3730. Aims to be chic but not expensive. To this end there is lavish decor, with mirrors and baby grand, a pianist nightly and a cabaret on Sun, yet the menu (changed weekly) is brief – six well-prepared English dishes with French accents. *Closed lunch.* ££.

Morning Coffee and Afternoon Tea

Kardomah; 81 Gloucester Rd SW7. 01-373 6900. Also snacks and light lunches.
Kensington Close Hotel; Wrights La W8. 01-937 8170. Tea, coffee and snacks in The Chandelier Coffee Shop.
London International Hotel; Cromwell Rd SW5. 01-370 4200. Try the Aviary Coffee House.
London Penta Hotel; Cromwell Rd SW7. 01-370 5757. Towering and ultra modern with its own Coffee Shop and Pub.
De Vere Hotel; De Vere Gdns W8. 01-584 0051. Order coffee or set tea in the Victorian lounge.
Kensington Palace Hotel; De Vere Gdns W8. 01-937 8121. Good coffee; cream, English or farmhouse tea.
Norfolk Hotel; Harrington Rd SW7. 01-589 8191. Go to The Big Apple for coffee, eggs benedict, waffles, strudels. A cup of tea any time, no set afternoon tea as such.

Map 11 SOUTH KENSINGTON

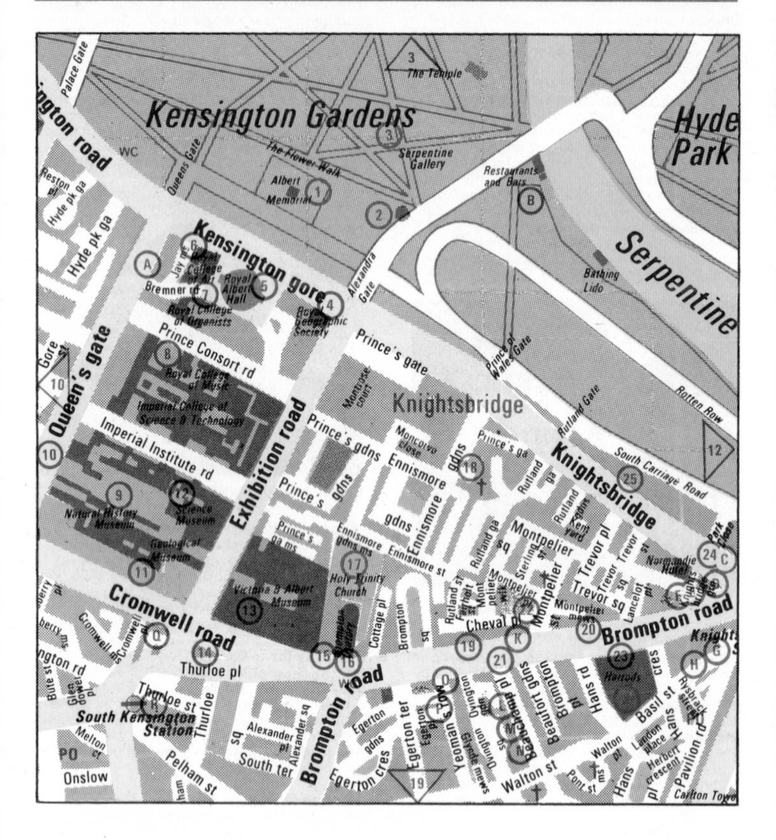

South Kensington has the greatest concentration of museums, colleges and academic institutes in London. The 88-acre site on which they stand was bought with the profits of the 1851 'Great Exhibition'. The complex was the brain-child of Prince Albert. It began to go up in his life-time, under his patronage, and continued after his death. The nearby Albert Memorial is specifically dedicated to him but in a sense the whole area is a memorial to his concern for education and the arts, and his name recurs all around it – Prince Consort Road, the Albert Hall, the Victoria and Albert Museum.

Brompton Road is mainly for shoppers with well-stocked wallets. It has high quality antique shops, galleries, clothes shops and, of course, the monumental Harrods, over-flowing with luxuries and confidently promising to supply almost anything.

The names of the early 19thC Montpelier Street, Square, Walk and Place come from a famous French health resort because this part of London was held to have very good air. By contrast, Knightsbridge Green was once a plague pit, shunned for many years for fear of lingering infection.

To the north of the map are several entrances to Kensington Gardens and Hyde Park, containing the Serpentine and The Long Water, The Flower Walk and Rotten Row – originally Route en Roi, the King's road to Kensington Palace. These acres of grass, trees and water attract walkers, workers in their lunch hours, tourists, children, dogs – a whole cross-section of London life looking for fresh air and relaxation.

PLACES OF INTEREST

1 **Albert Memorial**
Kensington Gdns SW7. A lavish Gothic monument built by Sir George Gilbert Scott in 1863–72. The bronze of the Prince, by Joseph Durham, sits under a canopy studying the catalogue to the Great Exhibition. Below him the steps and podium seethe with the works of various sculptors, which represent the continents, the arts and industry. The ultimate mid-Victorian memorial, though somewhat vulgar for modern taste.

2 **Hyde Park and Kensington Gardens**
SW7. To the right of the Alexandra Gate lies Hyde Park, once part of a forest where Henry VIII hunted wild boar, and a royal park since 1536. To the left lie Kensington Gardens, formal and elegant additions to the park, with Kensington Palace at the western end. *Gates close at dusk.*

3 **Serpentine Gallery**
Kensington Gdns SW7. 01-402 6075. The old Gardens Tea House, looking like a discreet Victorian lodge, has been taken over by the Arts Council as an attractive setting for changing exhibitions of contemporary prints, sculpture, paintings and drawings. *Closed 19.00 in summer, dusk in winter.*

4 **Royal Geographical Society**
1 Kensington Gore SW7. 01-589 5166. The variegated brick building, suitably adorned with statues of Shackleton and Livingstone, is by Norman Shaw. The fine map room is open to the public but the rest, including relics from great explorations, is for fellows and invited guests only. *Free. Closed Sat afternoon & Sun.*

5 **Royal Albert Hall**
Kensington Gore SW7. 01-589 8212. This superbly constructed vast red brick cylinder with its low iron and glass dome was designed in 1871 by Captain Fowkes, a Royal Engineer. It can accommodate 8000 for orchestral, choral and pop concerts, public meetings and the famous 'Proms'.

6 **Royal College of Art**
Kensington Gore SW7. 01-584 5020. Designed by Cadbury-Brown in the 1960s this dark brick and concrete building, with its distinctive glass penthouse studios, looks strikingly plain and modern in its Victorian-Gothic setting. Has occasional exhibitions of the work of students.

7 **Royal College of Organists**
Kensington Gore SW7. 01-589 1765. As decorative as an outsize jewel box, its façade covered in sgraffito and with a frieze of classical figures. Holds occasional recitals, see board outside for details.

8 **Royal College of Music**
Prince Consort Rd SW7. 01-589 3643. A wide range of recitals is laid on here – soloists, symphonies, full operas, all by students. The Donaldson Museum, with its collection of old musical instruments, including Handel's spinet, is open on Mon and Wed in term-time by appointment. *Free.*

9 **Natural History Museum**
Cromwell Rd SW7. 01-589 5323. This cathedral-like twin-towered building, in pale

Natural History Museum

terracotta and slate blue, with its realistic animal decorations, was built by Alfred Waterhouse in 1873–80. It houses the national collections of zoology, entomology, mineralogy, palaeontology and botany. The entrance hall is permanently awash with children, come to see the dinosaurs, whales, crystals, meteorites, dazzling butterflies and the exhibition on the biology of man. Don't miss the lovely Romanesque interior, best viewed from the second floor balcony. *Closed Sun morn. Free.*

10 **Baden-Powell House**
Queens Gate SW7. 01-584 7030. The HQ of the Scout movement, containing a permanent exhibition on its founding and on the life of B-P himself. *Free.*

11 **Geological Museum**
Exhibition Rd SW7. 01-589 3444. A 1930s building, with a classical look, houses the most ancient and fundamental exhibition of them all – 'Story of the Earth' which describes the origin of the universe itself. Riveting displays of fossils, a piece of moon rock, and also real gold, diamonds and gemstones, both in crude and in glittering form. *Closed Sun morn. Free.*

12 **Science Museum**
Exhibition Rd SW7. 01-589 3456. Serious and institutional-looking from outside – but inside it tells the story of science and its application to industry in vividly exciting terms. A raised walkway takes you up among the superb collection of early aeroplanes; also weighty steam engines, aged cars, a life-size reconstruction of a moon-landing and a genuine Apollo space capsule. *Closed Sun morn. Free.*

13 **Victoria and Albert Museum**
Cromwell Rd SW7. 01-589 6371. One of the most extravagant pieces of Victorian architecture in London, and a wonderfully rich museum of decorative art. Vast collections from all categories, countries and ages are displayed in more than 10 acres of museum, set around a peaceful garden presided over by a serene Buddha. There are extensive and choice collections of paintings, sculpture, graphics and typography, armour and weapons, carpets, ceramics, clocks, costume, fabrics, furniture, jewellery, metalwork, musical instruments, prints and drawings. Regular free lectures. *Closed Sun morn. & Fri. Free.*

Victoria and Albert Museum

14 Ismaili Centre
1–7 Cromwell Gdns SW7. At present still under construction but due to open in 1983 as the principal Islamic cultural and religious centre in Britain.

15 Cardinal Newman's Statue
Brompton Rd SW7. The cardinal was responsible, with Frederick William Faber, for introducing the Oratorians to Britain and was their first superior over here. His marble statue, by Bodley and Garner, 1896, stands outside the house which adjoins the Oratory and is the home of its priests.

16 Brompton Oratory
Brompton Rd SW7. Actually 'the Church of the London Oratory'. An Italianate Roman Catholic church by Herbert Cribble, 1878. The Oratorians are a community of priests who follow the teachings of the Florentine St Philip Neri. The Baroque interior is richly furnished with altars and statues from Italy.

17 Holy Trinity
Brompton Rd SW7. Behind the Oratory stands this Victorian Gothic parish church, consecrated in 1829. The choir, of mainly professional singers, gives concerts in and around London. There are sometimes exhibitions in the crypt.

18 Russian Orthodox Church
Ennismore Gardens SW7. The Patriarchal Church of the Dormition and All Saints was designed in the 1840s by Vulliamy in Early Christian style. The rich interior includes sgraffito work by Heywood Sumner, one of the leaders of the Arts and Crafts movement.

19 Crane Kalman Gallery
178 Brompton Rd SW3. 01-584 7566. Specialises in good 20thC British and European paintings.

20 Television Gallery
70 Brompton Rd SW3. 01-584 7011. Guided tour lasting 1½ hours gives an insight into the transmission of tv and radio programmes and a look at past and present technology. *By appointment. Min age 16. Free.*

21 Beauchamp Place
SW3. After the pomp and circumstance of the major museums, try a walk down this Regency street. It is crammed with attractive restaurants and bright little shops with small-scale delectable merchandise – clothes, jewellery, perfumes, old maps and prints, antique silver and high quality reject china.

22 W. & F. C. Bonham & Sons
Montpelier Galleries, Montpelier St SW7. 01-584 9161. Regular auctions of the necessities for elegant living – paintings, carpets, porcelain, furniture and wine.

23 Harrods
Knightsbridge SW1. 01-730 1234. World famous department store which prides itself on selling virtually everything. Especially worth a visit are the marble food halls, (where displays of fish have become an art form), the pets department and the gemstone section.

24 Pan
Bowater House SW1. Beneath Bowater House and apparently racing pell-mell towards Hyde Park, this bronze group of man, woman, child, dog and primitive god was Epstein's last work, finished in 1959.

25 Knightsbridge Barracks
Kensington Rd SW7. Austere brick quarters for the Household Cavalry. Designed by Sir Basil Spence and built in 1970.

EATING AND DRINKING

A Gore Hotel *Coffee House*
189 Queen's Gate SW7. 01-584 6601. Lavishly decorated with potted plants, an oasis among the grand stone frontages. Open to non-residents for morning coffee, lunchtime snacks and teas. £.

B Serpentine Complex *Restaurants*
Hyde Park W2. 01-723 8784. An elaborate modern structure by the water, made up of:
The Serpentine Restaurant, a carvery with a back-up à la carte menu. ££.
The Pergola Restaurant with its à la carte lunch menu. *Closed evenings and all winter.* £.
The Cocktail Bar open all year round during licensing hours.
The Plant Bar for summer drinking only and *The Serpentine Buffet,* a good cafeteria. *Closed 16.00 in winter, 18.00 in summer.* £.

C Sloane's *Café*
116 Knightsbridge SW1. 01-589 6873. Sandwiches, hamburgers, rich puddings or afternoon tea with cake. Cocktails are a speciality. Excellent club sandwiches to carry out to the park. £.

D Mr Chow *Restaurant*
151 Knightsbridge SW1. 01-589 7347. The modern decor, contemporary paintings, friendly service, Peking duck and sole in white wine are only part of the attraction – this is still one of those places where the smart set go to see and be seen. ££.

E Panzer *Delicatessen*
12 Knightsbridge Green SW1. 01-589 5613. Wondrous sandwiches, pitta bread split and stuffed with interesting fillings, pastries, apples, good coffee – all you need for a picnic in the park. *Closed evenings & Sun.* £.

F Tattersall's *Tavern*
Knightsbridge Green SW1. 01-584 7122. Built on the former site of Tattersall's offices, the racing world is evoked by the odd bridle and a replica of the Tattersall Yard Fountain. In the

cellar, *Tatters Wine Bar* offers 'never-ending steaks', daily specials and the usual choice of cold food. £.

G **Stockpot** *Restaurant*
6 Basil St SW3. 01-589 8627. Cheerful and always crowded. The international peasant food is reasonably priced. *Closed Sun.* £.

H **Upstairs and Downstairs** *Buffet & Wine Bar*
Basil St Hotel, 8 Basil St SW3. 01-730 3411. *Upstairs* is orange and white and runs a hot and cold buffet at lunchtime while *Downstairs* is a slick red and black wine bar with chiefly Mediterranean food on offer, in the evenings also. *Both closed Sun.* £.

J **Harrods** *Buffets and Restaurants*
Knightsbridge SW1. 01-730 1234. Here are four self-service buffets – *Leisure Circle* on the ground floor, *Dress Circle* on the 1st and *Upper Circle* and *Way In Circle* on the 4th. £. The ground floor also has the *Health Juice Bar* (between the Food Halls and Fruit and Flowers) and *The Green Man*, the first 'in-store' pub (near the Man's Shop). £. The 4th also has the *New Terrace Cocktail Bar*, the *Trafalgar Bar* and two restaurants: *The Georgian*, a carvery which also serves breakfast and afternoon tea, £££, and *The Knightsbridge* which has an à la carte menu, £££. *All closed 17.30 and Sun.*

Albert Memorial

K **Loose Box** *Wine Bar*
7 Cheval Pl SW7. 01-584 9280. You can get in from Brompton Rd but this is the pretty way, via the aptly named mews. Ample buffet and 90 wines. The upstairs restaurant serves home-cooked English food. *Closed Sun.* £.

L **Borshtch N' Tears** *Restaurant*
45 Beauchamp Pl SW3. 01-589 5003. Idiosyncratic Russian restaurant, loud with music, loved by the young and lively to the point, sometimes, of impromptu table-top dancing. *Closed lunchtime.* ££.

M **Grove** *Tavern*
43 Beauchamp Pl SW3. 01-589 5897. A small Victorian gas-lit tavern with a lunch-time wine bar above. £.

N **Bill Bentley's** *Wine Bar*
31 Beauchamp Pl SW3. 01-589 5080. Dark, cosy and relaxing, serving delicious snacks, with a good fish restaurant above and a pleasant garden out at the back. *Closed Sun.* £.

Royal Albert Hall

O **Bunch of Grapes** *Pub*
207 Brompton Rd SW3. 01-589 4944. Victorian, with gleaming wood and original snobscreens, real ale and home-cooked lunches (not Sun). £.

P **Luba's** *Bistro*
6 Yeoman's Row SW3. 01-589 2950. Spartan and basic but serving good, cheap Russian food. Bring your own wine, they don't charge corkage. *Closed Sun.* £.

Q **Incognito** *Restaurant*
38 Thurloe Pl SW7. 01-589 3663. Pretty little green and white place open daily from 12.00 to 24.00. Straightforward food, good coffee, very friendly. £.

R **Daquise** *Restaurant*
20 Thurloe St SW7. 01-589 6117. The haunt of Polish emigrés. You can eat stuffed cabbage or sausages very cheaply. Fine pastries. £.

Morning Coffee and Afternoon Tea

Gore Hotel; 189 Queen's Gate SW7. 01-584 6601. Coffee House.
The Serpentine Buffet; Hyde Park W2.
Sloane's Café; 116 Knightsbridge SW1. 01-589 6873. For tea only.
Basil Street Hotel; Basil St SW3. 01-581 3311. Coffee and teas in the first floor lounge.
Harrods; Knightsbridge SW1. 01-730 1234. Coffee and tea in all the buffets and full afternoon tea in The Georgian, 4th floor.
Grove Tavern; 43 Beauchamp Pl SW3. 01-589 5897. Morning coffee from 11.00.
Luba's Bistro; 6 Yeoman's Row SW3. 01-589 2950. Tea and cakes.
Daquise; 20 Thurloe Pl SW7. 01-589 6117. Coffee and tea with exceptional pastries.
Natural History Museum; Cromwell Rd SW7. Slightly claustrophobic tea bar.
Science Museum; Exhibition Rd SW7. Snack bar beyond the aeroplanes.
Victoria and Albert Museum; Cromwell Rd SW7. Large cafeteria (straight through, right at the stained glass and left at St George).

Map 12 HYDE PARK AND PARK LANE

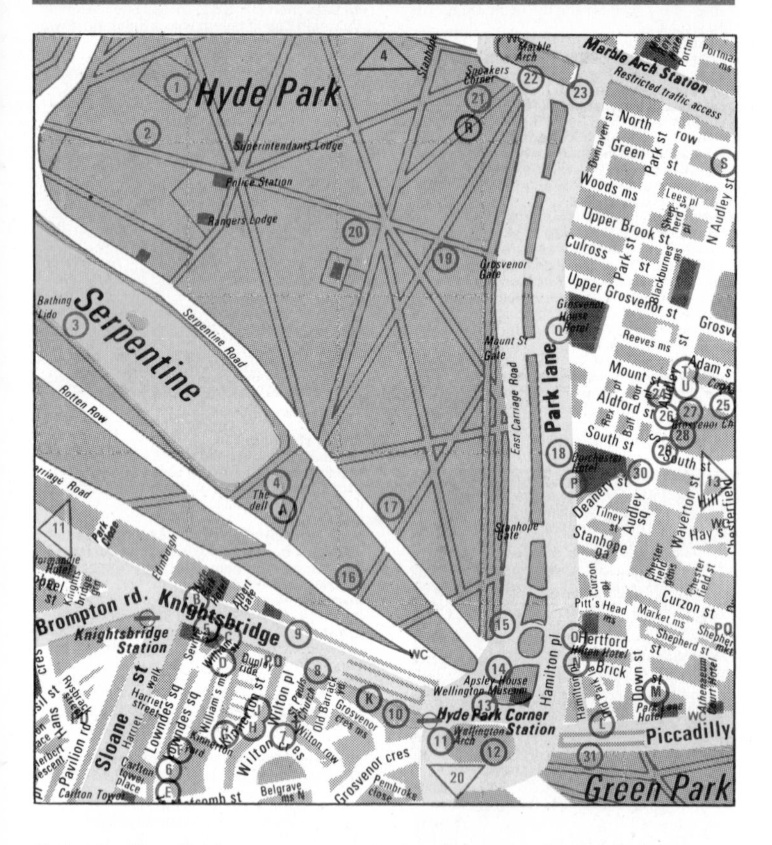

The broad and busy Park Lane cuts a great swathe through the map, its length defined by those two hefty landmarks, Marble Arch to the north and the Wellington Arch to the south. Along its eastern side stand some of London's principal luxury hotels, in buildings originally constructed as private mansions or even small palaces. Smart charity balls, or the slightly less smart annual dinners of City firms, are conducted in their opulent restaurants and lavishly decorated ballrooms, and the early evening frequently brings a stately influx of sleek cars from which the dinner jackets and long gowns glide serenely forth.

To the west are the wide green expanses of Hyde Park, appropriated by Henry VIII from the Abbot of Westminster and used exclusively as a royal hunting ground until it was opened to the public during the reign of James I. It went through a disreputable phase when footpads lurked at night and gentlemen fought duels at dawn, but it has also seen important celebrations and exhibitions. The most famous of these was The Great Exhibition of 1851, housed in Joseph Paxton's magnificent Crystal Palace which stood between Knightsbridge and Rotten Row, before its removal to south London and subsequent tragic destruction by fire.

To the south, Wilton Crescent marks the beginning of Belgravia with its elegant squares, charming mews and chic little galleries along Motcomb Street; and Sloane Street and Knightsbridge mark the beginnings of Knightsbridge itself, not only one of London's smarter addresses but one of her smartest shopping areas, too.

PLACES OF INTEREST

1 **Hyde Park**
W2. Despite the cultivated flowers and avenues of stately trees this is the most informal of the royal parks. Sheep grazed here as late as 1937. It has a wild bird sanctuary, varied sporting facilities, and is the venue for some impressive public spectacles – including the Household Cavalry Review in spring and the start of the London to Brighton Veteran Car Rally in autumn.

2 **Rima**
Hyde Pk W2. Jacob Epstein carved Rima, the Spirit of Nature, onto this primitive-looking stone slab in 1925 as a memorial to the naturalist and writer W. H. Hudson. The area behind her is a wild bird sanctuary, near the nurseries which grow plants for the central royal parks.

3 **Serpentine**
Hyde Pk W2. A fine artificial lake, created, together with The Long Water to the west, by damming the old Westbourne River. There is swimming from its south bank Lido, boats to hire from the north bank, modern restaurants at either end, fishing, and promenades and deckchairs all around.

4 **Dell**
Hyde Pk W2. A lushly green dip in the ground watered by the Westbourne. Dominated by a sombre standing stone brought from Cornwall in 1860 as part of a now defunct fountain.

5 **Sheraton Park Tower**
101 Knightsbridge SW1. 01-235 8050. A circular hotel by Seifert whose towering buildings have changed the face of London more than those of any other modern architect.

6 **Halkin Arcade**
SW1. From Lowndes Square, across Motcomb St to West Halkin St runs this expensive little covered way, with a fragrantly-overflowing flower shop and many antique shops and galleries.

7 **St Paul's Church**
32a Wilton Pl SW1. By Cundy Jnr, with a beautiful timbered ceiling and decorative interior. Notice the rich stained glass and the delicately coloured tile pictures by Daniel Bell, alternating with Gerald Moira's Stations of the Cross.

8 **Minema**
New Berkeley Hotel, 45 Knightsbridge SW7. 01-235 4225. Minute but luxurious cinema showing modern classics.

9 **German Food Centre**
44 Knightsbridge SW1. 01-235 5760. The complete range of German delicacies and wines. Sumptuous continental sandwiches to take to the park. *Closed Sun & Mon.*

10 **St George's Hospital**
Knightsbridge SW1. The early 19thC building by Wilkins is large enough to draw attention but has had no function since the hospital left in 1980.

11 **Royal Artillery Memorial**
Hyde Pk Corner SW1. One of the most dramatic of London's war memorials, by C. S. Jagger in 1925, its full-sized howitzer angled towards the Somme where so many gunners died in 1916.

12 **Wellington Arch**
Hyde Pk Corner SW1. This colossal arch is by Decimus Burton, who also designed the nearby screen leading to Hyde Park. A tiny police station is hidden in one massive leg. The bronze statue of Peace, her quadriga drawn by vigorously life-like horses, is by Adrian Jones, a cavalry officer and vet who entertained seven friends inside the structure before it was erected.

13 **Duke of Wellington**
W1. The bronze equestrian statue by Sir Joseph Edgar Boehm was cast from captured French guns. The horse is the famous Copenhagen (who was buried with full military honours).

14 **Wellington Museum**
Apsley House, 149 Piccadilly W1. 01-499 5676. The Duke of Wellington's house, known as No 1 London. Redecorated in 1982 to match original colours and style. Contains relics of his campaigns and his own fine collection of silver plate, porcelain and paintings – including three by Velasquez. *Closed Mon, Fri & Sun morn. Small charge.*

15 **Achilles**
Hyde Pk W2. London's first nude statue, which proved an embarrassment to the ladies of England who commissioned it in 1822 in honour of the Duke of Wellington. The sculptor was Sir Richard Westmacott; the material 33 tons of bronze from captured French guns, some taken at Waterloo.

Achilles

16 **Rotten Row**
Hyde Pk W2. The wide sandy ride, where those who have access to horses exercise daily, was originally *Route en Roi*, the King's road to Kensington Palace.

17 **Bandstand**
Hyde Pk W2. Military and brass bands play rousing music here on summer Sundays.

18 **Park Lane**
W1. In the 18thC, a most select lane bordered by small palaces and large mansions. Now a wide and busy dual carriageway with some of the mansions taken over by luxury hotels. The discreet Dorchester and Grosvenor House and the flashier London Hilton are here, each with ballroom, restaurants and glamorous cocktail bars.

19 **Joy of Life**
Hyde Pk W2. The large concrete fountain, surmounted by bronze nudes of a man and woman expressing their joy in abandoned dance, is by T. B. Huxley-Jones, 1963. One of three presented to the royal parks by Constance Guitz, who hoped to encourage public sculpture in memory of her artist husband, Sigismund.

20 Drinking Fountain
Hyde Pk W2. Jolly little squat figure by Theo Crosby, set up in 1981 after the park's International Year of the Child celebrations. Cunning levers allow you to drink – or squirt water at the person opposite!

21 Speaker's Corner
Hyde Pk W2. Every Sunday, in celebration of the British right of free speech, unknown orators express strong and often strange views on life, death and politics. At least half the wit and insight comes from the hecklers.

22 Tyburn Tree
W1. There is nothing to see now but a brass plaque on the road near Marble Arch but this was the site of the notorious gallows, so substantial it could dispatch 24 heretics, highwaymen and thieves at one go. In its day it stood beside the river Tyburn which has itself vanished and now flows underground, beneath the park.

23 Marble Arch
W1. The imposing arch with finely-wrought gates is a famous landmark – and a kind of failure. It was designed by Nash in 1828, as a gateway to Buckingham Palace; declared too narrow and moved here in 1851 as an entrance to Hyde Park; then left stranded when road-widening in the early 1900s pushed back the park boundaries.

24 James Purdey & Sons
57 South Audley St W1. 01-499 1801. Dignified and old-established (1814) firm of gunsmiths with solemn buffalo heads mounted on the walls and a portrait gallery of distinguished past patrons. *Closed Sat & Sun.*

Wellington Arch

25 Bonsack Baths
14 Mount St W1. 01-629 9981. Luxury baths and bathroom fittings, all custom-made although there are some seductive samples on view. *Closed Sat & Sun.*

26 Counter Spy Shop
62 South Audley St W1. 01-629 0223. Fancy 'phones and anti-bugging devices, as supplied to governments, embassies and other secretive organisations.

27 Hobbs
29 South Audley St W1. 01-409 1058. Cornucopia of cheeses, truffles, game pies, caviar and other gentlemen's relishes – the best of British and the rest from France.

28 Grosvenor Chapel
South Audley St W1. 01-499 5684. A simple colonial-style white chapel, with a vivid blue spire, by Benjamin Timbrell, 1730, the interior altered and decorated by Comper in 1913. John Wilkes, Lady Mary Wortley Montague and the Duke of Wellington's parents lie in the vaults, now locked away and inaccessible.

Grosvenor Chapel

29 Thos. Goode & Co
19 South Audley St W1. 01-499 2823. A super-abundance of antique and modern china and glass in what is probably the largest shop of its kind in the world – especially rich in glass suites, dinner services and crystal chandeliers. The magnificent seven-foot Minton elephants from the Paris Exhibition of 1889 are a trade mark and not for sale.

30 Alpine Club Gallery
74 South Audley St W1. 01-629 2280. A small art gallery, leased out for varied exhibitions of paintings, drawings and prints.

31 Porter's Rest
Piccadilly W1. A free-standing shelf designed so that a man with a load on his back could rest its weight without removing it. Nowadays, very handy for weary walkers with rucksacks.

EATING AND DRINKING

A Dell *Restaurant*
Hyde Pk W2. Superior star-shaped cafeteria with seats outside on the points that extend over the water. *Closed dusk & winter.* £.

B Hyde Park *Hotel*
66 Knightsbridge SW1. 01-235 2000. Drink in the gently military comfort of *The Cavalry Bar*, eat table d'hôte in *The Grill Room* or try buffet lunch and à la carte dinner in the more formal *Park Room* where they also do cream teas to piano accompaniment. ££.

C Sheraton Park Tower *Hotel*
101 Knightsbridge SW1. 01-235 8050. *The Trianon Restaurant*, its balcony overlooking Lowndes Square, offers a set lunch, ££, or international à la carte dinner, £££. *Closed Sat lunch. The Café Jardin* has snacks; the Bar has delectable lunchtime sandwiches. £.

D Upper Crust *Restaurant*
9 William St SW1. 01-235 8444. A family concern in a smart mock-farmhouse setting, serving extremely English food. Pies a

speciality – try turkey and apricot, steak and walnut or Fish Pie Belgravia. Puddings both solid and dreamy. Cream teas, too. ££.

E Carafe *Restaurant*
15 Lowndes St SW1. 01-235 2525. One of the chain of much-loved Wheeler's Fish Restaurants with the typical green exterior and excellent fish and shellfish. ££.

F Lowndes *Hotel*
21 Lowndes St SW1. 01-235 6020. It's utterly English in the *Adam Room* with heavy cutlery, starched cloths, roast beef and steak and kidney pudding. ££.

G Salloos *Restaurant*
62 Kinnerton St SW1. 01-235 4444. The luxurious oriental decor sets off the exquisite Pakistani cooking. Some original dishes from the era of the Mogul emperors. Also haleem akbari, chicken jalfrezi, tandoori quail and luscious oriental ice creams. *Closed Sun.* ££.

H Wilton Arms *Pub*
71 Kinnerton St SW1. 01-235 4854. Cheery and Victorian with real ale, hot lunches and salads in the evening. £.

J Nags Head *Pub*
53 Kinnerton St SW1. 01-235 1135. Looks like a tiny corner shop from outside, cosy and cottagey inside. Downstairs bar has regular darts matches. Not much food but two real ales and devilish Bloody Marys.

K Pizza on the Park *Restaurant*
11 Knightsbridge SW1. 01-235 5550. Lavish use of smoked glass tiles and giant parlour palms gives an appealing aquarium effect. Good hamburgers, pizzas cooked as you watch, welcoming staff and top-quality jazz downstairs on Mon through Sat evenings. £.

L Hard Rock *Café*
150 Old Park La W1. 01-629 0382. The long queues attest to the popularity of this vast and excellent hamburger joint with its blaring rock music, shorts bar and huge colour tv. Rich elaborate desserts. £.

M Park Lane *Hotel*
Piccadilly W1. 01-499 6321. The stately *Louis Room Restaurant* for lunch and dinner, ££, and breakfast at any time of day in *The Garden Room, closed evenings.* £. The coral and blue splendour of *Palm Court* is for afternoon tea and evening snacks, while a pianist plays 30s tunes.

N London Hilton *Hotel*
22 Park La W1. 01-493 8000. Fantastic views, buffet lunches and elaborate dinners with dancing in *The Roof Restaurant.* £££+. A grill menu in the mock-Tudor *London Tavern,* ££, snacks and coffee in *The Scandinavian Sandwich Shop, closed evenings,* £, and Polynesian food in the sultry South Seas setting of *Trader Vic's,* where cocktails come in bowls with floating flowers. £££+.

O Wolfe's *Restaurant*
34 Park La W1. 01-499 6897. More civilised than the average hamburger place with gentle lighting and music and a Supersalad Platter for non-carnivores. For dessert – try American Pecan Pie. £.

P Dorchester *Hotel*
Park La W1. 01-629 8888. Eat British in the *Grill Room,* ££, or dine and dance in the rococo *Terrace Restaurant* where chef Anton Mosimann is making his name with inventive,

Dorchester Hotel

handsome nouvelle cuisine, £££+. The light airy bar serves delicious platters, £; *The Promenade* is for elegant tea, with pianist.

Q Grosvenor House Hotel *Restaurants*
Park La W1. 01-499 6363. The exclusive *90 Park Lane* has nouvelle cuisine. £££+. The *Pavilion* is a coffee house-cum-brasserie with buffet meals and afternoon teas. ££. The informal *Pasta House* has fresh pasta daily. £.

R Hyde Park *Tea Bar*
Hyde Pk W2. Tea, soft drinks and sandwiches to take away. *Closed dusk & winter.* £.

S Marlborough Head *Pub*
24 North Audley St W1. 01-629 5981. Large and hospitable. The Dive Bar has a *Grill Restaurant* and cold collation counter. *Pub closed Sun.* £.

T Richoux *Patisserie*
41a South Audley St W1. 01-629 5228. Spoil yourself in this French patisserie where waitresses in pinnys and caps serve lunch, tea and snacks behind window displays of extravagantly boxed and mouth-watering chocolates. *Closed Sat afternoon.* £.

U Audley *Pub*
41 Mount St W1. 01-499 1843. Gracious Victorian pile with a permanent cold buffet, £, a *Steak Bar* for weekday lunches, ££, and a *Wine Bar* with satisfying home-cooking and good house wine. *Closed Sun.* £.

Morning Coffee and Afternoon Tea

Dell Restaurant; Hyde Park W2.
Harvey Nicholls; 109 Knightsbridge SW1. 01-235 5000.
Pizza on the Park; 11 Knightsbridge SW1. 01-235 5550.
Richoux Patisserie; 41a South Audley St W1. 01-629 5228.
Hyde Park Hotel; 66 Knightsbridge SW1. 01-235 2000.
Sheraton Park Tower Hotel; 101 Knightsbridge SW1. 01-235 8050.
Lowndes Hotel; 21 Lowndes St SW1. 01-235 6020.
Inn on the Park Hotel; Hamilton Pl W1. 01-499 0888.
London Hilton Hotel; 22 Park La W1. 01-493 8000.
Dorchester Hotel; Park La W1. 01-629 8888.
Grosvenor House Hotel; Park La W1. 01-499 6363.
Park Lane Hotel; Piccadilly W1. 01-499 6321.

Map 13 MAYFAIR AND SOHO

Mayfair is one of London's richest and smartest quarters, but its name comes from a different and disreputable past. The annual May Fair, held in a field now roughly covered by Shepherd Market, began in the late 17thC and became notorious for the wanton ways of those who took part. In the mid 18thC the West End, properly made up of the streets around Piccadilly and Bond Street, became a popular site for the town houses of the wealthy and their influence was successfully brought to bear to quell the uproarious fair – whose name lingered on as if to mock.

The Naval and Military Club in Piccadilly – known as the In and Out because of the bossy lettering on its gateposts – was one of these town houses. Originally built in the 1750s it was once home to Lord Palmerston. Burlington House, where the Royal Academy holds its exhibitions, is earlier. Though remodelled in the 19thC it was built for Lord Burlington in 1668, and the prohibition against unseemly noise in the nearby Arcade was intended to shelter the sensibilities of its inhabitants.

The West End is synonymous with theatres and the Lyric, the Apollo, the Globe and Queen's all stand along the north side of Shaftesbury Avenue with the venerable Criterion at Piccadilly Circus itself and the Prince of Wales down Coventry Street. In Argyll Street the London Palladium stages spectacular cabarets, down Sherwood Street the Piccadilly draws attention to itself with flaming torches, and in Wigmore Street the intimate Wigmore Hall offers chamber music and welcomes visiting musicians, who traditionally make their London debut within its walls.

PLACES OF INTEREST

1 United States Embassy
Grosvenor Square W1. 01-499 9000. The entire west side of London's largest square is taken up by Eero Saarinen's monumental building, topped by a somewhat threatening bald eagle with a 35 foot wing span. In the 6 acre square itself (sometimes called Little America) stands W. Reid Dick's lifelike statue of Franklin D. Roosevelt.

2 Oxford Street
W1. Like a huge, noisy valley – its gleaming walls made up of brilliantly window-dressed shops, punctuated by huge department stores, along which a river of people constantly surges. Clothes chains such as C & A and Marks & Spencer reappear periodically, as do shoe chains like Saxone, Dolcis and Ravel, while stores such as John Lewis and D. H. Evans hold their own on a single appearance. Here is the largest choice of modern mass-produced clothes and shoes in London.

3 Selfridge's
400 Oxford St W1. 01-629 1234. One of the most exciting of the large department stores with lavish food halls and glamorous displays of clothes, toys, furniture, household goods, perfumery, toys, the lot.

4 St George's Church
Hanover Sq W1. Imposing, porticoed and guarded by two cast iron dogs. Built by John James, 1721–4, and restored by Blomfield, 1894. The colourful painting of the Last Supper inside is attributed to Kent.

5 All Saints Church
Margaret St W1. A masterpiece of Gothic Revival architecture, by Butterfield in 1859. Breathtaking interior, rich in patterns, shapes, colours, textures, calmed by dim lighting and incense.

6 All Souls Church
Langham Pl W1. Very appealing round church with Corinthian columns, wearing its spire like a dunce's hat. Built by John Nash, 1822–4, when he designed the great curve of Regent Street, sweeping away to the south.

7 Broadcasting House
Langham Pl W1. 01-580 4468. The HQ of BBC radio dwarfs the church with its great height and rounded prow. Compared by some to an ungainly beached liner. Radios 1, 2, 3 and 4 each have very individual styles of broadcasting, ranging from the chatty to formal.

8 Academy 1, 2, 3
165 Oxford St W1. One: 01-437 2981. Two: 01-437 5129. Three: 01-437 8819. Three-screen cinema showing the latest continental and festival successes with occasional revivals.

9 Regent Street
W1. One great curve of elegance when built by Nash in 1813, now almost entirely rebuilt into a sedate shopping street for good clothes, china and glass. Aquascutum specialises in classical rain wear, Jaeger in cashmere and other pure woollen clothes, Hamleys in multitudes of toys and Wedgwood in china.

10 Liberty's
Regent St W1. 01-734 1234. Pretty department store, most famous for its own printed fabrics. Also china, glass, furniture, modern jewellery and fashions.

Liberty's

11 Soho
W1. London's oldest foreign quarter (see Map 14 for its other half) a curious mixture of charm and corruption. Here are excellent foreign food shops, patisseries, restaurants, foreign newsagents and the paper lanterns, supermarkets with a peculiar pong of dried fish and wind-dried ducks of Chinatown. Here also the porno movies, sex shops, topless bars and ladies offering a personal service.

12 Craftsmen Potters Shop
Marshall St W1. 01-437 7605. Pottery hand-made by craftsmen! – also books, tools and notices of relevant exhibitions.

13 Anything Left Handed
65 Beak St W1. 01-437 3901. For those with sinister bent – more than 100 tools and gadgets for south-paws.

14 Inderwick
45 Carnaby St W1. 01-734 6574. Tobacconist shop that's been going since the 18thC. Made pipes for Edward VII so there should be something good enough for anyone.

15 Berwick Street Market
W1. General market in the heart of Soho. Fruit and veg are good, and cheap. Food shops behind the stalls also worth a look.

16 Piccadilly Circus
W1. Celebrated confluence of roads, originally by Nash but 'developed' out of all recognition and now distinctly tawdry. Best after dark when neon lights give it a spurious glamour. But behind the hoarding at the foot of Shaftesbury Av cinemas and multi-storeyed shops are rising to smarten it up. Eros, the famous central cherub, isn't Eros at all but the Angel of Christian Charity, a memorial to the philanthropic Lord Shaftesbury. Youth both foreign and national chooses to congregate here.

17 Hatchards
187 Piccadilly W1. 01-439 9921. Reputable general bookshop. Also, some nice leather-bound editions.

18 St James' Church
Piccadilly W1. Large 17thC Wren church, badly war-damaged and restored by Sir Albert Richardson in 1954. Reredos and font garlanded by Grinling Gibbons. Houses the

London Brass Rubbing Centre with its replicas of engraved knights and animals.

19 Fortnum and Mason
181 Piccadilly W1. 01-734 8040. Most decorous of department stores with floor walkers in morning dress and food hall full of tinned and bottled exotica. Watch the outside clock on the hour, when 4-foot figures of Messers F and M emerge from doors and bow to each other to 18thC airs.

20 Royal Academy of Arts
Burlington House, Piccadilly W1. 01-734 9052. In the past sometimes exhibited a stuffy attitude to new art movements. Holds exhibitions of great international importance throughout the year and an annual summer show of the work of contemporary, but not necessarily the best, artists.

Royal Academy of Arts

21 Burlington Arcade
W1. Regency shopping arcade with original windows, full of jewellery and cashmere. You may not run, sing or whistle here and there's a uniformed beadle to see that you don't.

22 Museum of Mankind
6 Burlington Gdns W1. The British Museum's department of ethnography with spectacular displays from primitive cultures. One of the most fascinating museums.

23 Bond Street, Old and New
W1. Fashionable, expensive shopping street for good clothes, furs, Persian rugs, jewellery, pictures and prints. Many items are fit for the funds of middle eastern oil sheikhs. Look up to the second floor of the Time-Life Building, at 153, for the Henry Moore sculpture, Time-Life Screen, a little noticed frieze. In nearby Cork Street modern art dealers have their galleries.

24 Sotheby's
34–35 New Bond St W1. 01-493 8080. Began as auctioneers of rare books, now equally and internationally famous for antiques and works of art. At sale times, lots are allotted at dazzling speed.

25 May Fair Hotel
Stratton St W1. 01-629 7777. Smart, modern and a world in itself – inside you will find the elegant and intimate May Fair Theatre (01-629 3037), a tiny cinema (membership at the door), a classy Coffee Shop and the Aloha Bar with its simulated Polynesian storms, flower-decked cocktails and real crocodile grinning in the lagoon.

26 Culpeper House
21 Bruton St W1. 01-629 4559. Green and fragrant herbalist. Pomanders, pot pourri, pure cosmetics, nutmegs, honey and spices.

27 Berkeley Square
W1. The massive plane trees are nearly 200 years old and there are still some Georgian buildings in this grand, now rather commercial square, where the wealthy lose their money in smart gaming clubs or spend it on expensive cars.

28 Church of the Immaculate Conception
Farm St W1. Splendidly showy, by J. J. Scoles in 1844–9 with a high altar by Pugin and several lovely chapels. The London church of the Jesuits.

29 Trumpers
9 Curzon St W1. 01-499 1850. Gentlemen's hairdressers and perfumiers, by appointment to HM The Queen, with superb interior and windows full of real sponges and badger bristle shaving brushes.

30 G. Heywood Hill
10 Curzon St W1. 01-629 0647. Famous antiquarian and modern booksellers with literary connections – not least that Nancy Mitford once worked here.

31 Shepherd Market
W1. More or less on the site of the original May Fair. A picturesque little 18thC quarter of tiny streets and alleys and a diminutive piazza, with market stalls, antique shops, pubs and eating houses.

32 Denisa The Lady Newborough
Shepherd Mkt W1. Blue-blooded antique shop run by the widow of the 5th Baron, specialising in jewellery, netsuke, snuff boxes and other small and lovely things.

33 Curzon Cinema
Curzon St W1. 01-499 3737. Blissfully comfortable – good coffee in the foyer, good modern films inside.

EATING AND DRINKING

A Widow Applebaum's *Deli & Bagel Academy*
46 South Molton St W1. 01-629 4649. American-Jewish delicatessen decorated with mirrors and photographs of New York in the jazz age. Menu of 101 dishes ranging through matzo balls, pastrami, salads, burgers, home-made apple strudel. *Closed Sun.* £.

B Claridges Hotel *Restaurants*
Brook St W1. 01-629 8860. Traditional and discreetly luxurious. The small, light *Causerie*, with its extensive Smorgasbord, is especially popular at lunchtime. Elaborately elegant dining room serves haute cuisine while the sounds of a string quartet drift through the foyer. ££ or £££+.

C Cranks *Restaurant*
8 Marshall St W1. 01-437 9431. Stone-ground excellence at this earliest of London's health food restaurants. Go to the counter for fresh salads, vegetable dishes, fruit pies, yoghourt, sticky cake; to the juice bar for fruit juices, tea, coffee and other infusions. Light, piney decor with soft baroque background music. Waitress service *Tue–Sat eve. Closed 23.00, 20.30 on Mon, all Sun.* £.

Carnaby Street

D **Shakespeare's Head** *Pub*
Carnaby St W1. A bust of the man himself peers down in amazement on the colourful swirl of Carnaby Street where rails of cheap, bright clothes overflow from the shops and the ghost of the Swinging Sixties rattles its beads. Large, lively, crowded, with pavement tables and snacks. £.

E **Shampers** *Wine Bar*
4 Kingly St W1. 01-437 1692. Heartily popular with large range of wines, cold buffet, taped jazz and a heavy demand on the champagne – perhaps because of the 53 advertising agencies and several publishers within walking distance. *Closed Sat & Sun.* £.

F **Café Royal** *Restaurants*
68 Regent St W1. Two restaurants here – the lush, plush, rococo *Grill Room* (01-439 6320) unchanged since the days when Whistler, Wilde and Beardsley ate beneath the painted ceiling and reflected on the massive mirrors – and the smaller and more subdued *Le Relais* (01-439 6082). Franco-English food in the former – scampi Oscar Wilde, langoustines Noilly Prat – and a French prix fixé menu in the latter – cassolette de la mer, tournedos cordon rouge, packed cheese and sweet trolleys. *Closed alt Sat lunches.* £££.

G **Bentley's** *Restaurant and Oyster Bar*
11–15 Swallow St W1. 01-734 4756. Rather old world fish restaurant with excellent oysters, in season, from their own beds, and lobster, crab and fresh white fish all year round. The upstairs dining room is pleasant but the ground floor is more fun with its marble counter and tables in stalls. *Closed Sun.* £££.

H **Martinez** *Restaurant*
25 Swallow St W1. 01-734 5066. Graciously old-fashioned Spanish restaurant with a ground floor sherry bar from which an elegant staircase sweeps up to the thickly carpeted dining room. A guitarist plays in the evenings. Choose from a variety of paellas, octopus and other fish dishes, kidneys in sherry wine. ££.

J **Ritz** *Hotel*
Piccadilly W1. 01-493 8181. The very name is synonymous with grandeur and luxury. Go to the *Palm Court* for coffee, afternoon tea or cocktails; to the *Restaurant* for an international menu prepared by a British chef – try salmon with vermouth, chicory, fresh tomatoes and cream, tangy sorbet or a hot pancake with fresh mango and cointreau. Dance to a quartet on Fri and Sat night. £££.

K **Langan's Brasserie** *Restaurant*
Stratton St W1. 01-493 6437. Vast restaurant opened by Michael Caine and Peter Langan, with an atmosphere of decaying splendour, slightly eccentric service and a changing menu. If you don't spot faces famous from film and gossip column, you're just not trying. *Closed Sat lunch & all Sun.* ££.

L **I am the Only Running Footman** *Pub*
5 Charles St W1. 01-499 8239. Pub with the longest name in London, commemorating the servant who ran before his master's carriage, bearing a light and paying tolls. Real ale, good snacks. Often full of croupiers from the nearby clubs. £.

M **Tiddy Dols** *Restaurant*
2 Hertford St W1. 01-499 2357. Cheery eating place rambling through an 18thC house in Shepherd Market, named after a gingerbread maker of the same vintage. Traditional English food – fish pie, game, fruit fool. Live music nightly and a dance floor on which to move to it. *Closed Sat & Sun lunch.* ££.

N **Bunch of Grapes** *Pub*
16 Shepherd Market W1. 01-629 4989. Traditional and Victorian with the flavour of a village local. The main bar, with its 3 real ales, is linked to a carvery. Upstairs lunchtime restaurant is a boon to the greedy – pay a set price and take as much food as you want. £.

O **Shepherd's** *Tavern*
50 Hertford St W1. 01-499 3017. Comfortable and pretty with good home-cooking and stout English Sunday lunches. Though the Wedgwood pump handles are for ornament only, there is real ale. Upstairs, the Duke of Cumberland's old sedan chair contains a public telephone. £.

Piccadilly Circus

Morning Coffee and Afternoon Tea

Athenaeum Hotel; 116 Piccadilly W1. 01-499 3464. Coffee, tea, dainty sandwiches, cakes in the lounge.

Ritz Hotel; Piccadilly W1. 01-493 8181. Peaceful luxury in the Palm Court.

Cranks; 8 Marshall St W1. 01-437 9431. Strong coffee, tea both herbal and Indian. *Closed Sun.*

Ceylon Tea Centre; 22 Regent St SW1. 01-930 8632. Good variety of teas, gentle sari'd service, packets on sale to take home.

May Fair Hotel; Coffee Shop, Berkeley St W1. 01-629 7777.

Selfridges; Oxford St W1. 01-629 1234. Two coffee shops. *Closed Sun.*

Fortnum and Mason; 181 Piccadilly W1. 01-774 8040. Three restaurants, one open until 23.00 for coffee, tea, snacks and meals of an English and classy sort.

Map 14 SOHO AND BLOOMSBURY

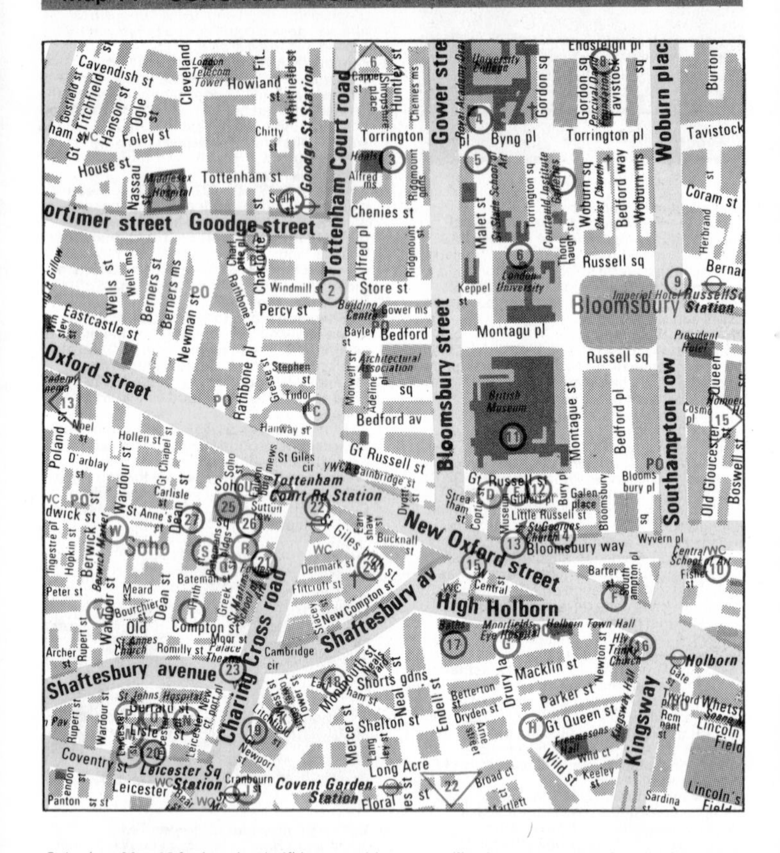

Soho (see Map 13 for its other half) has an odd, arty, seedily glamorous reputation which makes it at once appealing and unnerving. It is true that the eye is assaulted by sex in its most indelicate forms, and that those who succumb will find the experience extremely expensive. But it is also true that Soho is an intricate village packed with good, varied, reasonably priced restaurants, including the enormous variety in Chinatown, some nice old pubs, and several delicatessens and patisseries which serve as a pleasant reminder that this is London's oldest foreign quarter. What is more, it has collected many of the capital's most important theatres and cinemas around its edges.

Bloomsbury's reputation is very different – still glamorous, but rather literary and intellectual. Between the wars Virginia Woolf, Vanessa Bell and Lytton Strachey formed 'the Bloomsbury set', under the shadow of the unique and massive British Museum with its mighty, if dead, treasures, and its living heart – the domed reading room where so many influential writers have researched and written, and still do. Bloomsbury also has the most interesting architecture of the section with its Georgian terraces and generous leafy squares, most of them open to those in need of congenial surroundings in which to eat a lunchtime sandwich. Look at the 18thC Bedford Square, Montague Street built by Decimus Burton in 1800 and Gordon and Woburn Squares by Cubitt in 1820.

To the south is the rich conglomeration of Covent Garden (see Map 22) and to the north west another villagey area centred on the cheerful and somehow continental Charlotte Street, where those in search of a good cheap restaurant are spoilt for choice.

PLACES OF INTEREST

1 Pollocks Toy Museum
1 Scala St W1. 01-636 3452. Wander round two creaking floors of twisting stairs and tiny rooms, packed with Victorian cut-out theatres and old toys of all sorts, under the beady gaze of ancient dolls and decrepit teddies (the world's oldest, Eric, looks positively mummified). Lovely things for sale below, many of them tiny, exquisite and cheap. *Charge. Closed Sun.*

2 Tottenham Court Road
W1. Furniture shops, camera shops, but most of all – electronics. Hi-fis, videos and their relations can be priced, compared and cross-checked along one road.

3 Heals
196 Tottenham Ct Rd W1. 01-636 1666. Five floors of furniture, furnishings, pictures and kitchenware – the best of British and Continental designs. Don't miss the sinuously elegant pottery cat on the stairway who has become the shop's mascot.

4 Vanbrugh Theatre Club
62 Gower St WC1. Enquiries: 01-636 7076. Box Office: 01-580 7982. Two theatres, the Vanbrugh and the GBS, in which students of The Royal Academy of Dramatic Art take their finals in the form of experimental plays or revivals in front of an audience. High standards, low prices, membership cheap.

5 Dillons University Bookshop
1 Malet St WC1. 01-636 1577. Reliable and knowledgeable academic booksellers. Also of interest to the general book buyer.

6 University of London
Malet St WC1. Originally an examining body, which only became a teaching university at the turn of the century, its colleges are scattered around London. The main admin building is Senate House, whose distinguished library is open to visiting scholars. This was the first University to admit women on the same terms as men.

7 Courtauld Institute Galleries
Woburn Sq WC1. 01-580 1015. Charming fine art gallery, open to the public but somehow less famous than it should be. Samuel Courtauld's collection of French Impressionists and Post-Impressionists has the most important pictures but there is also Roger Fry's collection, Lord Lee's collection of 14thC–18thC paintings, the Witt collection of Old Master Drawings and the Mark Gambier Parry Bequest of early Italian paintings. The Princes Gate collection of Flemish and Italian Old Masters is on temporary exhibition. *Charge. Closed Sun morn & lunchtime.*

8 Percival David Foundation of Chinese Art
53 Gordon Sq WC1. 01-387 3909. In 1950 Sir Percival David gave a fine library and a priceless collection of Sung, Yuan, Ming and Ch'ing Dynasty Chinese ceramics to the University of London. They are housed here not solely for serious students but for anyone wanting to enjoy the cool serenity of their presence. *Opening times vary. Check.*

9 Imperial Hotel
Russell Sq WC1. 01-837 3655. Every third Mon and Tue in the month, provincial booksellers gather for a Book Fair of up to 20,000 volumes in the elaborate setting of the hotel's ballroom (which was originally designed as a Turkish bath, and looks it!).

10 Jeanetta Cochrane Theatre
Southampton Row WC1. 01-242 7040. Attached to the Central School of Art and Design, best known for student productions and the occasional experimental new play. Worth watching. During vacations such companies as the Theatre of the Deaf and Children's Music Theatre visit.

11 British Museum and British Library
Gt Russell St WC1. 01-636 1555. One of the greatest and most richly stocked museums anywhere, with exhibits from most countries of the world, most ages of history. Among the more damatic and famous – the Elgin marbles, the Egyptian mummies, the mighty Assyrian bulls and lions, the Rosetta Stone. But set aside time to explore the rest of the Greek, Roman, British, Oriental and Asian antiquities in Robert Smirke's massive classical building of 1823–47. Circular domed reading room by Sidney Smirke is for those with readers' tickets only. Regular film shows and lectures. *Free. Closed Sun morn.*

British Museum

12 Davenports
51 Gt Russell St WC1. 01-405 8524. An antidote to the splendid and dignified antiquities opposite – sneezing powder, masks, tricks, jokes and also some of the more elaborate and expensive deceptions used by professional conjurors. *Closed Sat.*

13 Louis Bondy
16 Little Russell St WC1. 01-405 2733. A shop for second-hand books, many of them for children, but most intriguing are the antique miniature volumes, none standing taller than 3½ inches, some as short as half an inch, some sold with an essential magnifying glass.

14 St George's Church
Bloomsbury Way WC1. 01-636 5572. George I in the guise of St George tops the spire of this early 18thC church by Nicholas Hawksmoor with its six-column corinthian portico and classical interior. Restored in 1870.

15 James Smith and Son
53 New Oxford St WC1. 01-836 4731. Behind its original showy Victorian shopfront is this famous old-established (1830) purveyor of umbrellas, shooting sticks and walking sticks to designs both ancient and modern. *Closed Sat & Sun.*

16 Holy Trinity Church
Kingsway WC2. 01-405 2315. Early 20thC church by Belcher and Joass that was never quite finished. The concave façade with its projecting portico was intended to be backed by a tower. The interior is plain, simple and peaceful.

17 Oasis Baths
Endell St WC2. 01-836 9555. Aptly named swimming baths, with an outdoor pool for good weather and baths, showers and saunas to aid recovery after the plunge.

18 British Craft Centre
43 Earlham St WC2. 01-836 6993. Showplace and saleroom for the work of British craftspersons in most of the traditional materials including clay, wood and wool. *Closed Sun.*

19 Smiths Snuff Shop
74 Charing Cross Rd WC1. 01-836 7422. Stockists of smokers requisites and, more importantly, of 53 varieties of their own snuff, most appealingly packaged for those with a nose for a nice present. *Closed Sun.*

20 Notre Dame de France Church
5 Leicester Pl WC2. The whole thing had to be rebuilt in the 50s, after war damage. Go inside to see the Aubusson altar tapestry and the large mural painted by Jean Cocteau.

21 Foyles
119–125 Charing Cross Rd WC2. 01-437 5660. The biggest of London's bookshops, which aims to stock virtually every British book currently in print. Not always easy to find the one you want. *Closed Sun.*

22 Centre Point
Tottenham Court Rd WC1. Richard Seifert's famous 34-storey office building, a towering landmark of the 60s, remained empty for years and aroused the ire of the homeless. (It is obviously coincidental that it stands on the site of an ancient curse, emitted by Sir John Oldcastle in 1417 as he was being burned for heresy in St Giles Circus.)

Centre Point

23 Palace Theatre
Shaftesbury Av W1. 01-437 6834. Became a musical comedy house in the 20s and still is, although occasionally plays are staged. Housed longest running musical in British theatre history – *Jesus Christ Superstar.*

24 St Giles in the Fields
St Giles High St WC2. 01-240 2532. An attractive church, well-restored in the 1950s, built by Flitcroft in 1731–3. A burial place of poets, including Andrew Marvell, and one of the regular stopping places for those en route to be hanged at Tyburn. Here they drank a last cup of ale.

25 Soho Square
W1. When the area was fields through which the gentry pursued foxes, the traditional hunting cry was 'So-Ho'. The half-timbered cottage in the centre of this square on Soho's periphery was a 19thC effort to hide the ventilation shaft of an electricity transforming station below.

Soho Square

26 House of St Barnabas
1 Greek St W1. An early Georgian town house at one corner of Soho Square with fine wood carving and rococo plasterwork inside. Now owned by a charity caring for London's destitutes. You may look around on Mon morning and Thur afternoon. A donation is appreciated.

27 St Anne's Church
57 Dean St W1. The Wren church was destroyed by bombing but Cockerell's early 19thC steeple remains, ivy-covered. In summer the stalls and music of the annual Soho Festival gather behind it.

EATING AND DRINKING

A Anemos *Restaurant*
34 Charlotte St W1. 01-636 2289/01-580 5907. Animated Greek restaurant with loud music, singing waiters, spontaneous dancing and plates occasionally smashed from sheer exuberance. Typical Greek food, Cypriot wine, retsina. *Closed Sun.* £.

B Bertorelli Bros *Restaurant*
19 Charlotte St W1. 01-636 4174. The family who make the famous ice-cream provide good Italian and international food in a 30s atmosphere with clear lighting and uniformed waitresses. *Closed 22.00 & all Sun.* ££.

C Mandeer *Restaurant*
21 Hanway Pl W1. 01-323 0660. Kitchen is on view to the diners in this popular vegetarian Indian restaurant. Food is cooked to a very high standard. All the curries are strongly spiced. *Closed Sun.* ££.

D Pizza Express *Restaurant*
30 Coptic St WC1. 01-636 2244. Cheap and cheerful – pizzas cooked as you watch. £.

E Museum *Tavern*
49 Gt Russell St WC1. 01-242 8987. The British Museum's local, once-patronised by Karl Marx. Pleasant Victorian interior, filling pub grub at lunchtime. £.

F My Old Dutch *Restaurant*
132 High Holborn WC1. 01-404 5008. Pine furniture, prints of Dutch masters, a plethora of potted plants and pancakes galore – sweet and savoury, huge and reasonably priced. £.

G White Hart *Pub*
191 Drury La WC2. 01-405 4061. Large lunchtime snack lounge is transmogrified into a music room at night, when it reverberates with good noisy jazz – trad from Mon–Wed, ragtime on Thur and modern from Fri–Sun. £.

H Freemason's Arms *Pub*
81 Long Acre WC2. 01-836 6931. Spacious, faintly tatty, often full of publishing types who appreciate good beer – four real ales and three draught lagers are on tap. Snacks at lunchtime, folk singing on Sun. £.

J Cork and Bottle *Wine Bar*
44–6 Cranbourn St WC2. 01-734 7807. Popular basement wine bar with a wide range of reasonably priced wines. Quality cold food, a theatrical and publishing clientele and a nightly guitarist. *Closed Sun.* £.

K Ivy *Restaurant*
1 West St WC2. 01-836 4751. Famous and old established theatrical restaurant. Part Italian, part French menu, good wines. *Closed Sat lunch & all Sun.* £££.

L Manzi's *Restaurant*
1–2 Leicester St WC2. 01-734 0224. Dim, busy, old-established Italian fish restaurant where you can partake of oysters, with champagne, in season. Also white fish, grilled or poached, with the rich creamy warmth of zabaglione to follow. *Closed Sun lunch.* £££.

M Joy King Lau *Restaurant*
3 Leicester St WC2. 01-437 1132. Four floors of simple elegance. Cantonese cooking. An abundance of delicious dim sum (served from 11.00 to 17.30), including duck web in black bean sauce and king prawn dumpling. £.

N Ganges *Restaurant*
40 Gerrard St W1. 01-437 6284. A most warmly welcoming Indian restaurant with authentic and interesting meals, both set and à la carte. *Closed Sun.* £.

O Lee Ho Fook *Restaurant*
15 Gerrard St W1. 01-734 9578. If dipping into Chinatown, eat where the Chinese eat. Always crowded, which makes service slow, but the food is excellent. Try duck stew with abalone, sliced steak in black bean sauce or dim sum – steamed savouries. £.

P Dumpling Inn *Restaurant*
15a Gerrard St W1. 01-437 2567. Lively and crowded. Pekinese food. Good pork dumplings, prawns in chilli sauce, fried seaweed. ££.

Q Au Jardin des Gourmets *Restaurant*
5 Greek St W1. 01-437 1816. The gourmets come in search of the fine old claret as much as the classical French cooking. Particularly interesting cheese board. *Closed Sat lunch & all Sun.* ££.

R Gay Hussar *Restaurant*
2 Greek St W1. 01-437 0973. Cosy and much-loved Hungarian restaurant with a sophisticated, discreetly arty clientele whose loyalty means you must book. Stuffed cabbage, saddle of carp, rich puddings with much cream. *Closed Sun.* £££.

S Ronnie Scott's *Restaurant*
47 Frith St W1. 01-439 0747. The best jazz in London from the big names – mostly U.S. imports. Food good but not amazing – steak, chicken, salads – the music's what it's all about. Always crowded. ££.

T Jimmy's *Restaurant*
23 Frith St W1. 01-437 9521. Engagingly scruffy setting in which to eat large quantities of Greek Cypriot food and drink ferocious Cypriot wine for little outlay. *Closed Sun.* £.

U Tracks *Wine Bar*
Soho Sq W1. 01-439 2318. Smart café-style wine bar serving breakfasts, lunches, teas and snacks – with French wines within licensing hours. Pavement tables in summer. £.

V Duke of Wellington *Pub*
77 Wardour St W1. 01-437 2886. Attractive old pub with panelled walls and leaded windows. The beer is from a Scottish brewery and the decor includes famous tartans and coloured clan crests. £.

W Intrepid Fox *Pub*
99 Wardour St W1. 01-437 5025. Named for the Whig statesman, Charles James Fox. Commodious and cheerful with well-kept real ale and good lunches. £.

Gerrard Street, Chinatown

Morning Coffee and Afternoon Tea

Tracks; Soho Sq W1. 01-439 2318.
Cranks Restaurant; on top floor of Heals, 196 Tottenham Court Rd W1. 01-636 1666. Tea, coffee, infusions, juices, healthy snacks. *Closed Sun.*
British Museum; Smart brown cafeteria. Also licensed snacks. *Closed Sun morn.*
Patisserie Valerie; 44 Old Compton St W1. 01-437 3466. Coffee, tea, hot chocolate, cream cakes (also to take away). *Closed Sun.*
Café de Paris; 3 Coventry St W1. 01-437 2036. Tea dances every day. Don't wear jeans.

Map 15 BLOOMSBURY AND CLERKENWELL

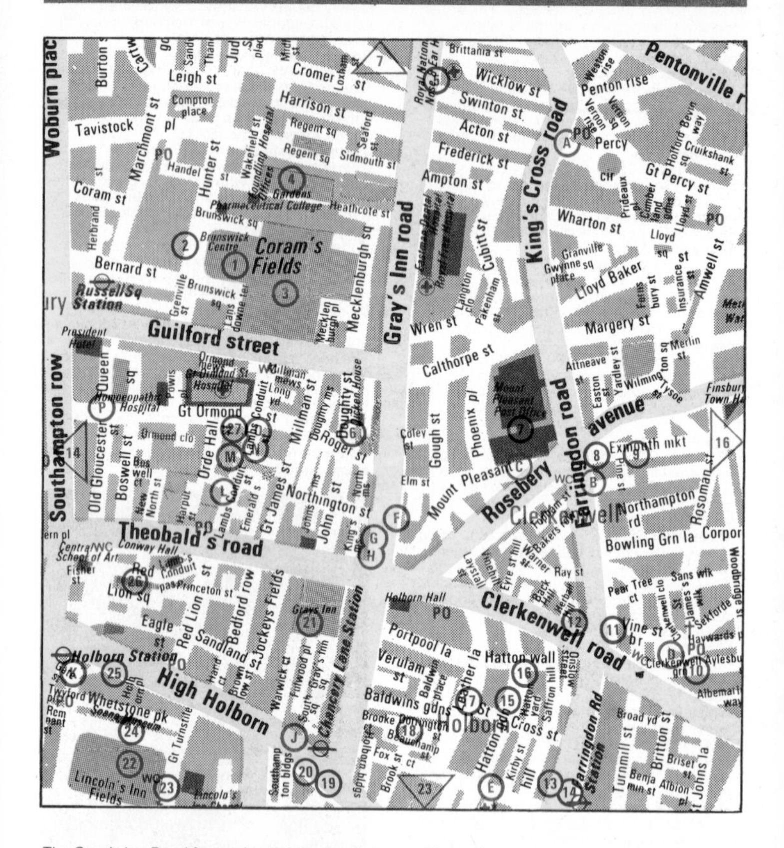

The Gray's Inn Road forms the dividing line between Bloomsbury to its west and Clerkenwell to its east. Clerkenwell, despite its busy roads and tiny active market, has a slightly forsaken feel to it. During the late 18thC and early 19thC it was a fashionable place to live, and the gentry who built large houses here left their names in its squares – Lloyd, Brunswick, Claremont, Wilmington. But by the end of the last century its heyday was over and, despite its Georgian houses, it remains impoverished.

The northern part of Bloomsbury has a generous supply of hospitals – the Homeopathic, the Great Ormond Street Hospital for Children, The Dental and The Royal Free just east of Gray's Inn Road, and in Queen's Square the pretty Italian Hospital and the rather menacing frontage of the Examination Hall of the Royal College of Surgeons. White-coated doctors, and nurses in fancy caps, buzz through the surrounding streets like bees around their hives, and the bookshops tend to specialise in medical matters. The southern part impinges on Legal London with the discreet buildings and gardens of Gray's Inn, one of the four great Inns of Court, which are to the Law what colleges are to the universities. Along High Holborn and Chancery Lane (see Map 23) are the specialist suppliers of wigs, gowns and legal tomes.

The central slice, Gray's Inn and Farringdon Roads, has to do with communication. Here are the offices of the Sunday Times and Guardian, the print shops, bulk stationers, second-hand bookstalls, and, squatting in the centre, the PO's principal parcels sorting office at Mount Pleasant.

PLACES OF INTEREST

1 **Gate Two**
Brunswick Centre WC1. 01-837 1177. Cinema club (membership available at the door) in a large, modern, windswept scheme of shops and flats. Shows quality modern classics.

2 **Thomas Coram Foundation for Children**
40 Brunswick Sq WC1. 01-278 2424. The new offices of the old Foundling Hospital, which still looks after children in distress, contains a reconstruction of the 18thC courtroom from the old building. Here you can see paintings by Hogarth and Gainsborough, an original MS score of Handel's Messiah and a poignant collection of tokens left with abandoned children. *Small charge. Closed 16.00, weekends, public hols & when conferences in progress.*

3 **Coram's Fields**
WC1. Now a large children's playground. Once the site of the Foundling Hospital, set up in 1739 by Capt. Thomas Coram for abandoned infants. *Closed Dusk.*

4 **St George's Gardens**
Off Sidmouth St WC1. One of the most magical of lost churchyards, made dim by towering trees. Headstones lean on the walls, fern-covered tombs slant at slight angles, old trees weigh on crutches and old men sit on benches and perhaps consider mortality.

5 **Pindar of Wakefield**
328 Gray's Inn Rd WC1. 01-837 7269. On Thur to Sat evening inclusive it is *the* place for Old Time Music Hall. Excellent shows, packed with participating regulars and basket meals served while you watch (though you don't have to eat). Book on 01-722 5395.

6 **Dickens House Museum**
48 Doughty St WC1. 01-405 2127. Preserved more or less as it was when he lived here, writing Oliver Twist and Nicholas Nickleby in the small study. The best Dickens library in the world: also letters, MSS, pictures and personal effects. *Charge. Closed Sun.*

7 **PO Mount Pleasant**
109 Farringdon Rd EC1R 3BT. 01-837 6888. The biggest parcel sorting office in the country. More than a million arrive here each week, travelling on their own underground railway system which connects with mainline stations and main post offices. Write to the Superintendant for permission to view.

8 **Exmouth Market**
EC1. One of London's smallest general markets. Cheery, busy and over by 15.00.

9 **Church of the Holy Redeemer**
Exmouth Mkt EC1. Heavy, overpowering Romanesque church, begun by John Sedding in 1888 and completed after his death by H. Wilson, who added the Lady Chapel, Clergy House and dominating campanile. Italian interior with carved capitals by F. W. Pomeroy.

10 **Clerkenwell Green**
EC1. A misnomer; it hasn't been green for 300 years. Its two major buildings are the solidly Palladian Session House, built at the end of the 18thC by Thomas Rogers, now the Freemasons' HQ; and the imposing St James' Church by James Carr in 1788–92, restored by Blomfield in 1882. *See Map 16.*

11 **Clerks Well**
16 Farringdon Rd EC1. Clerkenwell takes its name from a well first mentioned in documents in 1174. In a hangover from early British well-worship the parish clerks (most ancient of City Companies to form a Guild or Fraternity) traditionally met here to perform miracle plays. Recent building has preserved the well for public viewing.

12 **St Peter's Church**
Clerkenwell Rd EC1. Pale and pretty Italian church cramped between dark brick buildings. Built by John Brydon in 1863 with a bright frieze without and baroque painting and Italian statues within.

St Peter's Church

13 **Fullerscopes**
Telescope House, 63 Farringdon Rd EC1. 01-405 2156. Scientific instrument manufacturers specialising in telescopes and other astronomical devices, custom-built or gleaming in the showroom, awaiting purchase.

14 **Farringdon Road Market**
Farringdon Rd EC1. Old and rare books tantalisingly mixed with old and ordinary ones. *Closed by 16.00 & all Sun.*

15 **Hatton Garden**
EC1. The centre for serious jewellery buyers and major diamond traders, on the site of the rose-filled gardens of the Bishop of Ely's town house. Windowfuls of lavish glitter lie ready for wholesale, retail and export.

16 **St Andrew's National School**
43 Hatton Gdn EC1. A 17thC charity school, essential before the days of free State education, badly damaged in the Second World War. Don't miss the two charity children, in niches on the façade, whose presence formerly announced that education here was free to the deserving poor.

St Andrew's National School

17 Leather Lane Market
Leather Lane EC1. Once specialised in the sale of cured skins – now a busy general market with few leather stalls left. *Open 11.00–15.00 Mon–Sat.*

18 St Alban's Church
Brooke St EC1. At one corner of the neat, discreet Brooke Court, with its patch of green and small-scale buildings. Originally by Butterfield, in 1859, but almost entirely rebuilt after much bomb damage. Inside, the huge mural is by Hans Feibusch.

19 Dragons
High Holborn EC1. The two shining, shield-bearing dragons, on plinths on either side of the road, guard the boundary between Westminster and the City of London.

20 John Brumfit
337 High Holborn WC1. 01-405 2929. Most suitably ensconced in a half-timbered building which leans with age is this old-established purveyor of snuffs, pipes and rich tobaccos. Legal London shops here.

John Brumfit's tobacco shop

21 Gray's Inn
Holborn WC1. 01-405 8146. An Inn of Court since the 14thC, although the oldest surviving buildings are 17thC. Francis Bacon had chambers here from 1577 until his death. It is said that he laid out the gardens and planted the catalpas, now exceedingly venerable and supported on crutches. Gardens open on summer weekday afternoons; Hall open by appointment only.

22 Lincoln's Inn Fields
WC2. Central London's largest square, laid out by Inigo Jones in 1618. Nowadays most of the large surrounding houses hold the offices of solicitors. On Tue lunchtimes during summer military bands take to the outdoor stage and entertain office workers and pigeons. Off the map to the south lies the Inn of Court itself, a compact Dickensian world of squares, gardens and barristers chambers. Its Hall, and Chapel by Inigo Jones, can be viewed on application to the Gatehouse in Chancery Lane. *See Map 23.*

23 Royal College of Surgeons
Lincoln's Inn Fields WC2. 01-405 3474. The porticoed building, somewhat altered since G. Dance Jnr designed it in 1806, contains the Hunterian Museum, the collection on anatomy, physiology and pathology assembled by the 18thC surgeon John Hunter. (Don't miss his massive bust by Nigel Boonham in Lincoln's Inn Fields opposite). *Closed Aug & weekends. By appointment only. No children under 14.*

24 Sir John Soane's Museum
13 Lincoln's Inn Fields WC2. 01-405 2107. The eccentric and inventive Neo-Classical architect (1753–1837) has here designed his own house to accommodate a uniquely obsessive collection of antiquities and architectural models. Most immediately exciting are the 1370BC sarcophagus of Seti I, the 12 paintings by Hogarth – the Rake's Progress and The Election – and the intricate interior itself. *Closed Sun & Mon.*

25 Russian Shop
278 High Holborn WC1. 01-405 3538. For those who enjoy dolls within dolls within dolls. Immense stock of souvenirs from Russia, some of the nicest hand-carved in wood.

26 Red Lion Square
WC1. Before it became a square legends say the bodies of Cromwell, Ireton and Bradshaw were here exposed to public gaze and, possibly, buried (though Cromwell, like Boadicea, is buried in many parts of London!) Don't miss No 17 where Rossetti, William Morris and Burne-Jones lived. You can't miss the appealing nude Pocahontas, reclining outside the former offices of Cassells who commissioned her from David McFall in 1956.

27 Workshop 83
Lamb's Conduit St WC1. 01-242 5335. Small accessible gallery of lively prints, run by Mel Calman. Stacked with his wry, funny cartoons, both reproductions and originals.

EATING AND DRINKING

A Royal Scot *Hotel*
King's Cross Rd WC1. 01-278 2434. Four opportunities to eat and drink under one roof. *Charlie's Bar* – casually smart with modern wood panelling and electronic games. *Charlie's Diner* – green and cream with art deco lights, masses of plants, imaginative snacks and uniquely succulent Danish pastries. Upstairs, *Bugatti's Bar* – all cocktails and art deco sophistication. *Bugatti's Restaurant* – (the only one to close for weekend lunches) – flashily elegant with lavish cold table, good carvery, pretty sweet trolley. £ or £££.

B Quality Chop House *Restaurant*
94 Farringdon Rd EC1. Behind a window proclaiming 'Progressive Working Class Caterer' you will find great high-backed wooden settles, shining wooden tables on cast-iron stands, and utterly English food – all the way from a fried egg sandwich to roasts, pies and marmalade roll. Breakfasts exceptional. *Closed 16.30 & all weekend.* £.

C Pillar Box *Pub*
59 Mount Pleasant WC1. 01-837 6114. The perfect local for the PO's main parcels sorting office. Trace the history of pillar box shapes on the walls. Much darts played upstairs, much food consumed downstairs. £.

D Café St Pierre *Restaurant and Brasserie*
9 Clerkenwell Grn EC1. 01-251 6606. Ground floor brasserie is welcoming and airy with jazz-funk background music, huge windows and mirrors, fresh flowers. Coffee, wine, salads, mussels in mayonnaise and mustard, good cheeses. In the upstairs restaurant try deep fried camembert, and turbot in white wine sauce. Rich sweets, port, brandy and cigars. £ or £££. Winner of the Standard 'Wine Bar of the Year' award 1982.

E Olde Mitre *Tavern*
Ely Court, Ely Place EC1. First find the gas lamp in Ely Place, turn the corner and you face this charming 16thC inn. But note, it closes at 20.00 and all weekend.

Gray's Inn

F Saraceno *Restaurant*
182 Gray's Inn Rd WC1. 01-837 9281. Small upretentious and Italian. Pleasant place for a quick cheap meal. *Closed weekends.* £.

G Polly's *Wine Bar*
39–41 Gray's Inn Rd WC1. 01-405 6410. A large, rambling brick-walled place with low-key lighting. Usual wine bar menu, but the crab salad and apple strudel are rather special. *Closed weekends.* £.

H Yorkshire Grey *Pub*
2 Theobald's Rd WC1. 01-405 2519. Old, wood panelled and welcoming, with live music at weekends – usually country and western or jazz – and 7 different real ales. Lunchtime snacks. £.

J Holborn Bars *Pub*
22–3 High Holborn WC1. 01-242 7670. Late 17thC and one of the longest bars in London. Wood-panelled with massive wooden casks looming above the counter. Discreet cubicles down one side where lawyers used to exchange confidences. Snacks, wine, real ale. *Closed Sun.* £.

Dragon marking City boundary

K Ship *Tavern*
12 Gate St WC2. 01-405 1992. Founded in 1549 and rebuilt in 1923 – though the cellar with its priest's hole hasn't been changed. The legal profession from nearby Lincoln's Inn Fields sups real ale here. Grills and steaks at lunchtime. *Pub closed weekends.* £.

L Sun *Inn*
63 Lamb's Conduit St WC1. 01-405 8278. A place of pilgrimage for real ale drinkers – the immense old vaulted cellars can store up to 70 of them, and there are 20 on draught at any one time including little known but excellent 'guest beers'. Home delivery by the barrel can be arranged! Snacks, too. £.

M Swiss *Coffee House*
38 Lamb's Conduit St WC1. More of a café than a coffee house, but a superior one. Simple, immaculately clean with really good hot dishes of the day – casserole, liver, lasagne – fresh vegetables and home-made puddings. *Closed 17.30 & all weekend.* £.

N Good Food Shop and *Restaurant*
86 Lamb's Conduit St WC1. 01-242 4119. Ground floor shop sells wholemeal bread, good cheeses, cakes like grandmother should have baked. Spacious basement restaurant specialises in healthy salads with two or three hot dishes of the day. £.

O Lamb *Pub*
94 Lamb's Conduit St WC1. 01-405 5962. Suitably mild, with good bitter, wood panelling, Hogarth prints, the original snobscreens and strong game pie. £.

P Queen's Larder *Pub*
1 Queen Sq WC1. 01-837 5627. On the corner of an attractive square with gardens and Italianate piazza where George III, when mentally ill, was cared for by one Dr Willis. The pub is on the site of a cellar rented by the Queen as a store for special delicacies. It is large and pretty with real ale and a lunchtime wine bar upstairs offering its own delicacies. £.

Morning Coffee and Afternoon Tea
Grand Hotel; 126 Southampton Row WC1. 01-405 2006. In the Coffee Shop. Also substantial snacks.
Royal Scot Hotel; King's Cross Rd WC1. 01-278 2434. Charlie's Bar.
Mount Pleasant Hotel; 53 Calthorpe St WC1. 01-837 9781. In the new Coffee Shop. Snacks too.
Café St Pierre; 9 Clerkenwell Grn EC1. 01-251 6606. Coffee not tea.
Swiss Coffee House; 38 Lamb's Conduit St WC1. *Not weekends.*

Map 16 THE ANGEL

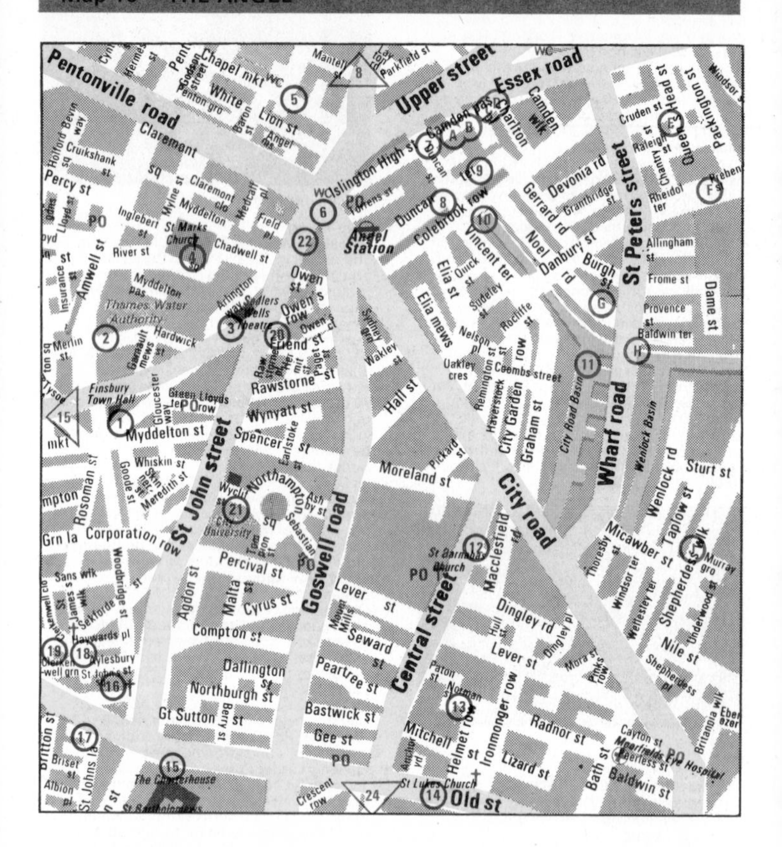

Bounded by Islington to the north and the City to the south, partly in the borough of Islington and partly in the old borough of Finsbury which has now been amalgamated with it, the Angel can be seen as something of a no-man's-land. To those who pass through it, on any one of its powerfully busy main roads, it is part concrete jungle and part dereliction, not the most instantly appealing of combinations. But its water and trees, old wells, churches, restful squares and historic buildings are there to be found – off the beaten track.

The first major buildings went up in the 11thC – the Priory of the Order of St John of Jerusalem of which a little still remains, and the Benedictine Nunnery of St Mary, of which nothing is left. They were followed in the 14thC by a Carthusian Priory, the Charterhouse. They stood in countryside, with the damp wastes of Moor Fields to their south, and attracted a few dwellings. But it was refugees from the Plague and the Fire of London who first began seriously to settle the area. Then the medicinal springs were found and spas, pleasure gardens and yet more accommodation sprang up. By the 18th and 19thC the residential streets and squares were being laid out with determination and new churches provided. The Angel was established as a mixed residential, business and light industrial area – attracting makers of clocks, optical instruments and jewellery.

At the top of the map, like an intricate and wholly intriguing crown, lies the narrow Camden Passage, an enclave of small but well and variously stocked antique shops. (Don't miss the few 'escapes' along Islington High Street and Upper Street.)

PLACES OF INTEREST

1 Finsbury Town Hall
Rosebery Av EC1. 01-837 2121. Built by C. Evans Vaughan in 1895. No longer in use as a town hall but the Registrar's Office is here and the main hall, with its great arched ceiling and ornate plasterwork is worth a look. Can be hired for weddings by those who feel the family could rise to its baroque expectations.

Thames Water Authority

2 Thames Water Authority
Rosebery Av EC1. Grandiose neo-Georgian building of the 1920s on the site of a 17thC waterhouse at the head of Sir Hugh Myddleton's New River, which brought water to London from the Lea Valley. The boardroom of the original building, with its richly ornamental plasterwork and wood carving, has been preserved.

3 Sadler's Wells Theatre
Rosebery Av EC1. 01-837 1672. In 1684 Mr Sadler discovered a well of pure water and developed it into a spa. The well still exists, under a trapdoor at the back of the stalls, in this 1931 building incorporating part of an older theatre, where Joey Grimaldi played in the mid 18thC. The birthplace of the Royal Ballet Company, now used by visiting opera and dance companies.

Sadler's Wells Theatre

4 St Mark's Church
Myddleton Sq EC1. A stock-brick Gothic church of 1826, prettily pinnacled, especially on the west tower, built by the surveyor of the New River Estate, W. Chadwell Mylne.

5 Chapel Market
Chapel Mkt N1. Busy general market for fruit and veg with the addition of a few knick-knacks on Sat. First received its trading charter in the 18thC.

6 The Angel
N1. Now a name for an underground station and a road junction, once a famous inn and landmark dating from the 17thC. Manorial courts were held in it, travellers from the north took rest and refreshment at it, Hogarth depicted its yard in 'A Stage Coach'. A late 19thC terracotta building with a cupola stands on its site (once Lyons Corner House, about to be offices) and a 19thC green, onion-domed clock, in the centre of the junction, is the area's remaining landmark.

7 Camden Passage
N1. A paradise for lovers of antiques – a full day is scarcely enough to examine everything. The narrow paved street is lined with small shops, both general and specialist, and unexpected arcades open off it filled with yet more treasures. You will find silver, lace, furniture, prints, fob watches, snuff, porcelain, militaria, maps, jewellery and much more. On Wed morning and all Sat market stalls appear at each end, piled with antiques and bric-a-brac. On Thur and Fri, second-hand book stalls hold sway. *Closed Sun.*

8 Duncan Terrace
N1. When writer Charles Lamb lived at No 64 the long line of houses faced Colebrooke Row across the New River but the water has now been sent underground at this point and the square landscaped into a pleasant place to rest or picnic.

9 St John the Evangelist Church
Duncan Ter N1. Large, important-looking Roman Catholic church with twin towers, one higher than the other as though the edifice is raising an eyebrow. Designed by J. J. Scoles in the 1840s. The architect Pugin, initiator of the Victorian Gothic revival, slated it as 'the most original combination of modern deformity that has been erected for some time past'.

10 Regent's Canal and Islington Tunnel
Vincent Ter N1. At Vincent Terrace the Regent's Canal – an extension of the Grand Union Canal – emerges from 970 yards of early 19thC tunnel and fills the City Road basin before crossing East London to the Thames at Stepney. Its towpaths are being patched and made public – already the walker can follow it for most of its length.

Regent's Canal

11 City Road Basin
N1. A three-acre branch of the Regent's Canal, bounded by towpaths. Limited greenery competes with the concrete view but the art of coarse fishing may be practised here. (First get your licenses, one from The London Anglers Assoc, 01-520 7477, one from The Thames Waterways Board, 01-837 3300.)

12 St Barnabas Church
King Sq EC1. Square church with an imposing portico and finely tapering spire. By Thomas Hardwick, 1826, but restored since his day.

St Barnabas Church

13 Finsbury Leisure Centre
St Luke's Sports Hall, Norman St EC1. 01-253 4490. Good modern facilities for squash, roller-skating and other sporty indoor pursuits. *Charge.*

14 St Luke's Church
Old St EC1. Built in 1732 and now partially demolished, but the obelisk-like tower, most controversial in its day, still stands. Students of ecclesiastical architecture are aware of the echoes of another controversy – was it by John James or G. Dance the Elder and was the tower by Hawksmoor or only 'after' him?

The Charterhouse

15 Charterhouse
St John St EC1. Historically the most important building in the area, which has served various purposes; established as a Carthusian Priory in 1371, dissolved by Henry VIII, used as a private mansion by the earls of Norfolk and Suffolk, turned into an almshouse and school (later the famous public school), taken over by Merchant Taylors' School, severely bombed in World War II, and finally adapted as a medical school for St Bartholomew's Hospital.

16 St John's Church
St John's Sq EC1. Mostly 18thC but the crypt is part of the original 12thC Priory Church of the order of St John of Jerusalem, whose brothers were known as the Knights Hospitallers. Within the church, a lovely alabaster monument with suitably impressive title – Juan Ruyz de Vergara, Proctor of the Langue of Castile in the Order of St John.

St John's Gate

17 St John's Gate
St John's Sq EC1. The old gatehouse of the Priory of St John of Jerusalem became a watchhouse and a tavern and is now a museum on all aspects of the Knights Hospitallers. In the hands of the Order of St John, revived in 1834 as a purely national body. Admission on application to 01-235 5231.

18 Session House
Clerkenwell Grn EC1. This solid Palladian building is now the HQ of the Freemasons, but it was built as a courthouse towards the end of the 18thC, by Thomas Rogers.

19 St James' Church
Clerkenwell Grn EC1. Imposing building with a balustraded tower sporting stone vases at the corners, originally by James Carr in 1788–92 but restored by Blomfield in the 1880s. Gloomy monument inside to Sir William Weston, Prior of St John, showing him long-dead and enshrouded.

20 Armalette and Armalene
320 St John St EC1. Small studio pottery where you can watch work in progress. Original mugs, jugs, jars and suchlike for sale. A friendly artisan enclave. *Closed lunchtime, Sun & Mon.*

St James' Church

21 **City University**
St John St EC1. 01-253 4399. Principally housed in what was Northampton Institute, an Edwardian baroque building by Edward Mountford, better known for designing the Old Bailey. Specialises in technical subjects, especially engineering.

22 **Old Red Lion Pub**
418 St John's St EC1. 01-837 7816. From Tue to Sun you can watch lunchtime and evening performances in the studio theatre upstairs. Mixed bag of plays presented by a company of four who bring in other professionals as necessary. Pub itself offers full lunches, evening snacks and a patio for summery drinking.

EATING AND DRINKING

A **Frederick's** *Restaurant*
Camden Passage N1. 01-359 2888. Large and smart with an intimate dining room opening on to a conservatory with oil paintings which leads to a garden room with indoor trees, which in turn leads on to a pretty patio. Wherever you sit you may eat deep fried mushrooms, carré d'agneau, breast of duckling with wild mushrooms followed by one of the pastry chef's triumphs. *Closed Sun.* £££.

B **Carrier's** *Restaurant*
2 Camden Passage N1. 01-226 5353. The well-known cookery writer conceived this one with as much attention to decor as food. Sit in the pink room, the mirror room or the lush ivy-covered Gothic greenhouse at the back. Imaginative menu with the emphasis on rich sauces. Attentive service, excellent claret, luxurious ambiance. *Closed Sun.* £££.

C **Trattoria Aqualino** *Restaurant*
31 Camden Passage N1. 01-226 5454. Simple Italian-run restaurant offering good, satisfying meals at prices that won't make your hair stand on end. Lots of pasta, pizza and spare ribs. Related to the more expensive Portofino next door. *Closed Sun.* £.

D **Portofino** *Restaurant*
39 Camden Passage N1. 01-226 0884. Large, sophisticated and friendly, made dim by plant clogged windows. Don't miss the hors d'oeuvre trolley, succulent with seafood. Lots of veal dishes, calves liver with sage and butter, lobster in summer, and fresh fruit to follow. *Closed Sun.* ££.

E **Ram and Teazel** *Pub*
39 Queen's Head St N1. 01-226 4830. Victorian pub, into live entertainment – every evening except Tue groups sing numbers that tend to appeal to the over-30s. Snacks as well. £.

F **Nevada Bar** *Pub*
Prebend St N1. 01-226 3194. The former Giles has been transmogrified into a pub-sized version of Las Vegas with pinball machines, videos and other electronic games of chance. Food midday only. £.

G **Island Queen** *Pub*
87 Noel Rd N1. 01-226 0307. Very popular local with distinctly surreal decor. Vastly larger-than-life dolls hang from the ceiling or flop in corners, currently dressed as a Moulin Rouge dancer, a naval captain and a 20-foot long Margaret Thatcher. Good bar food or go 'Upstairs' to the French à la carte restaurant (which is closed Sun & Mon). £ or ££.

The Angel

H **Narrow Boat** *Pub*
119 St Peters St N1. 01-226 3906. From outside, ordinary and unassuming – but go in and you'll find yourself overlooking the canal, with a lovely large waterside verandah for fine days. Friendly atmosphere and nice 'homey' food (mainly in the week). £.

J **Eagle** *Pub*
2 Shepherdess Walk N1. 01-253 3561. This is the Eagle they go in and out of in the somewhat esoteric nursery rhyme *Pop Goes The Weasel*. Once a Victorian music-hall pub, the decor includes pictures of old music-hall stars and a scale model of itself as it once was. Snacks and basket meals at every session. £.

Map 17 FULHAM

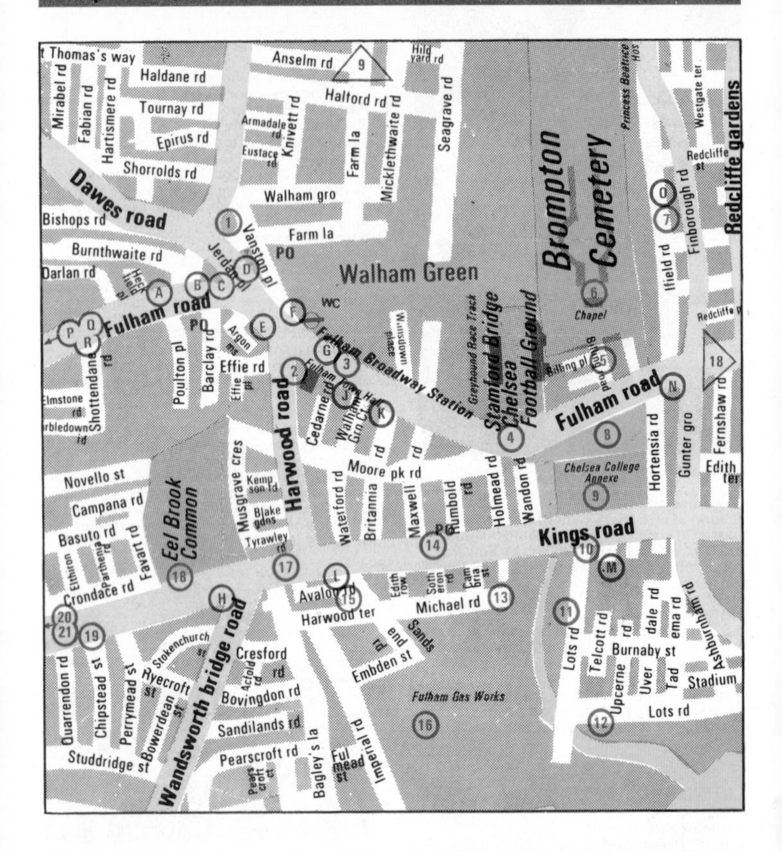

Fulham began as three separate villages – Fulham itself, Walham Green and, to the west, Parsons Green – each with one or two mansion houses standing at its perimeter. The fertile marshy ground grew such quantities of vegetables that the area came to be regarded as London's kitchen garden. The clay-rich earth was also suitable for making pots and in 1671 John Dwight founded Fulham Pottery, whose one remaining bottle kiln can still be seen at the western end of New King's Road. The Lords of the Manor of Fulham were the successive bishops of London. The palace north of Putney Bridge was their official residence until 1973.

The rural atmosphere of Fulham was obliterated by a rapid urbanisation which began in 1850 and was complete by 1900. The villages were joined by terraced housing, all but one of the manor houses were demolished and almost all the gardens and commons disappeared beneath brick and concrete. Eel Brook Common is one that survived but Walham Green is green no more and the church of St John stands on the site of its village pond.

Yet Fulham has largely been spared high-rise estates and the scale is human and accessible. The rich scramble of busy streets between the industrialised Chelsea Canal with its power station and gasworks, and the North End Road with its food shops and market, has a vigour all its own. Fulham Road itself has live-music pubs, the Chelsea football ground and the splendidly Gothic Brompton Cemetery. King's Road, on the other hand, is smarter, flanked by antique shops as if conscious that it leads through the more fashionable 'village' of Chelsea.

PLACES OF INTEREST

1 **St John's Church**
Walham Green SW6. Large, heavy, towered church built by J. H. Taylor in 1827, on the site of the old village pond.

2 **Fulham Town Hall**
Fulham Rd SW6. Built by G. Edwards in the late 1880s. No longer council offices, but the Concert Hall and Grand Hall (entrances on Harwood Rd) are used by amateur and professional groups to present a variety of entertainment throughout the year – musicals, tea dances, jazz and poetry festivals, children's workshops. Details from the box office at Hammersmith Arts and Entertainment Office, 181 King St W6. 01-741 3696. *Charge.*

3 **Chelsea Football Souvenir Shop**
468a Fulham Rd SW6. 01-385 4913. For a suitable souvenir of the area, how about a Chelsea Football Club rosette? Also stocks training shoes, football boots and the regulation shorts and shirts of all the best known teams. Popular with overseas visitors. *Closed Thur afternoon & Sun.*

4 **Stamford Bridge Football Ground**
Fulham Rd SW6. 01-385 5545. During the season the high blue gates admit devotees of soccer to the home of the Chelsea Football Club. While matches are being played you can hear the roar of the assembled fans for miles. Football fever can lead rapidly to fights and drunkenness, and police come out in force to control the crowds. Great matches.

5 **The Billings**
SW6. A wholly unexpected little group of culs-de-sac of small pastel-washed terraced houses with brightly painted shutters. Diminutive pub, The Fox and Pheasant, completes the 'toy town' effect.

The Billings

6 **Brompton Cemetery**
SW6. Massive Victorian necropolis crowded with ornate tombs and ranks of tall gravestones, the stands of the football ground looming over the wall in a nice juxtaposition of the quick and the dead. The domed chapel is no longer open but its flanking WCs are. Gates close at dusk and just as well.

7 **Mind the Shop**
63 Ifield Rd SW10. 01-352 4285. Second-hand clothes and oddments, in good condition, sold in aid of the Mental Health Association for Kensington and Chelsea. There's a chance you might find something you've always wanted. Upstairs, voluble volunteer ladies serve coffee, tea and sandwiches in a good cause.

8 **Octagon Library and Chapel**
Fulham Rd SW6. Two listed buildings, both designed by Edward Blore in 1843 and both belonging to Chelsea College. The chapel is closed, awaiting renovation, temporarily colonised by flocks of London pigeons, but the library, whose eight walls allow maximum shelf space, is used by the students.

9 **Chelsea College Annexe**
King's Rd SW6. On land which was once part of St Thomas More's extensive Chelsea estate. The oldest building is the 17thC Stanley House with its Georgian extensions and memories of celebrated guests – Fanny Burney mentioned it in her diaries and Spenser wrote part of *The Faery Queen* in its grounds. The remaining buildings date from the 18thC. Now inhabited by the University of London's Department of Applied Zoology and Biology.

10 **Furniture Cave**
533 King's Rd SW10. 01-352 3187. Massive old brewery premises converted to the sale of second-hand and antique furniture. Huge selection of pine, period and reproduction pieces and a special architectural section for large items. *Closed Sun.*

11 **Lots Road Galleries**
71 Lots Rd SW10. 01-352 2349. An aptly named site for a firm of auctioneers. They specialise in redistributing the contents of affluent houses, and fine pictures, ornaments and period furniture change hands here. *Viewing between 09.00–17.00 Mon, 09.00–18.00 Tue. Sales Tue, 18.00–21.00.*

12 **Lots Road Power Station**
SW10. One of the landmarks of London, this plain-faced giant was opened in 1905 and is now the property of London Transport, supplying almost all the power for the London Underground. The floods of the '50s immobilised all routes not on the national grid. No longer at risk now the Thames Flood Barrier is in place downriver as protection from high tides.

13 **Sandford Manor**
Michael Rd SW10. The last remaining manor house in Fulham and a haunting, ragged sight despite its preservation order. It was built in the 17thC, rumour says for Nell Gwynne, but has been altered during the intervening years. May soon be renovated and used as offices. No public access.

Christopher Wray's Lighting Emporium

14 Christopher Wray's Lighting Emporium
600 King's Rd SW6. 01-736 8434. The largest and most glittering of the four shops that make up Christopher Wray's empire. More than 2,000 old, converted, or reproduction oil lamps. The other shops, within sight of this but on the opposite side of the road, have the same telephone number. They are:
The Tiffany Shop at 593. A glimmering Aladdin's cave of reproduction Tiffany lamps.
The Lamp Workshop at 613. For spare parts, shades and advice on restoration.
The Pot Shop at 606. Stacks of richly-red hand-thrown terracotta pots, the largest stored outside in a cage-like enclosure.

15 Armstrong-Waterford Garden Centre
110 Waterford Rd SW6. 01-731 4717. Massed supplies of burgeoning plant life, with the heady scent of herbs in summer. While picking your way through the petunias don't miss the eccentric frontage of the Gasworks Restaurant opposite, with its oak doors, stained glass and cluttered Victorian roof garden (so exclusive that you may only eat there if the management already knows you!).

Fulham's most exclusive eating house

16 Fulham Gas Works
SW10. Between Lots Road and Imperial Road stand the old works which have not created gas since the advent of the North Sea supply. They still act as holders to top up the grid when demand increases. Built in 1824 they include the oldest gas holder in the country, possibly in the world; now out of use and deflated but recognisable by its fancy superstructure.

17 King's Road
SW10. This section of the three mile road, which until 1829 formed part of the royal route from St James's Palace to Hampton Court, is most notable for its shoulder-to-shoulder antique and specialist furniture shops. Rich in bulk – dining tables, hefty carvings, three-foot high jardinieres, capacious sideboards, desks riddled with intriguing little drawers.

18 Eel Brook Common
SW10. A truly ancient piece of common land, once marshland cut across by a ditch where families of eels made their homes. In 1866 it was declared unhealthily damp, drained and made into a public pleasure ground. It's now a grassy park, shaded by statuesque plane trees and visited each summer by a travelling circus.

19 Peterborough Estate
SW10. Much of the area west and south of Chipstead Street was built, in 1900–02, on the site of the vanished house and grounds of the earls of Peterborough. The parapets and balustrades which decorate the amply proportioned mansion blocks are literally infested with small stone lions, the trade mark of the builder who ordered ten times more than he needed, by mistake.

Off the Map
Two places of particular interest lie half a mile along the New King's Road.

20 Fulham Pottery
184 New King's Rd SW6. 01-731 2167. John Dwight's 1671 pottery is commemorated by a carefully preserved bottle kiln. Now supplies only clay and advice to local studio potters.

Fulham Palace

21 Fulham Palace
SW6. The oldest visible parts of the calm two-storey house and intimate collegiate courtyard are Tudor. The extensive riverside grounds, now a public park, contain a magical herb garden, secreted behind a high wall and discovered through a narrow Tudor arch. Fourteen past bishops lie in the nearby yew-shadowed churchyard of All Saints.

EATING AND DRINKING

A Fawlty Towers *Restaurant*
Fulham Rd SW6. 01-736 0240. A cocktail bar, two restaurants, a dance floor, a cabaret and an unending supply of Barnum's Carnival Novelties; spiders will drop on your head, flies will float in your drink and anyone rash

Fawlty Towers Restaurant

enough to order 'Soup in a Basket' will have it poured over his head through a colander. The steaks are good and the prices reasonable, but be ready for relentless fun. *Closed lunchtime & Sun.* ££.

B New Golden Lion *Pub*
490 Fulham Rd SW6. 01-385 3942. The whole place is designed to accommodate the various rock groups who play live every night, so lunchtime is quiet, but the food is home-cooked and good. £. Or try the *Dandy Lion* wine bar – don't worry, it serves a variety of wines, and no dandelion brew.

C Windmill Wholefood *Restaurant*
486 Fulham Rd SW6. 01-385 1570. Affable little vegetarian restaurant, all wood and basketwork, with a short menu of excellent food – crisp salads, wholesome savouries, gooey gateaux – at low prices. The shop at the back sells bread, pulses, free-range eggs and honey, and the embryonic bookshop above specialises in health, mysticism and nuclear disarmament. *Closed Sun lunch.* £.

D Scamps *Wine Bar*
32 Vanston Pl SW6. 01-381 3782. The red brick walls and green plants flourishing under the skylight make the place cosy and airy at the same time. There is a cold buffet and six or seven hot dishes of the day. On Thur, Fri and Sat a DJ entertains. *Closed Sun lunch.* £.

E Swan *Pub*
1 Fulham Bdwy SW6. 01-385 1757. Real ale, traditional pub games and hot lunches on weekdays. A new venue for the rock bands, on Thur, Fri and Sat. £.

F King's Head *Pub*
474 Fulham Rd SW6. 01-385 3209. Enormous, dwarfing the next door tube station, with live music every night but Mon. Jazz, country and western and rock groups come and go – see details in the bar. There's always food. £.

G A La Pizza *Restaurant*
51 Fulham Bdwy SW6. 01-381 2042. Freshly made pizzas and an interesting salad bar. Take away or eat here. £.

H Peterborough Arms *Pub*
65 New King's Rd SW6. 01-736 2837. Huge popular pile at the edge of the Peterborough estate, with good lunches and one real ale. £.

J Blues Trattoria *Restaurant*
Walham Green Court SW6. 01-381 3735. Small, simple, friendly, Italian and very reasonable. *Closed lunchtime & Sun.* ££.

K Britannia *Pub*
515 Fulham Rd SW6. 01-385 4502. Pop groups play live on Fri, Sat and Sun evenings and the large bar serves full lunches on weekdays. Can get rather lively, not to say rowdy, when Chelsea plays on its home ground opposite.

L Imperial Arms *Pub*
577 King's Rd SW6. 01-736 1105. Lunches on weekdays and a beer garden at the back. £.

M The Click *Restaurant and Disco*
533 King's Rd SW10. 01-352 3063. Tucked away behind the Furniture Cave is this bouncy mix of wine bar, restaurant and club (no membership necessary). There's live music while you eat and the disco starts at 23.00 and throbs on until 02.00. Plenty of wines, cocktails and food ranging from a cheeseburger to a full meal. *Closed lunchtime & Sun.* ££.

N September *Restaurant*
457 Fulham Rd SW6. 01-352 0206. Natty, green shuttered exterior and an unusual interior designed around a glass atrium, open to the sky and packed with plants. The predominantly French menu changes with the seasons but always includes vegetarian dishes. *Closed lunchtime except Sun.* ££.

O Nikita's *Restaurant*
65 Ifield Rd SW10. 01-352 6326. Flamboyantly painted doorway looks as though it might lead into the Tunnel of Love. In fact you'll find a small bar, and traditional Russian dishes downstairs. Staff most willing to explain the food to the uninitiated. *Closed lunchtime & Sun.* ££.

Off the Map
A short trip off the map, along the Fulham Road towards Putney, will bring you to three eating places, each well worth the effort.

P Red Onion *Bistro*
636 Fulham Rd SW6. 01-736 0920. Pleasantly basic and good value. Eat in French, English or Italian. *Closed lunchtime & Sun.* £.

Q Carlo's Place *Restaurant*
855 Fulham Rd SW6. 01-736 4507. French food in a happy atmosphere, surrounded by stove pipes, naked bulbs and cuckoo clocks. On a varied menu you will always find salmon mousse, butterfly prawns, duck, and chicken with interesting sauces. *Closed Sun.* ££.

R Fingal's *Restaurant*
690 Fulham Rd SW6. 01-736 1195. Young, informal kind of place with the added joy of a garden for summer and an open fire for winter. There's always game, poultry and fish in some form and a rather special rack of lamb. *Closed Sat lunchtime & Sun.* ££.

Where it all happens – Chelsea football ground

Map 18 CHELSEA

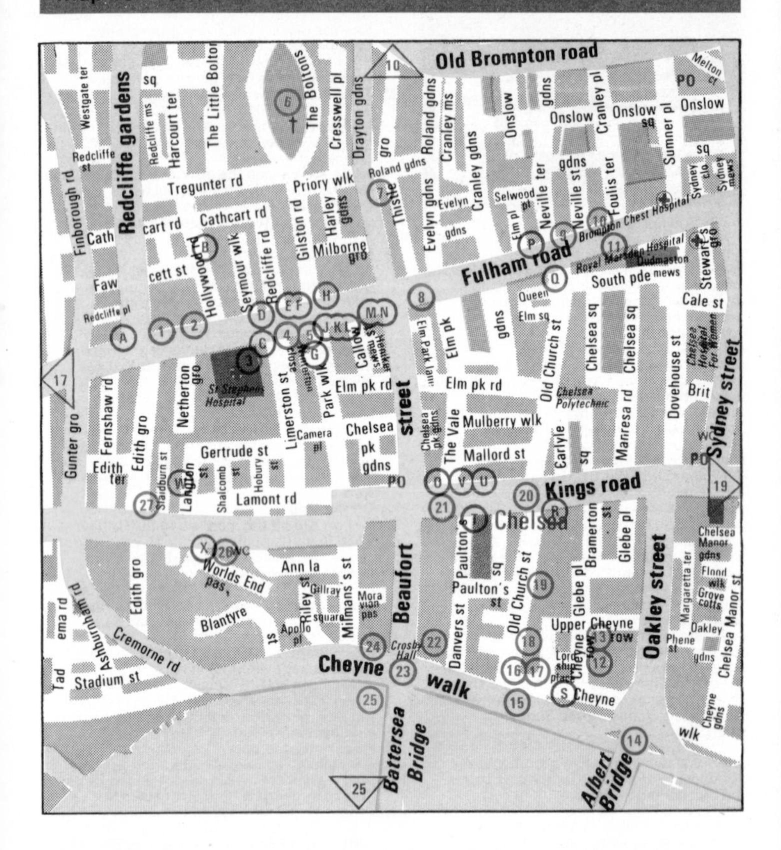

Chelsea resonates with the names of celebrated writers and painters, especially at its heart between Beaufort and Oakley Streets. Thomas Carlyle 'the sage of Chelsea' lived and worked in Cheyne Row. The pre-Raphaelites congregated at Rossetti's house in Cheyne Walk, its garden clamorous with peacocks. Turner and Whistler, each so controversial in his day, both lived in Chelsea and so did the ill-fated Oscar Wilde, Leigh Hunt, and Augustus John, who received his famous sitters at 33 Tite Street.

The tradition lingers on, though Chelsea's elegant houses and pretty squares are now too expensive for beginners or the unsuccessful. Alongside its dreamy, eccentric, even scandalous artistic side runs a flamboyantly commercial one, epitomised in the King's Road, with its small but lavishly stocked shops and lively, popular restaurants. Fulham Road, which divides Chelsea from Kensington, is a paler echo. It doesn't have the same historical precedent for eccentricity, and its preponderance of large hospitals gives it a more serious air, but it does have an abundance of good restaurants and cafés, and antique shops to rival any to its south.

The most powerful ghost of Chelsea is Sir Thomas More, beheaded by Henry VIII for refusing to publicly acknowledge his divorce and subsequent marriage to Anne Boleyn. His mansion and grounds covered a large area, now cut through by Beaufort Street. A plaque on the wall of the convent chapel half-way up the east side of the street marks its approximate centre, and the mulberry tree glimpsed through the fence is said to be the one beneath which he meditated.

PLACES OF INTEREST

1 **Servite Church and Priory**
St Mary's Priory, 264 Fulham Rd SW10. 01-351 1037. The home of the Servite Friars, a mendicant order founded in 1233 by seven merchants of Florence. The present church was built in 1875, in early English Gothic style, by Charles Hansom, the Catholic architect and designer of the famous Hansom cab.

2 **Knightsbridge Coffee Centre**
248 Fulham Rd SW10. 01-352 8466. Top-quality coffees, teas and related equipment – grinders, pots, percolators, fancy sugars.

3 **St Stephen's Hospital**
Fulham Rd SW10. 01-352 8161. Has a Dickensian past as a workhouse infirmary. Now a general hospital with a 24-hour casualty department.

4 **Wainwright and Daughter**
359 Fulham Rd SW3. 01-352 0852. Ultra smart family butcher with the best of British meat, poultry, game and fish – fresh and smoked salmon, quail, venison or a simple lamb chop.

5 **L'Herbier de Provence**
341 Fulham Rd SW10. 01-352 0012. Deliciously aromatic little shop where sacks and baskets overflow with sun-dried herbs and the shelves are piled with fragrant pomanders, sachets, oils and soaps.

St Mary the Boltons

6 **St Mary the Boltons**
The Boltons SW10. Pretty church in the tree-shaded centre of the fashionable Boltons. Originally by Godwin in 1850, its unusual angel-encircled spire added later, and the whole much restored after bomb damage. Excellent choir and active Music Society responsible for public recitals.

7 **Paris Pullman**
65 Drayton Gdns SW10. 01-373 5898. Small elderly cinema showing good foreign films, new releases and revivals, mostly subtitled.

8 **Mr Light**
275 Fulham Rd SW10. 01-352 7525. Luminous displays of lamp bases, shades and fittings, for indoors and out.

9 **Fulham Road Antique Shops**
SW10. Between Neville Terrace and Neville Street stand several dignified, spacious antique shops specialising in period furniture, often displayed as though still standing in some elegant living room.

10 **Brompton Hospital**
Fulham Rd SW10. 01-352 8121. Built in grand Tudor style in the 1840s for the care of consumptives, and still ministering to afflicted chests.

11 **Royal Marsden Hospital**
Fulham Rd SW3. 01-352 8171. The first in London to specialise in the treatment of cancer. Built in the 1850s and extended in the 1880s by A. Graham, a close friend of Florence Nightingale.

12 **Carlyle's House**
24 Cheyne Row SW3. 01-352 7087. Thomas and Jane Carlyle lived in this modest 18thC terraced house from 1834 until their respective deaths. The interior is so little changed there is an awesome sense of the immanence of the writer, especially in the attic study where his desk, pens, inks and manuscripts wait. Don't miss Robert Tait's painting *A Chelsea Interior*, in the parlour, an almost eerily exact reflection of the room as it is now, but with its remarkable owners in their places. *Closed Mon, Tue & end October to April. Charge.*

13 **Church of the Holy Redeemer and St Thomas More**
Cheyne Row SW3. Catholic church dedicated to the most local of saints. When closed its blue-grey interior, dotted with little golden statues, is protected from vandals by a massive grille inside the doors. By George Goldie, 1895, on the site of one of William de Morgan's potteries.

14 **Albert Bridge**
SW3. Fairytale cantilever and suspension bridge by Ordish, 1873, its delicate structure still threatened by the weight of modern traffic despite recent measures to strengthen it.

15 **Cheyne Walk**
SW3. This picturesque riverside road with its appealing Georgian houses and ferocious modern traffic is part of the heart of old Chelsea – and great names shimmer in the air. George Eliot died at No 4, Rossetti and Swinburne lived at No 16, Whistler worked his way through 21, 96 and 101, Mrs Gaskell was born at 93, and Turner spent his later years at 119.

Rossetti's house

16 **Chelsea Old Church, All Saints**
Chelsea Embankment SW3. Rich in evocative memorials – the 17thC Sara Colville arising in

her shroud, Lord and Lady Dacre's baroque monument, the Chapel built by Sir Thomas More in 1528, incorporating a 14thC archway; in the wall are plaques to Henry James and William de Morgan; in the churchyard is Sir Hans Sloane's commemorative urn. Unexpectedly modern brick exterior – the church was blitzed in 1941 and restored in the 50s.

17 Margaret Roper Gardens
Chelsea Embankment SW3. In memory of Sir Thomas More's eldest daughter who collected her father's head after his execution and buried it in the Roper family vault in Cambridge.

18 H. Allen Smith
7–11 Justice Walk SW3. 01-352 4114. The remains of the old courthouse, which later became one of the first Wesleyan Chapels in the country, has been a wine merchant's since 1832. Through the barred gates and down the stone steps lie their ancient cellars, once the cells of prisoners awaiting trial. They have a fascinating collection of old wine making equipment and signed Royal Warrants among the modern bins.

19 David Thomas Design
46 Old Church St SW3. 01-352 8671. Look up and acknowledge the cow's head mounted high on the wall – a sign that the building was once a dairy. The sun symbolises gold – David Thomas's elegant modern jewellery has supplanted butter and cream.

20 King's Road
SW3. Still one of the most exciting of London's roads, especially on a Saturday when traffic slows almost to a halt down its narrow length and the young and colourful fill the boutiques and antique shops and drink coffee and wine at pavement cafés as they watch each other go by. No sign of the recession here. Hard to believe it once stood aloof as a private royal track from St James' towards Hampton Court Palace.

21 Chelsea Rare Books
313 King's Rd SW3. 01-351 0950. Excellent browsing ground for antiquarian and second-hand books. Good stock of 18th and 19thC English literature. The Beaufort Gallery, below, has prints, maps and watercolours, especially of Chelsea and environs.

22 Crosby Hall
Cheyne Walk SW3. Magnificent 15thC Great Hall with vaulted ceiling, fading tapestries and a copy of Holbein's painting of Sir Thomas More and family. Part of the Bishopsgate mansion of Sir John Crosby, which was occupied by Richard III when Duke of Gloucester, and bought by More in 1523. Threatened with demolition in 1910 it was moved, piecemeal, to this site, once part of More's gardens. Now the dining hall of the British Federation of University Women. *Closed lunchtime, 17.00 & some weekends. Free.*

23 Battersea Bridge
SW3. In 1890 Joseph Bazalgette's strong, iron structure replaced the romantic but unsteady gaslit wooden bridge, whose memory is preserved forever in the paintings of Whistler and Turner.

Crosby Hall

24 Lindsey House
Cheyne Walk SW3. Chelsea's only 17thC mansion, elegant but not entirely original; reconstructed in 1752, subdivided in 1774 and slightly altered in the 19th and 20thCs. In the 18thC it was the English HQ of the Moravian sect. Both Brunels lived here and so, briefly, did Whistler.

25 Chelsea Houseboats
Battersea Bridge SW3. A permanent village of assorted houseboats, jumbled cheerfully together, demonstrating an attractive alternative life-style to the massive red towers and walkways of World's End Estate to the east of them.

26 World's End Nurseries
441 King's Rd SW10. 01-351 3343. More like a true garden than most, with long greenhouses, creepers climbing across pergolas and shrubs flourishing in tubs along the aisles.

27 Strangeways
502 King's Rd SW10. 01-352 9863. Glossy little gift shop with slightly surreal presents and unusual cards. Pick up a large china goose, a toastrack made of pottery toast or a shiny aeroplane-shaped cushion.

EATING AND DRINKING

A Carlos 'n' Johnny's *Restaurant*
268 Fulham Rd SW10. 01-352 0379. Junk shop items depend from the ceiling, as though a bedroom above has just fallen through. Bright and bouncy with loud music and fast food American and Mexican style – burritos, tacos, burgers, club sandwiches. Cocktail bar is open to all – no need to eat. £.

B Hollywood Arms *Pub*
Hollywood Rd SW10. Big Victorian pub astride a mews, with cosy nooks, glowing wood and gleaming brass. Food at lunchtime. £.

C Pizza Express *Restaurant*
363 Fulham Rd SW10. 01-352 5300. One of a cheerful chain. Watch your pizza cooked in the centre of the room.£.

D Salamis *Restaurant*
204 Fulham Rd SW10. 01-352 9827. Tranquil, friendly setting in which to enjoy Greek and Mediterranean dishes – lamb with herbs, giant prawns in garlic butter, lemon soufflé, and the golden finale, a wondrous stuffed pancake with Grand Marnier sauce. *Closed Sun.* £.

E Davico's *Wine Bar*
198 Fulham Rd SW10. 01-352 0251. Polished pine decor and 40 French wines. Good cold beef salad, hot 'specials' and a roof terrace for clement weather. £.

F Hungry Horse *Restaurant*
196 Fulham Rd SW10. 01-352 7757. Bustling, unassuming restaurant for thoroughly English appetites – saddle of lamb, roast beef, chops, puddings, pies, treacle tart and spotted dick. *Closed Sat lunchtime.* £.

G The American *Restaurant*
335 Fulham Rd SW10. 01-352 7555. That seminal hamburger joint, The Great American Disaster, has changed hands and name but not menu or popularity. Hamburgers, chilli and spare ribs served with relishes, salads and taped rock. £.

H Finch's (King's Arms) *Pub*
190 Fulham Rd SW3. 01-352 7469. Solid Victorian interior with engraved glass partitions, good pub grub, real ale and the full range of Irish whiskeys. £.

J Goat in Boots *Pub*
333 Fulham Rd SW10. 01-352 1384. Young, lively and French-managed with the usual lunchtime food, crêpes in the evening and a popular cocktail bar. £.

K Busabong *Restaurant*
331 Fulham Rd SW10. 01-352 4742. Gentle, attentive service and delicate Thai dishes. There is a western-style dining room or a red and subtly glittering room where you sit on the floor to eat while formal Thai dancers entertain. ££.

L Up All Night *Restaurant*
325 Fulham Rd SW10. 01-352 1998. Youthful and casually fashionable. You really can eat hamburgers, steaks or spaghetti all night. £.

M BJs *Restaurant*
313 Fulham Rd SW10. 01-352 8493. Fast food with a difference – huge helpings of beef, turkey, tuna or ham toasted in a bun and dished up with french fries and salad. £.

Albert Bridge

N Parsons *Restaurant*
311 Fulham Rd SW10. 01-352 0651. Cool, pale American café with massive mirrors and elegant parlour palms. Spaghetti, quiche, steak, cauliflower cheese, salads. £.

O Queenies *Restaurant*
338 King's Rd SW3. 01-352 9669. 1920s style extravaganza with pink marble decor, potted plants and a pianist playing 20s and 30s tunes in the evening. Classy English food. £££.

P Il Girasole *Restaurant*
126 Fulham Rd SW6. 01-370 6656. The name is Italian for sunflower, and sunflowers bloom in boxes around the forecourt and blaze on blinds and menu. Enjoy the luxury of good Italian food – and real table linen! *Closed Mon.* £.

Q Queen's Elm *Pub*
241 Fulham Rd SW3. 01-352 9157. Genial, slightly grubby place, popular with writers and publishers, which sells books signed by their authors over the bar – try for Laurie Lee's or the landlord's own.

Houseboats and high rise blocks

R Borshtch N'Cheers *Restaurant*
273 King's Rd SW3. 01-352 5786. Quirky, lively Russian restaurant with loud music, much fraternising between tables, and some dancing on top of them. *Closed lunchtime.* £.

S King's Head and Eight Bells *Pub*
50 Cheyne Walk SW3. 01-352 1820. 400 years old, with gracious 18thC decor and famous locals among its regulars. Nice snacks. £.

T King's Road Jam *Restaurant*
289a King's Rd SW3. 01-352 5390. Mainly for the lithe – tables are in narrow alcoves on different levels of a scaffolding structure. Adjust your own lights and music and eat smoked mackerel, chilli, or steak followed by luscious profiteroles. *Closed lunchtime.* £.

U Kennedy's *Restaurant*
316 King's Rd SW3. 01-352 0025. Immense Franco-American restaurant with live jazz most evenings, a slick modern cocktail bar downstairs and pavement tables in summer. ££.

V Bistro Bistingo *Restaurant*
332 King's Rd SW3. 01-352 4071. One of an extremely reasonably priced chain. Flowers on the tables, space between them, reliable prix fixé meals. Also fresh sardines, scampi, veal, fruit in season. £.

W La Famiglia *Restaurant*
7 Langton St SW10. 01-351 0761. Friendly white-walled Italian restaurant with a pretty rear garden for summer eating. Southern Italian cooking includes grilled monk fish, sea bass in garlic and rosemary, and 14 different shaped pastas to excite the most jaded appetite. ££.

X World's End *Pub*
459 King's Rd SW10. 01-352 7992. What better place for a final drink? Infinitely more robust than its name, with as much Victorian glass and wood as survived the war-time bombing and a steady flow of hot meals. £.

Map 19 CHELSEA AND BROMPTON

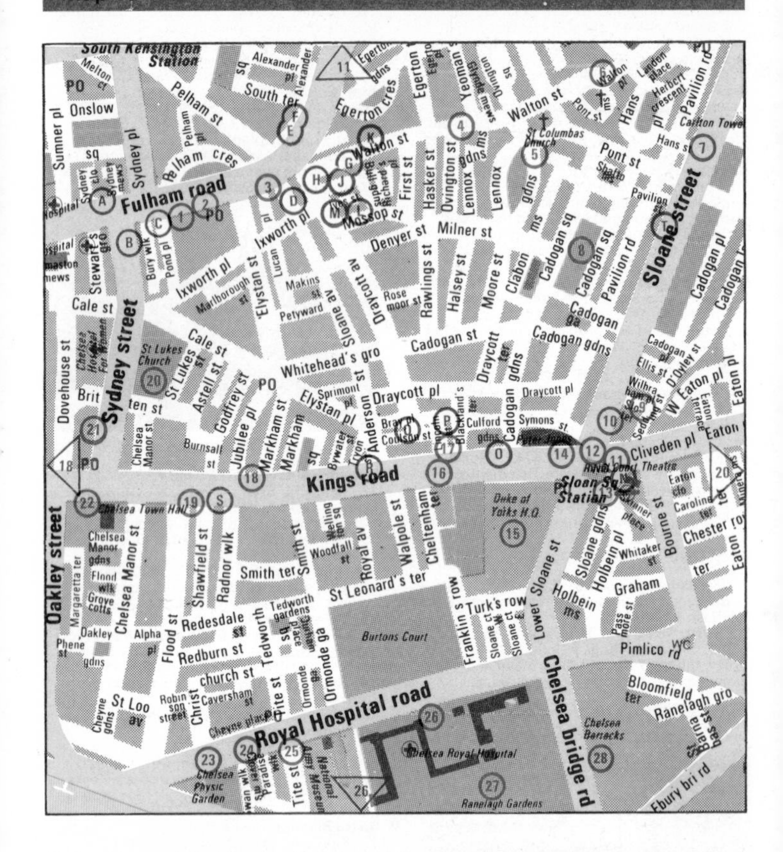

Chelsea has two distinct flavours. The one which flows up and down the King's Road is somewhat narcissistic, fed by the boutiques, pavement cafés, antique shops full of jewellery and lace, and the endless procession of young, avant-garde fashion. North and south of the road it is contrastingly dignified and elegant. This is still one of the best addresses in London and two or three steps are enough to take you from the lively, tawdry glamour into a quietly prosperous leafy square.

Chelsea began as a riverside village whose steady growth was pushed ahead by sudden surges of building activity. There was a major one in the late 19thC when Chelsea spread inland to join Brompton and Kensington and the high brick terraces, in the style known as 'Pont Street Dutch', arose in the Cadogan Square area. Another was in 1777 when the architect Henry Holland began the development known as Hans Town, north west of Sloane Street. Sir Hans Sloane, whose name is given to these roads and streets, was an 18thC physician. He bought Henry VIII's manor house, which once stood to the south of Chelsea Manor Street, and his rich personal collection formed the nucleus of the British Museum.

Sloane Street divides Chelsea from Belgravia and is an extension of the smart Knightsbridge shopping area. To the north lie the Brompton Road shops, particularly good for furnishings and objets d'art, and the small Walton Street galleries. To the south is Chelsea Royal Hospital, from which the aged Pensioners emerge in their scarlet coats, most willing to settle in a local pub and comment on the state of the world for the favour of a pint of best bitter.

PLACES OF INTEREST

1 Laura Ashley
157 Fulham Rd SW3. 01-584 6939. Romantic printed cotton and corduroy dresses for girls who dream of drifting through fields of buttercups. Distinctive fabrics at 71 Lower Sloane St SW1, 01-730 1771. Furnishings at 183 Sloane St SW1, 01-235 9728.

2 Whittards Fine Teas and Coffees
111 Fulham Rd SW3. 01-589 4261. All the classical infusions together with intriguing exotica. How about mango or kwai flower tea?

3 Michelin House
81 Fulham Rd SW3. Don't miss Edouard Montaut's engaging tile pictures of early motoring enthusiasts which decorate the outer wall of the tyre company's elaborate 1910 art-deco building.

Michelin House

4 Walton Street
SW3. It's well worth wandering along this quiet, narrow street for the sake of its small but interesting picture and print galleries. Linger at Maria Andipa's Icon Gallery, No 162, full of darkly gleaming Byzantine treasures, and at Dragons, No 25, with traditional wooden furniture, including chairs in children's sizes, all handmade by country craftsmen.

5 St Columba's Church of Scotland
Walton St SW3. 01-584 2321. A pale, almost Moorish outline combined with kirk-like simplicity of design by Edward Maufe, 1950–55. Cool cream and blue pillared interior decorated only with the heraldic shields of Scotland.

6 St Saviour's Church
Walton Pl SW3. Designed in 1840 by George Basevi, who died five years later falling off Ely Cathedral. Renovations have altered the original appearance somewhat.

7 Sloane Street
SW1. On a more imposing scale than much of Chelsea; fashionably residential in its central stretch with some tall elegant 19thC buildings and lovely, if private, gardens opposite. At its extremities are smart shops for clothes, furnishings, presents. The Princess of Wales' wedding list was at The General Trading Company, No 144; at No 166 Taylor of London distil and sell English country fragrances and dispatch them to other shops in a 19thC horse-drawn brougham.

8 Cadogan Square
SW3. A typical 19thC square of red-brick mansions in a style Pevsner calls 'semi-Dutch, semi-Queen Anne'.

9 First Church of Christ Scientist
Sloane Ter SW1. Large white turn-of-the-century church designed by Robert Chisholm as the first London base of the Christian Science movement.

10 Holy Trinity Church
Sloane St SW1. A living and lovely church and also a shrine to the Arts and Crafts movement of the 1890s. The graceful design is by one of its principal ecclesiastical exponents, J. D. Sedding, and his pupil Harry Wilson. Notice the east window, planned by Burne-Jones with glass by William Morris.

11 Royal Court Theatre
Sloane Sq SW1. 01-730 1745. Avant-garde theatre in which major new waves of drama have twice broken. At the beginning of the century audiences were shocked by George Bernard Shaw – in the late 50s they were shaken by John Osborne's Look Back In Anger. Still stages experimental plays.

12 Sloane Square
SW1. The traffic may be hectic but the wide central island is a haven with its graceful plane trees, its calm fountain (by Gilbert Ledward) and its sudden, bright flower stall.

13 Westbourne River
Sloane Sq Stn SW3. The large metal pipe that passes above the tracks at the underground station carries the old Westbourne river on its secretive way to the Thames.

14 Peter Jones
Sloane Sq SW1. 01-730 3434. One of the most architecturally successful of London's department stores with its clear, curved glass frontage. Good general stock at fair prices and a cafeteria at tree-top height.

15 Duke of York's Headquarters
King's Rd SW3. Built in 1801 as a school for the children of soldiers' widows but now the HQ of the Territorial Auxiliary and Voluntary Reserve Association for London. Look through the palings across the large parade ground to a neo-classical front.

16 King's Road
SW3. One of the places where the Swinging Sixties swung, and still alive with the more bizarrely fashionable young. Shop here for clothes – floaty or denim, smart or down-right eccentric!

17 John Sandoe
10 Blacklands Ter SW3. 01-589 9473. Courteous and well-stocked modern bookshop.

18 The Pheasantry
King's Rd SW3. A modest 19thC house with an over-dramatic entrance arch. It became famous from the 30s to the 60s as a club frequented by Diaghilev, Dylan Thomas, Augustus John and others, and was snatched from the jaws of the developers in the 70s. It reopened in 1982 as a brasserie and cocktail bar (01-351 3085) with the avowed intention of recreating its past glamour.

19 Antiquarius Antique Market
135–141 Kings Rd SW3. 01-351 1145. Covered complex of small purpose-built stalls where

it's a pleasure to get lost amongst the fine and applied arts, silver, antique jewellery, Edwardian silk blouses, Victorian dolls' house furniture and bric-a-brac.

20 St Luke's Church
Sydney St SW3. Charles Dickens was married in this tall and faintly forbidding Gothic revival by Savage. Started in 1820 it was the first church to go up in the great 19thC Chelsea rebuild.

21 Jack Beanstalk Garden Centre
Sydney St SW3. 01-352 5656. Fascinating, if self-consciously wholesome, 'shopping village' – plants, shrubs, sheds and chalets, aquaria, farm eggs, English cheeses, live (though doomed) trout, good wines and the Café Du Chalet for healthful snacks.

22 Chelsea Old Town Hall
King's Rd SW3. 01-352 1856. Attractive listed building of the late 1880s by John Brydon, its Ionic façade added in 1908 by Leonard Stokes. Contains the Registrar's offices, an indoor swimming pool and sports centre and the local library and lays on some highly-thought-of annual exhibitions. Especially good are the Chelsea Antiques Fair in March and September, and the Chelsea Arts Society and Craftsmen's Fair in October.

23 Chelsea Physic Garden
Royal Hospital Rd SW3. 01-352 5646. Partly visible through its wrought iron gates lies the second oldest botanical garden in the UK (Oxford is older). It was founded by the Society of Apothecaries in 1673. Plants are grown for research and teaching purposes and entry is by appointment only.

24 National Army Museum
Royal Hospital Rd SW3. 01-730 0717. March in and marvel at the story of the British Army from 1480 to 1914. Medals, weapons, personal effects. Push buttons produce soldiers' songs and the electronic rifle range is often in working order. *Closed Sun morn. Free.*

White House, Tite Street

25 Tite Street
SW3. One of several in Chelsea famous for their elegant late-Victorian architecture and the aura of aesthetic endeavour left by past tenants. J. S. Sargent died at 31, Oscar Wilde lived at 34, and Whistler, who painted so much of Chelsea and worked his way through 8 addresses, had The White House designed for him by Godwin.

26 Chelsea Royal Hospital
Royal Hospital Rd SW3. 01-730 0161. Unique retirement home founded by Charles II for aged and infirm soldiers – Chelsea Pensioners – whose scarlet frock coats and black tricorns dazzle visitors. The building, by Wren, has a small museum and the grounds hold the famous massed blooms of the Chelsea Flower Show each May. *Closed Sun morn. Free.*

27 Ranelagh Gardens
SW3. Once part of the Earl of Ranelagh's estate. Famous in the 19thC as a 'pleasure park' with a central rotunda in which masques were mounted and the 8-year-old Mozart once played the harpsichord. Now part of the Royal Hospital grounds, and open to the public, though no traces of the rotunda or the lavish masques remain. *Free.*

28 Chelsea Barracks
Chelsea Bridge Rd SW3. Sleek, early 60s building which is one of the homes of the Grenadier, Welsh, Scots and Coldstream Guards. Some weekdays they parade at 10.20 and leave at 10.55 to relieve the Guard at Buckingham Palace. On other days, and at weekends, they leave from Wellington Barracks, where details of their movements are posted outside.

EATING AND DRINKING

A San Frediano *Restaurant*
62 Fulham Rd SW3. 01-584 8375. Chaotic and popular trattoria with a beautifully laid out cold table – tagliatelli with cream and mushroom sauce, clam salad, snails. Also – good veal and liver, skewered quails, monk fish in fresh tomato and basil. *Closed Sun.* ££.

B Chelsea Rendezvous *Restaurant*
4 Sydney St SW3. 01-352 9519. Sophisticated Chinese restaurant with Pekingese and Shanghai dishes. Crispy duck, Peking duck, deep-fried shredded beef in a chilli sauce. Toffee apples or bananas for a lovely, sticky finish. ££.

C Meridiana *Restaurant*
169 Fulham Rd SW3. 01-589 8815. Attractive, white, Moorish-looking building with a first floor terrace green with plants. Appetising hors d'oeuvres display, beautiful fresh home-made pastas, and a passion fruit truffle dessert that is out of this world. £££.

D Poissonerie de l'Avenue *Restaurant*
82 Sloane Av SW3. 01-589 2457. Friendly, intimate French fish restaurant; sole, turbot, brill, shellfish in season and a richly-flavoured bouillabaisse maison. In their next-door fish shop silvery heaps of fish and scallops compete with tiled pictures of similar displays. *Closed Sun.* ££.

E La Brasserie *Café*
272 Brompton Rd SW3. 01-584 1668. Long, fan-cooled French café with newspapers to read while you enjoy coffee and hot croissants at the front, or a light meal under the potted palms at the back. Well-stocked bar and gruff French table service. ££.

F Wheeler's George and Dragon *Restaurant*
256 Brompton Rd SW3. 01-584 2626. One of a much-loved chain of fish restaurants, born in Soho more than 100 years ago. Fish in sauce, shellfish in season, fruit or cheese to follow. *Closed Sun.* ££.

Chelsea Pensioners

G Walton's *Restaurant*
121 Walton St SW3. 01-584 0204. Sumptuous, luxurious and traditionally English with some unusual 18thC delights on the ambitious menu. How about collop-in-the-pan – pan-fried steak with madeira sauce and pickled walnuts – noisette of lamb with lobster and Béarnaise sauce – or a burnt cream sweet from an original recipe from Trinity College. £££+.

H Daphne's *Restaurant*
112 Draycott Av SW3. 01-589 4257. Small, gently-lit and relaxing, with good home-cooking. Try haddock mousse, carré d'agneau, poulet fumé et avocat, followed by crême brulée or soufflé Grand Marnier. ££.

J Le Suquet *Restaurant*
104 Draycott Av SW3. 01-581 1785. A charming, French, seafood restaurant famous for its massive plateau de fruits de mer. Plentiful choice of fish dishes; grilled sea bass stuffed with fennel is one of the top favourites. Mixed sorbet with sauce to follow. *Closed Mon & Tue lunch.* ££.

K San Martino *Restaurant*
103 Walton St SW3. 01-589 1356. Noisy, friendly restaurant with a bar and bright Italian paintings around the walls. All the pasta is home-made and all the fresh herbs are grown on the roof. Amazing speciality – Spaghetti San Martino – a bag of pasta which spills forth prawns, mussels, scampi and spaghetti in wine and garlic. *Closed Sun.* £.

L Nineteen *Restaurant*
19 Mossop St SW3. 01-589 4971. Bistro-style with scrubbed tables, candles, and interesting food at low prices. Try filet au poivre vert, succulent calves liver, chicken Kiev and the ever-popular ginger syllabub. *Closed Sat lunch.* £.

M Admiral Codrington *Pub*
17 Mossop St SW3. 01-589 4603. Good 'up-market' Chelsea local with wood-panelling, gas-lighting, antique mirrors and a large garden with a grape vine and barbecues in good weather. Reliable Grill-and-Carvery (though that's closed Sun). £.

N Sloane's *Wine Bar*
52 Sloane Sq SW1. 01-730 4275. Spread throughout the vast cellars of the King's Arms pub. Candlelit and meandering with a good range of wines, delicious snacks and a sprinkling of famous faces. £.

O Blushes *Wine Bar*
52 King's Rd SW3. 01-589 6640. Rosy-pink luxurious bar, with huge mirrors reflecting the parlour palms and tables which spill on to the pavement in good weather. Run café-style – coffee, tea and patisserie are available outside licensing hours. £.

P English Garden *Restaurant*
10 Lincoln St SW3. 01-584 7272. In a pretty 19thC terraced house with a lavish decor, decked with plants and plant prints. Informal menu of English food served with French delicacy of style: try Elegant Fish and Chips – sticks of sole rolled in crushed hazelnuts and deep fried with mini chips and a tomato-based Béarnaise sauce. Real trifle and home-made ice cream. £££.

Q Charco's *Wine Bar*
1 Bray Pl SW3. 01-584 0765. Rustic in design with a stable-like interior and walls covered with antique sugar moulds. Dim lighting and art nouveau prints in the basement. More than 90 wines, interesting salads, seafood, game pies. *Closed Sun.* £.

R Queen's Head *Pub*
27 Tryon St SW3. 01-584 8374. An almost entirely gay pub. Both men and women welcome. Regular snacks. £.

S Chelsea Potter *Pub*
119 King's Rd SW3. 01-352 9479. Named in honour of the old Chelsea Pottery. The olde worlde oak interior has become a trendy meeting place and the massive outdoor tables are good vantage points for viewing the King's Road scene. Good lunches. £.

A rainy day in Sloane Square

Morning Coffee and Afternoon Tea
Cadogan Hotel; 75 Sloane St SW1. 01-235 7141. Good coffee, set tea.
La Brasserie; 272 Brompton Rd SW3. 01-584 1668. Coffee anytime.
King's Road Café; Habitat, 206 King's Rd SW3. 01-351 1211. Snacks, too.
Peter Jones Cafeteria; Sloane Sq SW1. 01-730 3434. Also snacks.
Blushes; 52 King's Rd SW3. 01-589 6640. Coffee and patisserie, set tea.

Map 20 BELGRAVIA AND VICTORIA

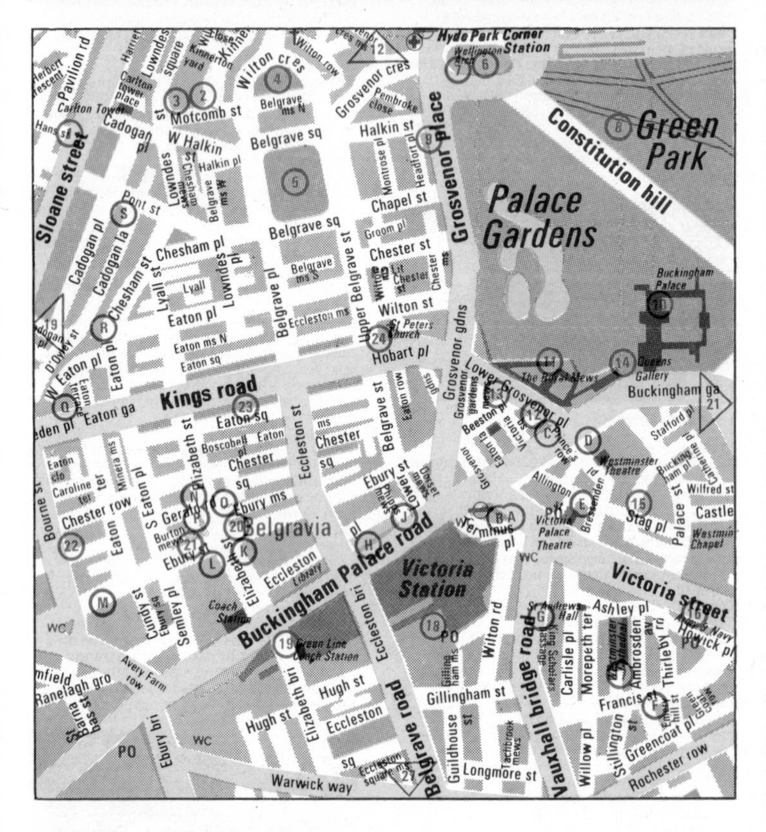

Belgravia has come a long way since it was an area of fields and footpads, where fog hovered over marshy patches and travellers heading for London moved in mutually protective groups. It began to come up in the world in 1821 when George IV made his London home at Buckingham House, which he later had remodelled into a palace by John Nash. Almost immediately after this Thomas Cubitt, whom Pevsner calls 'the prince of Builders', began his crowning achievement on this unpromising property of Lord Grosvenor. He filled in the marsh with earth excavated from St Katharine's Dock and within a very few years had built the now familiar grand squares and sweeping crescents of monumental white stuccoed buildings, softened by pretty mews and smaller scale Georgian terraces, and rich in graceful central gardens with splendid trees and ornamental shrubs.

The alluring tract of greenness to the north east of the map is chiefly taken up by the 40 private acres belonging to the Palace, screened by high walls, seen only by those select few fortunate enough to receive a prestigious invitation to a garden party. But east of Constitution Hill (where Charles II took 'constitutionals') the simple grassy expanses of Green Park are open for all.

Victoria rail and coach stations dominate the south of the map, set in a tangle of confusing streets. The two most useful landmarks are the sky scraping office block of the Portland Cement Company, rooted in Stag Place, and the slender red and cream tower of Westminster Cathedral – it is well worth the fee to take the lift to the top of the latter and get London into perspective.

PLACES OF INTEREST

1 Sloane Street
SW1. Runs wide and straight from Sloane Square to Knightsbridge, bounded by some elegant 19thC buildings and lovely, though private, gardens. This end has smart clothes shops, Taylors for perfumes and pomanders, Bendicks for classy chocolates, the Danish House for gifts and Laura Ashley for dream-like dresses.

Laura Ashley

2 Motcomb Street
SW1. Small, stylish galleries and fine art shops, where you can find antique jewellery, exquisite miniature carriage clocks, prints, pictures, ceramics and small furniture. Here too is Sotheby's of Belgravia, 01-235 4311, auctioneers of glass, ceramics, Arts Deco and Nouveau, furniture, fabrics, bronzes and silver.

3 Halkin Arcade
SW1. From Lowndes Square, across Motcomb Street to West Halkin Street runs this expensive little covered way sheltering several antique shops and galleries including Baynton-Williams, 01-235 6595, who stock thousands of antique maps, prints, plans and charts.

4 Wilton Crescent
SW1. An elegant entry to Belgravia, not by Cubitt who built so much of the area, but by Seth-Smith, another builder and contractor. Mostly early 19thC, although the northern side is a dignified 20thC replacement.

5 Belgrave Square
SW1. The central sunken gardens cover almost 10 acres. Many of George Basevi's surrounding calm terraces are now occupied by embassies since few private owners can afford their running costs. The highly individual corner houses are by Hardwick (SE), Kendall (SW) and Smirke (NW).

6 Wellington Arch
Hyde Pk Cnr W2. The colossal arch is by Decimus Burton, who also designed the nearby screen leading to Hyde Park. It has a tiny police station concealed in one massive leg. The surmounting bronze of Peace, her quadriga drawn by vigorously life-like horses, is by Adrian Jones, a cavalry officer and vet who entertained seven friends within the structure before it was erected.

7 Royal Artillery Memorial
Hyde Pk Cnr SW1. One of the most dramatic of London's War Memorials, by C. S. Jagger in 1925, its full-sized howitzer angled towards the Somme where so many gunners died in 1916.

8 Green Park
SW1. A simple green space with trees for shade and deckchairs for comfort. Henry VIII enclosed it as a deer park. Later, in the 18thC, the fashionable gentry strolled within its bounds. The delicate gates opposite Buckingham Palace were made by Jean Tijou around 1690.

9 33 Grosvenor Place
SW1. It's worth rubber-necking to get a view of the sculpture high on the front of the 1956 British Steel building (architectural consultant Sir Albert Richardson) where large smug powers of light persecute small demonic powers of darkness.

33 Grosvenor Place

10 Buckingham Palace
SW1. The sovereign's London residence. Built in 1705 as the Duke of Buckingham's house, remodelled into a palace by Nash in 1830, refaced by Sir Aston Webb in 1913. Its 40 acres of grounds are the setting for summer garden parties – by invitation only. The military pomp and pageantry of the changing of the Guard starts daily at 11.30; (alternate days in winter) and the royal standard flies to proclaim the royal presence.

11 Royal Mews
Buckingham Pal Rd SW1. 01-930 4832. The home of the royal horses and of the state coaches, including the elaborate golden coronation coach and the fairytale glass coach. *Open 14.00–16.00 Wed & Thur but not during Royal Ascot week. Charge.*

12 J. A. Allen & Co Ltd
1 Lower Grosvenor Pl SW1. 01-828 8855. Perfectly placed booksellers specialising in everything to do with horses and their trappings.

13 Marshall Foch's Statue
Grosvenor Gdns SW1. The equestrian statue of the Supreme Commander of the French and British forces in the First World War, by G. Malissand, faces Victoria Station, terminus of the rail link with Paris. It was presented by the French government who also put up the two tiny houses, encrusted with Normandy seashells, now repositories for gardener's tools.

Buckingham Palace

14 Queen's Gallery
Buckingham Palace, Buckingham Pal Rd SW1 01-930 4832. Has its own entrance so you will not meet the lady herself. Pictures and works of art from the extensive royal collection, which tell the tale of how wealth attracts lots more wealth. *Open 11.00–17.00 Tue–Sat, 14.00–17.00 Sun. Charge.*

15 Stag
Stag Pl SW1. The aluminium stag with the wind-blown antlers is by E. Bainbridge Copnall and marks the site of the long defunct Stag Brewery.

16 Army and Navy Stores
105 Victoria St SW1. 01-834 1234. Suppliers to the services in the 1890s. Now a generously stocked department store with self-service restaurants on the 1st and 2nd floors and a coffee and croissant bar on the ground floor.

17 Westminster Cathedral
Ashley Pl SW1. 01-834 7452. This most important of England's Roman Catholic churches has a striking exterior of red brick with pale stone stripes and a tall slim campanile with magnificent views (a lift operates daily, for a small charge). The unfinished interior, its exquisite marble facings and darkly gleaming mosaics fading into the plain dark brick of the domed ceiling, has a true atmosphere of sanctity. Amidst the Byzantine beauty, by John Francis Bentley, 1895–1903, don't miss Eric Gill's stone reliefs of the Stations of the Cross.

18 Victoria Station
SW1. The gateway to the Continent. Built for the London, Chatham and Dover, and the Great Western Railways in 1862, on piles over the basin of the old Grosvenor Canal. Modernisation creeps steadily around its concourse.

19 Sloane Cycles
17–19 Elizabeth St SW1. 01-730 6716. Will hire you a bike by the day, week or month; also sell and repair same.

20 Justin de Blank
114 Ebury St SW1. 01-730 2375. Plants and herbs, growing and dried, exotic spices and fresh flowers delivered weekly if you wish.

21 180 Ebury Street
SW1. The 8-year-old Mozart composed his first symphony here in 1764.

22 St Mary the Virgin Church
Bourne St SW1. Built in 1927, like a brick liner with a tiny bell tower. The plain brick interior contrasts effectively with the gilded trappings of Christianity.

23 Eaton Square
SW1. So big you could almost miss it! Not a square at all, but four great rectangles, cut through by roads, their beautifully cultivated vegetation and luxuriant trees bringing the scent of the countryside to the heart of Belgravia.

24 St Peter's Church
Eaton Sq SW1. By Hakewell in the 1820s with a massively colonnaded portico, its interior refurbished by Blomfield in 1872–5. Has memories of many a society wedding.

EATING AND DRINKING

A Overton's *Restaurant*
4 Victoria Bldgs, Terminus Pl SW1. 01-834 3774. Unhurried yet efficient courtesy in an excellent fish restaurant with its oyster bar, cocktail bar and dining room. The best seafood, perfectly prepared, with delicate crêpes to follow. *Closed Sun.* £££.

B Grandma Lee's Bakery and *Eating Place*
22 Terminus Pl SW1. 01-834 7602. Friendly take-away or eat-in place with good, fresh-baked bread and cakes, fresh coffee, home-made casseroles, hot pots, apple pies – all served on cardboard 'crockery' with salt and sugar in packets and plastic spoons. A bit like eating farmhouse food in a grounded airliner. £.

C Bag o' Nails *Pub*
6 Buckingham Pal Rd SW1. 01-834 6946. Originally called The Bacchanals but the mispronunciation stuck. Boozy and darts-playing with real ale. Good place to watch the Guard pass after it has changed at Buckingham Palace. Snacks. £.

D Gates Wine Bar and *Restaurant*
43 Buckingham Pal Rd SW1. 01-834 0119. Get yourself past the strangely cemeterial gates which dominate the windows to find a pleasant new wine bar cum restaurant where you may drink without eating or eat steak, trout, sole and the usual quiche and salad. *Closed Sat evening & all Sun.* £.

Stag by E. Bainbridge Copnall

E Stag *Pub*
25 Bressenden Pl SW1. 01-828 7287. Octagonal pub on the site of Watneys old Stag brewery. You can drink Stag Bitter and, if it doesn't seem too heartless, eat venison in the smart upstairs restaurant. Filling snacks in the bar every day. £. Restaurant *closed Mon evening, Sat lunch, all Sun.* ££.

Westminster Cathedral

F Cardinal *Pub*
23 Francis St SW1. 01-834 7260. A fittingly ecclesiastical title for a pub behind the Cathedral. Daily lunches. £.

G Yasmine *Restaurant*
278–280 Vauxhall Br Rd SW1. 01-834 5413. The tandoori oven was imported from India to ensure the authenticity of the cooking. Serious food, light-hearted menu which includes a special lunch for 'poor millionaires'. *Closed Sun.* ££.

H Bumbles *Restaurant*
16 Buckingham Pal Rd SW1. 01-828 2903. Seating in booths amid brown and gold decor. Food purports to be English but has a distinctly Continental air. Try shallots with herbs, tomatoes and garlic to start; go on to steak with blue cheese or boned leg of lamb; end with rich syllabub. *Closed Sat lunch & all Sun.* ££.

J Victoria *Tavern*
56 Buckingham Pal Rd SW1. 01-730 1683. Cosmopolitan free house with 5 real ales to offer, snacks at every session and traditional roast Sunday lunches. £.

K Ebury *Wine Bar*
139 Ebury St SW1. 01-730 5447. Old world dark green bar with cane chairs and cast iron sewing machine tables. Full lunches, good evening snacks and sporadic live entertainment of a calm and classical kind. ££.

L Mijanou *Restaurant*
143 Ebury St SW1. 01-730 4099. Pretty little place with two dining rooms – one for smokers, one for non-smokers. Inventive French-accented menu changes all the time; you might find fresh salmon with seaweed sauce, venison with elderberries, gateaux without flour – if not, there will be something equally interesting. Everything home-made including the bread and ice cream. *Closed weekends.* ££.

M La Poule au Pot *Restaurant*
231 Ebury St SW1. 01-730 7763. Busy, jolly French restaurant where you can eat poule au pot itself or one of a range of other solid provincial dishes. Less choice at lunchtime but still good. *Closed Sun.* ££.

N Mimmo d'Ischia *Restaurant*
61 Elizabeth St SW1. 01-730 5406. Sprightly Italian restaurant with signed photos of the famous on its walls. Lovely mixed seafood starter, a 'special' of veal with mozzarella, courgettes and tomato, and diet-defying puddings. *Closed Sun.* £££.

O Prince of Wales *Pub*
44 Elizabeth St SW1. 01-730 5437. Tucked between a marvellous wet fish shop and the cobbled charm of Ebury Mews is this amiable Victorian pub which will feed you any day of the week. £.

P Eatons *Restaurant*
43 Elizabeth St SW1. 01-730 0074. Small, French and cosy. Start with home-made soup or blinis; go on to lamb and kidneys provençale, chicken supreme; end with home-baked gateaux. *Closed weekends.* ££.

Q Antelope *Pub*
22 Eaton Ter SW1. 01-730 7781. 18thC inn, pretty and dainty outside, hearty and companionable inside with rugger-types among the regulars. Wine bar on the first floor has hot and cold food Mon to Sat. £.

Belgrave Square

R Lowndes Arms *Pub*
37 Chesham St SW1. 01-235 2595. The 160-year-old remains of a coaching inn, in a cul-de-sac off a tangle of streets of tall white stuccoed buildings. Its wood glows, its brass gleams, its tiny back garden blooms, its lunches are home-cooked. £.

S Drones *Restaurant*
1 Pont St SW1. 01-235 9638. Belgravia's answer to the hamburger joint – smart decor, framed pictures, lavish foliage and young, well-heeled customers. The usual hamburgers, salads and ices plus some more ambitious dishes. ££.

Morning Coffee and Afternoon Tea
Victoria Station; Snack Bars.
Cadogan Hotel; 75 Sloane St SW1. 01-235 7141. Good coffee, set tea.
Goring Hotel; 15 Beeston Pl SW1. 01-834 8211. Coffee and afternoon tea in the lounge.
London Belgravia Hotel; 20 Chesham Pl SW1. 01-235 6040. Take tea in the lounge bar.

Map 21 ST. JAMES'S AND WHITEHALL

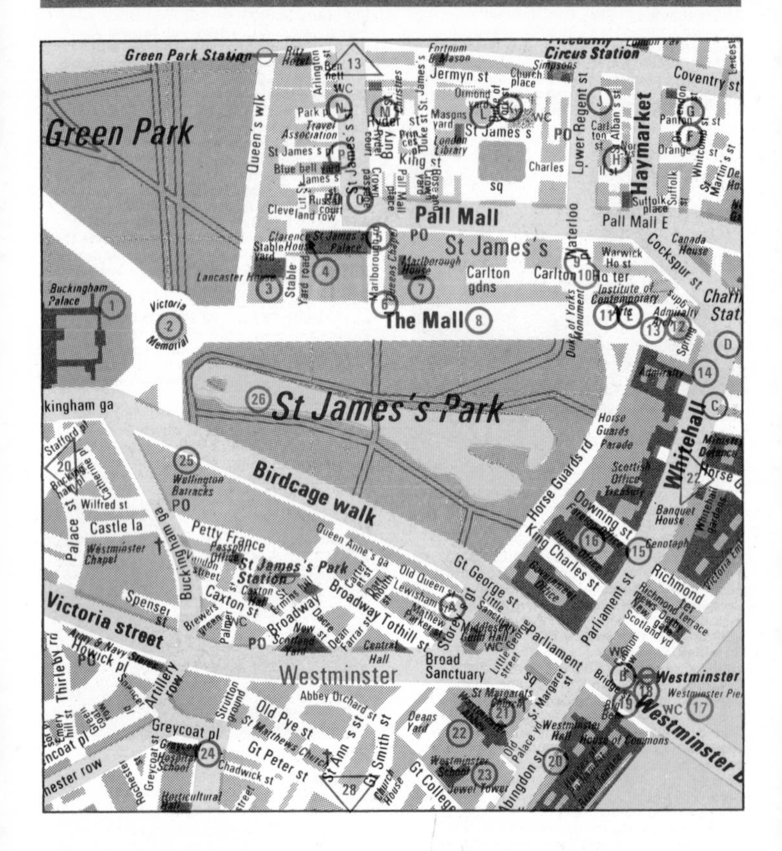

Here is the most majestic quarter of London. Whether you believe Britain to be governed from Buckingham Palace, from the Houses of Parliament, from the offices and Ministries along Whitehall, or from the discreet and sober confines of the gentlemen's clubs of St James's – it all happens within the boundaries of this map.

St James's, bordered by Piccadilly to the north and the Mall to the south, is dignified by the exclusive clubs which occupy so many of its grand 18thC houses. Among them is the Tory White's, the oldest, used once by Swift, Steele and Pope, and its rival Brooks's, leading Whig meeting place of the 1770s. Look too at 19thC club architecture in the neo-classical United Service Club and harmonising Athenaeum, and Italian Renaissance style Travellers' and Reform clubs. A different kind of club is the London Library, one of the largest private subscription libraries in Britain, founded by Carlyle in 1841. It borders on St James's Square, the oldest square in the West End, its equestrian statue of William III complete with the molehill which tripped his horse and killed him.

The imposing buildings of Whitehall face each other across the processional way which leads to those twin Gothic splendours – the New Palace of Westminster, otherwise known as the Houses of Parliament, and Westminster Abbey, treasury of history and riches.

One of the most beautiful and most delicately landscaped of London's parks – St James's – fills the centre of the area with calm greenery, flowers and birds. On the site of a 13thC hospice for leprous maidens, its casually formal lake now offers sanctuary to waterfowl.

PLACES OF INTEREST

1 **Buckingham Palace**
SW1. The sovereign's London residence. The royal standard flies on the flagpole to announce the royal presence. Royal processions lead from it down the Mall on ceremonial occasions, attracting cheering crowds. Daily at 11.30 in summer, (alternate days in winter) the guard is changed with many a military flourish. (*See Map 20.*)

2 **Victoria Memorial**
The Mall SW1. Dazzling white marble and gilded bronze allegorical group, designed by Sir Aston Webb, with the Queen seated at its centre. Good vantage point for the changing of the guard at the Palace.

3 **Lancaster House**
Stable Yd SW1. A palace of a house, solid and decorous without but lusciously, ripely baroque within. Designed by Smirke for the Duke of York in 1820 but largely redesigned by Benjamin Wyatt in 1825. Breathtaking staircase, lavishly painted ceilings, sumptuous furnishings. Now used as a Government hospitality centre but open on weekend afternoons from Easter to October.

4 **Clarence House**
Stable Yard Gate SW1. The residence of the Queen Mother. When she is at home a lone piper plays in the garden daily at 09.00. Originally built by Nash in 1825 for the Duke of Clarence, later to become William IV.

5 **St James's Palace**
Pall Mall SW1. In warm red brick with blue diapering, its Tudor gatehouse giving on to courtyards and buildings planned for Henry VIII, but with important additions by Wren and others. Still officially a royal residence – foreign ambassadors and commissioners are always 'accredited to the Court of St James'.

6 **Queen's Chapel**
Marlborough Rd SW1. Designed by Inigo Jones in 1623 for Charles II's Queen. Beautiful timber ceiling. Open for Sunday services from Easter to August.

7 **Marlborough House**
Marlborough Gate, Pall Mall SW1. 01-930 8071. Charming 18thC red brick Wren building with additions by Pennethorne in the 19thC. Built for the first Duke of Marlborough and now the Commonwealth Centre. The state apartments are open on weekend afternoons from Easter to September.

8 **The Mall**
SW1. Wide avenue leading to Buckingham Palace, with moveable lampposts and traffic islands to accommodate royal processions. Laid out for Charles II and used in his time for the ball and mallet game of 'pall mall'.

9 **Guards Memorial**
Waterloo Pl SW1. The memorial to the guards who died in the Crimean War was cast from captured cannon. The chilling pile of cannons at the back were all fired at Sebastopol.

10 **Carlton House Terrace**
SW1. The triumphal termination of Nash's Regent Street scheme (See Map 13), built on the site of the Prince Regent's Carlton House. At the top of the steps the Regent's brother, the grand old Duke of York, is commemorated in a seven ton bronze statue by Sir Richard Westmacott, atop a granite column 137½ feet high.

Changing Guard

11 **ICA**
Nash House, The Mall SW1. 01-930 6393. The Institute of Contemporary Arts mounts challenging exhibitions of paintings and photography in a young, relaxed atmosphere. Also has two cinemas, a theatre, video reference library, arts bookshop, bar and a health food restaurant. *Closed Mon.*

12 **Admiralty Arch**
The Mall SW1. Sir Aston Webb's massive memorial to Queen Victoria bestrides the beginning of the Mall, a weighty triple arch erected in 1910.

13 **Captain Cook**
The Mall SW1. Sir Thomas Brock's statue of 1914 shows the Captain in an unseamanlike stance, one foot precariously placed on a coil of rope.

14 **Whitehall**
SW1. Impressive, governmental and sometimes imperialist architecture fronts on to this wide processional way leading to the Houses of Parliament. Principal buildings are:
The Old Admiralty by T. Ripley, 1725–8 with a fine Adam columnar screen of 1760. The new Admiralty of 1887 lies behind.
The Horse Guards by William Kent, 1750–60. Try not to miss the changing of the guard at 11.00 Mon–Sat and 10.00 on Sun. *Horse Guards Parade* is the scene of the ceremony of Trooping the Colour every June.
The Old War Office, William Young, 1898–1907.
The Ministry of Defence, designed by Vincent Harris in 1913 and finished in 1959. Incorporates Henry VIII's wine cellar, actually built for Cardinal Wolsey and open on Sat afternoons, on application only.
The Banqueting House by Inigo Jones, its ceilings painted by Rubens, open from 10.00 to 17.00 in the week and Sun afternoons.
Dover House (The Scottish Office) by Paine in 1755–8, the entrance screen and rotunda by Henry Holland in 1787.
The Treasury by Sir Charles Barry, 1846.
The Foreign Office and *Home Office*, mostly by Gilbert Scott in mid-Victorian palazzo style.
The New Government Offices, late Victorian, by J. M. Brydon.
World War Two Operational HQ, a 6-acre

underground honeycomb of corridors and rooms, Churchill's secret HQ, still with war-time furnishings. Closed in 1982 for conversion into a museum. Due to reopen Autumn 1983.

15 The Cenotaph
Whitehall SW1. Lutyens' simple memorial to the dead of two World Wars. The annual service of remembrance takes place here in November.

The Cenotaph

16 Downing Street
SW1. 17thC houses built by Sir George Downing. Here are two famous official residences – the Prime Minister's at No 10, and, less famous, the Chancellor of the Exchequer's at No 11.

17 Westminster Pier
Victoria Embankment SW1. 01-839 2349/01-930 4097. The main starting point for boat trips east through the City and docks to the Tower and Greenwich; and west to the exotic greenery of Kew and the Palace at Hampton Court. The River Boat Information Service (01-730 4812) has full details.

18 Queen Boadicea
Westminster Bridge SW1. Statue by Thomas Thornycroft, 1902. The Queen of the Iceni appears to direct her horses by willpower since she has no reigns.

19 Big Ben
Houses of Parliament SW1. The name not of the clock but of the bell, cast at Whitechapel in 1858, whose hourly chimes are broadcast to the nation.

20 Houses of Parliament
St Margaret St SW1. 01-219 3000. Strictly – the New Palace of Westminster, by Barry and Pugin in 1840–68. A grand and glorious Gothic structure built around the late 11thC Westminster Hall whose 14thC timber roof rivals any in Europe. You may tour the building when the house is not sitting, or listen to debates when it is. Write to your MP for an invitation or join the queue outside. *Free. Closed Sun.*

21 St Margaret's Church
Parliament Sq SW1. 01-222 6382. The parish church of the House of Commons, rebuilt in the 16thC. Don't miss the lovely modern stained glass by John Piper.

22 Westminster Abbey
(The Collegiate Church of St Peter in Westminster) Broad Sanctuary SW1. 01-222 5152. Magnificent repository of much of the royal history of Britain. Original church by Edward the Confessor, 1065, rebuilt by Henry III, completed in 1376–1506, with the towers finished by Hawksmoor in 1734. In fine perpendicular with a mighty and soaring Gothic nave, lavish and beautiful side chapels and displays of riches, elaborate tombs and prestigious monuments. Superb, ornate vaulting in Henry VII Chapel. Scene of the coronation, burial and sometimes marriage of England's sovereigns. *Free. Charge* to see Royal Chapels and museum of plate and effigies asks small entry *charge.*

23 Jewel Tower
Old Palace Yd SW1. 01-937 9561. This 14thC fragment of the Old Palace of Westminster displays medieval carvings and 11thC capitals from Westminster Hall. *Free. Closed 16.00 & all Sun.*

24 Greycoat Hospital School
Greycoat Place SW1. Appealing early 18thC building restored by Laurence King after war damage. The wooden 'charity children' above the door were symbols of a free school.

25 Guards Chapel
Wellington Barracks, Birdcage Walk SW1. Austere replacement for the original, destroyed in 1944 with the loss of 121 lives. Small museum tells the story of the Brigade of Guards. *Charge.*

St James's Park

26 St James's Park
SW1. The oldest royal park and one of the prettiest and most romantic with its long lake, delicate bridge and weeping willows. Especially rich in bird life, including 20 species of ducks and geese.

EATING AND DRINKING

A Westminster Arms *Pub*
9 Storey's Gate SW1. 01-222 8520. Pleasant watering-hole for political journalists and for MPs, who can be recalled to the House by a division bell. Big Ben Bar and Queen Anne Bar both serve real ales and snacks and Storey's Wine Bar (closed weekends) will do you a steak and kidney pie, ham salad and the like. *Closed Sun evening.* £.

B St Stephen's *Tavern*
10 Bridge St SW1. 01-930 3230. The second of the only two pubs with a division bell to call MPs back to the House. Good river views and hearty English restaurant with cartoons of bygone MPs. *Closed Sun evening.* ££.

C Clarence *Pub*
53 Whitehall SW1. 01-930 4808. 18thC gaslit house with wooden pews and sawdusted floor. Popular with civil servants from the

Ministry of Agriculture next door – who may be drawn by the old farm equipment on the beams, but are more likely to come for the 7 real ales. Food at every session and a strolling minstrel most evenings. £.

D Silver Cross *Pub*
33 Whitehall SW1. 01-930 8350. 13thC building, with a preservation order on its fine Italian waggon-vaulted ceiling, which was licensed as a brothel by Charles I. Open all day serving English breakfasts, lunches, afternoon teas and evening snacks in a cheery, friendly atmosphere. *Closed Sun evening.* £.

Horse Guards Parade

E Justin de Blank at the ICA *Restaurant*
Nash House, The Mall SW1. 01-839 6762. This split level restaurant, complete with tree, in the Mall's small but active arts centre, still has some of the relaxed, arty flavour of the 60s. Food is mainly vegetarian, hot and cold, with fresh salads. Snacks only at night. *Closed Mon.* £.

F Slatters *Wine Bar*
3 Panton St SW1. 01-839 4649. Soothing chocolate brown decor with a vividly red overflow bar at the top of a spiral stairway. The Tom Merrifield prints on the walls are for sale. Hot food undistinguished, cold food very good. *Closed Sun.* £.

G Stockpot *Restaurant*
40 Panton St SW1. 01-839 5142. Cheap and cheerful international peasant food. Speedy service, and they quite like their customers to be quick, too. £.

H Captain's Cabin *Pub*
7 Norris St SW1. 01-930 4767. Three-bar pub with a nautical theme and a lunchtime fish restaurant with its own cocktail bar. ££.

J Hunting Lodge *Restaurant*
16 Lower Regent St SW1. 01-930 4222. Flamboyant red and black decor with many a reference to the chase, including sporting guns and the kind of food you might expect to shoot – jugged hare, duckling, game in season. End the meal in masculine style with cheese or a savoury. *Closed Sat lunch & all Sun.* £££.

K Wheeler's *Restaurant*
Duke of York St SW1. 01-930 2640. One of a chain of affable fish restaurants with the usual green-painted exterior, panelling, plush and prints. Oysters in season, white fish in sauce, fruit or cheese to follow. *Closed Sun.* ££.

L Red Lion *Pub*
2 Duke of York St SW1. 01-930 2030. A gem of a Victorian gin palace with mahogany panelling and mirrors engraved with British flowers. Lovely weekday lunches, especially on Friday when the excellent fish shop next door provides the traditional main course. £.

M Wilton's *Restaurant*
27 Bury St SW1. 01-930 8391. Eat the best oysters in London in a charming, Art Nouveau decor. Or, according to season, spoil yourself with one or other of the outstandingly well-prepared nobly British dishes – crab, salmon, sausages and mash, pheasant, partridge, port and stilton. *Closed Fri evening, all Sat & Sun.* £££+.

N Suntory *Restaurant*
72 St James's St SW1. 01-409 0201. Authentic Japanese restaurant, popular with ministers and officials from the nearby Japanese Embassy, with two main dining areas and private rooms kept aside for parties. Gracious service, and guidance through the menu if required. Try fillet steak with shrimps and fresh fruit salad with seaweed jelly. *Closed Sun.* £££+.

O Overton's *Restaurant*
5 St James's St SW1. 01-839 3774. A sedate and traditional fish restaurant with a handsome oyster bar at the front and cocktail bar and restaurant behind. First class fish converted into traditional dishes, oysters and lobsters in season, crêpes or savouries to follow. Courteous service and fine wines. *Closed Sun.* £££.

P Dukes Hotel *Restaurant*
35 St James's Pl SW1. 01-491 4840. A quiet hotel whose small restrained dining room, tastefully furnished with antiques, offers an ever-changing menu of English and French specialities. £££.

10 Downing Street

Morning Coffee and Afternoon Tea
Fortnum and Mason; 181 Piccadilly W1. 01-774 8040. Three restaurants, one open until 23.00 for coffee, tea, snacks, meals. *Closed Sun.*
The Ritz Hotel; Piccadilly W1. 01-493 8181. Peaceful luxury in the Palm Court.
The Tevere; Gt Peter St SW1. 01-222 4901. Also substantial snacks and meals. *Closed 17.30 & all weekend.*
The Silver Cross Pub; 33 Whitehall SW1.
Justin de Blank at the ICA; Not Mon.

Map 22 COVENT GARDEN AND THE STRAND

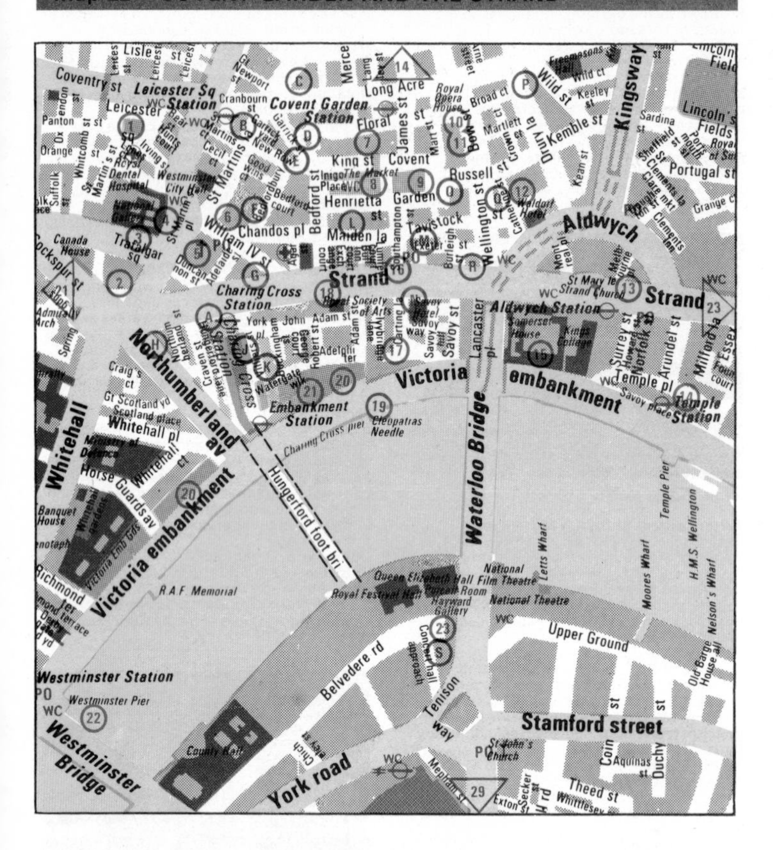

Here is the cultural centre of London, bordered on the west by the majestic government buildings of Whitehall and on the east by legal London and the Temple. This square mile contains the majority of the West End theatres and cinemas, the Royal Opera House, the London Coliseum, the National Gallery and the massive concrete structure of the South Bank Arts Centre, which is the home of the National Theatre, the National Film Theatre and three major concert halls. Charing Cross Road is rich in second-hand bookshops and St Martin's Court and Cecil Court offer venerable books, sheet music and old prints. Traces of an earlier past linger in the York Watergate and Goodwin's Court which allow glimpses, still, of the 17thC.

North of the Strand lies Covent Garden, which will never be quite the same now the great fruit and veg market has moved to Nine Elms and late night opera-goers no longer share mobile tea bars with early morning porters. With the passing of the market, various grand schemes were put forward for the area. These were opposed by the tenants who had hoped for more social amenities and fresh opportunities for small businesses, but much of their opposition was worn down by time and the result is a compromise but great fun. The new GLC housing and office blocks are stark and the market buildings themselves have been face-lifted into a mock-Georgian shopping arcade. However, the area remains exciting and genuinely alive with street theatre, galleries, publishing houses, rehearsal rooms, and new enterprises moving into the converted warehouses, where craftsmen setting up workshops continue a pattern established generations ago.

PLACES OF INTEREST

1 **Leicester Square**
WC2. Pedestrianised and commercial, flanked by four major cinemas, the Swiss Centre and several eating places with their sights set on tourists. The first statue of Charlie Chaplin stands to the west, under trees raucous with starlings in the bright night lights.

2 **Trafalgar Square**
WC2. Commemorates Nelson, the focal point being the 185ft column topped by the Admiral and guarded by Landseer's amiable lions. Well-known for its fountains, pigeons, political gatherings and annual Christmas tree from Norway. Less well-known for the fire damage at the column's base, caused when the 1918 Armistice celebrations got out of hand; the Imperial Standards on the north wall, decreeing the lengths of inches, etc; and the minute police station *inside* a stone lamp on the east side.

3 **National Gallery**
Trafalgar Sq WC2. 01-839 3321. One of the richest collections of paintings in the world, with magnificent Leonardos, Raphaels, Botticellis, Titians, Rembrandts, Rubens, Van Dycks, El Grecos, Constables, Turners, Gainsboroughs and Reynolds. Spare a glance for the entrance floor where some famous faces are set in mosaic; among them Greta Garbo as the 'Tragic Muse'. *Closed Sun morn. Free.*

4 **National Portrait Gallery**
2 St Martin's Pl WC2. 01-930 8511. Each of the portraits of the great and notorious was painted during the subject's lifetime, so the likenesses are probably accurate. Often an itinerant artist outside who will draw your image for a fee. *Closed B hols. Free.*

5 **St Martin-in-the-Fields**
Trafalgar Sq WC2. 01-930 1862. Built by James Gibbs in 1722–4. This is the parish church of Buckingham Palace (though not used as such) and above the congregation is a royal box, complete with fireplace. On Mon and Tue lunchtimes, young musicians perform free, and the Crypt Folk Club entertains below on Sun evening. *Collection.*

6 **London Coliseum**
St Martin's La WC2. 01-836 3161. Splendidly lavish theatre designed by Oswald Stoll in 1904, with the first revolving stage in Britain, and a majestic arched and columned interior. The home of the English National Opera since the 60s. International ballet companies perform for limited seasons when the Opera is on tour during the summer.

7 **Dance Centre**
12 Floral St WC2. 01-836 6544. For those inspired to emulate the professional dancers. For minimal daily membership and a less minimal class fee anyone can join a tap, ballet or modern dance class. They sell leotards, too.

8 **St Paul's Church**
Covent Gdn WC2. 01-836 5221. An archway in Henrietta St leads to a small garden, once the burial ground for St Peter's Hospital, and to the 'actors' church'. Built by Inigo Jones in the 1630s it contains memorials to Marie Lloyd, Boris Karloff, Sybil Thorndike, Lewis Casson and many more. Grinling Gibbons, buried in the crypt with his wife, is remembered by a wreath he carved himself.

9 **Covent Garden Complex**
Market Hall WC2. In 1979 the main hall became the antithesis of the old lusty, vulgar market. It shelters shops for clothes, herbs, pretty shoes, books and chocolates and stalls for arts and crafts. Wandering musicians entertain. There are health foods, crêpes, hamburgers or full meals, often at outdoor tables. The Punch and Judy pub is near the site of the first puppet show and the Crusting Pipe is a good wine bar. Attractive, but all a bit precious and over-priced. The London Transport Museum has a collection of historic road and rail vehicles.

Covent Garden

10 **Royal Opera House**
Covent Gdn WC2. 01-240 1066. A sumptuous domed building with lush cream, gold and red interior, by Sir Edward Barry (1857–8). A mecca for grand opera and the home of the Royal Ballet.

11 **Bow Street Police Station**
28 Bow St WC2. 01-434 5212. London's oldest police station and the birthplace of the Bow Street Runners. There's no traditional blue lamp outside because Queen Victoria thought it vulgar so near the Royal Opera House.

12 **Theatre Royal, Drury Lane**
Catherine St WC2. 01-836 8108. Known as 'Drury Lane', though in fact it's round the corner. The royal box has accommodated every monarch since Charles II, and Nell Gwynne, Garrick, Mrs Siddons and Edmund Kean played here. The 'Man in Grey' (who appears where building work has uncovered a male skeleton) is one of the best-loved theatre ghosts – he traditionally heralds a successful musical.

13 **St Mary-le-Strand**
Strand WC2. A perfect small Baroque church, built 1714–17 by James Gibbs, on an island in the middle of the road.

14 **Lord Astor's House**
Temple Pl, Embankment WC2. A delicate, early Elizabethan style town house (by J. L. Pearson, built 1895). Look through the gates at the lamps flanking the door for the unexpected sight of a cherub making a telephone call.

15 **Somerset House**
Strand WC2. Built by Sir William Chambers in 1776, and now used entirely for Government

offices, with occasional public exhibitions in the 'Fine Rooms'. The name is synonymous with the Register of Births, Marriages and Deaths in England and Wales, but the Registrar's Office has moved to St Catherine's House, 10 Kingsway WC2, 01-242 0262, where those wishing to search into their pasts should apply.

16 Strand
WC2. Once truly a strand, a riverside walk, before the river was embanked and pushed southwards. With Fleet Street as its continuation, it links the City with Westminster. In Tudor times great mansions stood along it, their gardens reaching to the Thames. One of these was York House and when George Villiers, Duke of Buckingham, had to sell it to pay his debts, he asked to be remembered in the streets on the site. This accounts for George Court, Villiers St, Duke St, York Place (formerly Of Alley) and Buckingham St.

17 The Lamp That Never Goes Out
Carting La WC2. Behind the Savoy Hotel, one street lamp burns continually with the vague glow of gaslight. It is one of the last of London's sewer lamps, and it feeds upon the effluent of that smart hotel.

18 Royal Society of Arts
6–8 John Adam St WC2. Established in 1754, in Somerset House, to encourage art and industry. Now occupying a fine Adam house built in 1774. Entry on application only.

19 Cleopatra's Needle
Victoria Embankment SW1. Has nothing to do with the lady herself. One of a pair of obelisks from an Egyptian temple, c1450 BC, it is a gift from Egypt, mounted here in 1877. Two jars under the pedestal contain some things the Victorians felt would excite future archaeologists – including a picture of Queen Victoria, a box of hairpins and Bradshaw's Railway Timetable. Presumably they'll be noted down as 'ritual objects'.

20 Victoria Embankment Gardens
WC2. Stretch both sides of Charing Cross Station. In summer leading military bands and light orchestras play at the bandstand near Watergate Walk (at lunchtime on weekdays and early afternoon at weekends).

21 York Watergate
Watergate Walk, off Villiers St WC2. When built in 1626, the gate stood on the bank of the Thames, at the river entrance to the Duke of Buckingham's York House. It hasn't moved – the Embankment Gardens have been reclaimed from the river. The sadly eroded lions support the Villiers' family arms.

22 Westminster Pier
Victoria Embankment SW1. 01-839 2349/01-930 4097. The Thames is the heart of London, whose history lines the riverbanks as if waiting to be admired from an unhurried motor launch. The main starting point for trips east through the City and docks to the Tower and Greenwich; and west to the exotic greenery of Kew and the Palace of Hampton Court. The River Boat Information Service (01-730 4812) has full details.

23 South Bank Arts Centre
Between Hungerford and Waterloo Bridges, SE1.

National Theatre

The National Theatre Company stages a wide variety of plays in the apron-staged *Olivier*, the conventional *Lyttleton* and the adaptable *Cottesloe*. Booking on 01-928 2252.
The Royal Festival Hall and *Queen Elizabeth Hall* offer symphony, orchestral and choral concerts and the *Purcell Room* chamber music and soloists. Booking on 01-928 3191.
The National Film Theatre shows rare and classic films. Booking on 01-928 3232.
The Hayward Gallery mounts major art exhibitions. Details on 01-928 3144.
The complex includes bookstalls, bars, snack bars and live entertainment in the theatre foyers, a restaurant and a riverside terrace.

EATING AND DRINKING

A Charing Cross Hotel *Carvery*
Strand WC2. 01-839 7282. One of the best carveries in London for a hungry luncher – at reasonable prices. Help yourself to traditional British roast beef, lamb and pork with all the things that go with them, like Yorkshire pudding and roast potatoes. ££.

B Salisbury *Pub*
90 St Martin's La WC2. 01-836 5863. Gleaming brass, red plush and cut glass mirrors in an Edwardian bar with a very superior food counter. Full of theatre-goers in the early evening. Famous meeting place for male gays. £.

C Peppermint Park *Restaurant*
13 Upper St Martin's La WC2. 01-836 5234. Pink, green, young and lively with loud background music. They make a speciality of parties, sticking sparklers in the food and singing relevant songs. Cocktails, burgers, salads, 12" hot dogs and puddings aptly, if inelegantly, known as Belly Busters. ££.

D Lamb and Flag *Pub*
33 Rose St WC2. 01-836 4108. While enjoying lunch in the 300-year-old Lamb, you may care to know it wasn't always so mellow. Called The Bucket of Blood when bare fist fights were staged upstairs, it made a mark on the world of literature when the poet Dryden was beaten up outside. £.

E Regency *Café*
Corner New Row/Bedfordbury WC2. Small and unpretentious with good snacks. Popular with dancers and impecunious actors. *Closed Sun.*

F Lemon Tree *Pub*
4 Bedfordbury WC2. 01-836 1864. Drink here in memory of old Covent Garden Market where, in the 18thC, the first landlord ran a stall of imported Italian lemons. The local for the orchestra, chorus and staff of the Coliseum. Bar food. *Closed Sun.*

G Lyons Corner House *Restaurant*
450 Strand WC2. 01-930 9381. Famous English institution, now happily revived. Coffee Shop for breakfasts, coffees, teas and snacks. Downstairs licensed restaurant for lunch or early dinner. *Open 08.00–20.00.* £.

H Sherlock Holmes *Pub*
10 Northumberland St WC2. 01-930 2644. This was the Northumberland Arms Hotel, mentioned in *The Hound of the Baskervilles.* Fans of the fictitious detective will recognise the mementoes in the bar, including the pawprint of the dreaded dog. Upstairs there's a reconstruction of Holmes' study, next to the restaurant. *Restaurant closed Sat D & Sun.* ££.

J Duke of Buckingham *Pub*
8 Villiers St WC2. 01-930 4728. Real ale, live music most evenings and food always.

K Gordon's *Wine Bar*
47 Villiers St WC2. 01-930 1408. Down some steps from Villiers St to Watergate Walk stands an unprepossessing door which leads into a 300-year-old candlelit cellar. Here you can drink excellent wine, eat game pie and cheese, and enjoy the sensation of having escaped the world. *Closed 21.00 & Sat & Sun.*

L Rules *Restaurant*
35 Maiden La Strand WC2. 01-836 5314. A slice of Edwardian London to be savoured. Edward VII dined Lily Langtry in an upstairs room. Thackeray and Dickens ate here. Electric chandeliers now, but authentic panelling, pictures and playbills. Roast beef and jugged hare recommended. *Closed Sat & Sun.* ££.

St Martin-in-the-Fields

M Joe Allen *Bar*
13 Exeter St WC2. 01-836 0651. Fashionable, fun and very much on the lines of the New York and Paris versions. First-rate cocktail bar; blackboard menu of burgers, steaks, salads and pecan pie. Very crowded, especially when the theatres empty. ££.

N Savoy *Restaurant*
Strand and Embankment WC2. 01-836 4343. Deservedly world-famous hotel with stylish decor, lovely river views and famous faces at the tables. A choice of *Grill Room* or the restaurant where a dance band plays every night but Sunday. The cocktails in the snazzy *American Bar* are so popular, a book of their recipes is sold in the foyer. £££.

O Tuttons *Wine Bar*
11–12 Russell St WC2. 01-836 1167. A wine bar above and a restaurant below offering breakfast, imaginative snacks or dinner. ££.

Westminster Pier

P White Hart *Pub*
191 Drury La WC2. 01-405 4061. Large lunchtime snack lounge becomes a music room every evening for good, noisy jazz.

Q Opera Tavern *Pub*
23 Catherine St WC2. 01-836 7149. Victorian, with elaborate façade. Popular with actors from nearby theatres. Pool, darts and hints of a ghost downstairs . . . Nice food. *Closed Sun.*

R Balls Bros *Wine Bar*
142 Strand WC2. 01-836 0156. Run by a firm of shippers and merchants. Reliable snack counter and a selection of about 70 tried and true wines. *Closed 19.30 & all weekend.*

S Archduke *Wine Bar*
Concert Hall Approach SE1. 01-928 9370. Flee from the South Bank Arts Centre to this cheery railway arch with ground floor wine bar and upstairs restaurant. Live jazz or blues, and amazing sausages, in the eve. ££.

Morning Coffee and Afternoon Tea
Charing Cross Hotel; Strand WC2. 01-839 7282. Coffee or tea in the first-floor lounge.
Savoy Hotel; Strand and Embankment WC2. 01-836 4343. Afternoon tea in the Thames Foyer to piano or harp.
At the *South Bank Arts Centre*:
National Theatre's Lyttleton Foyer; serves tea, coffee and cakes all day except Sun.
National Film Theatre's Buffet; serves tea and cakes every afternoon.
Royal Festival Hall's Cafeteria; serves tea, coffee, cakes and snacks with river views. *Closed Sun morn.*
Strand Palace Hotel; Strand WC2. 01-836 8080. Hotel Coffee Shop open 7 days a week.
Waldorf Hotel; Aldwych WC2. 01-836 2400. Coffee or elegant afternoon tea in the Palm Court Lounge.

Map 23 FLEET STREET AND THE CITY

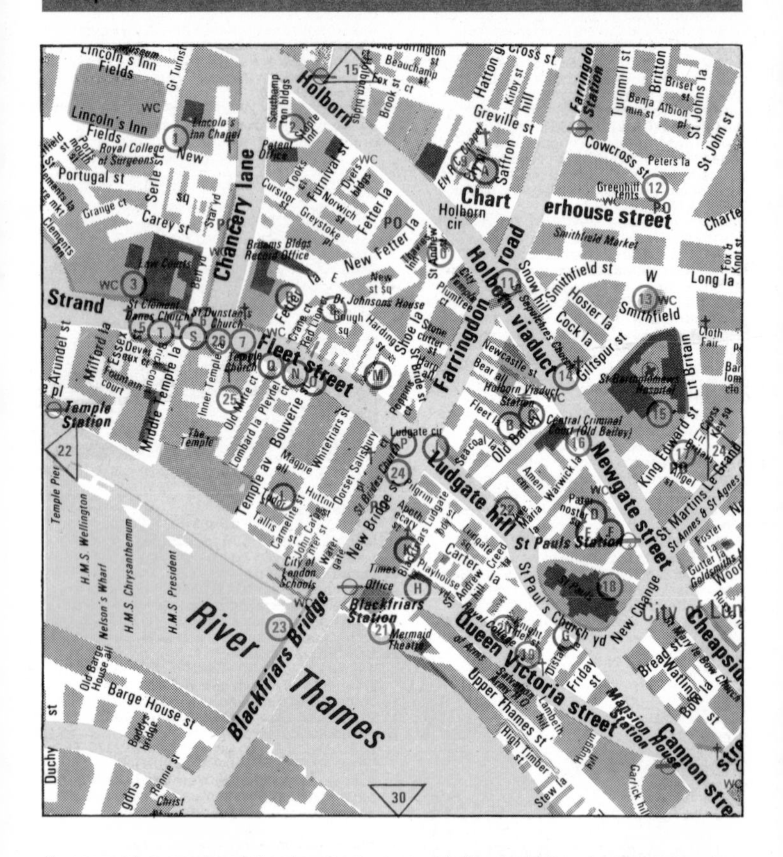

Here as much as anywhere in London, street names evoke the past. Holborn is a contraction of Hollow Bourne, the valley through which the Fleet River flowed before it was culverted and sent beneath Fleet Street to join the Thames near Blackfriars Bridge. The Temple stands on land which once belonged to the controversial crusading order of the Knights Templar, dissolved in 1312. The Knights who rode down Knightrider Street are of less sombre memory – they were en route from the Tower to Smithfield to take part in jousts and tournaments. And the ubiquitous name 'Blackfriars' recalls a 13thC order who flourished in their rich priory south of Ludgate Hill until they fell foul of Henry VIII.

To the west is much of legal London, with two of the four great Inns of Court – Lincoln's Inn and the Temple – flanking the Royal Courts of Justice. The Central Criminal Court, better known as the Old Bailey, stands in the City itself on the site of the notorious Newgate Prison. The Magpie and Stump opposite still has a room in which the gentry hired window space to watch public hangings.

Fleet Street, famous for newspaper offices and printing works, is in every way a communications link between the rest of London and the square mile of the City itself, which spreads its riches onto maps 24 and 31. The two structures most often encountered here are Wren churches and old pubs. Spend time in the latter to get the flavour of the area, imbibing with lawyers, journalists, printers and City gents – but bear in mind that the City closes down in the evening and at weekends and its hostelries have shorter hours than most.

PLACES OF INTEREST

1 Lincoln's Inn
WC2. One of the four great Inns of Court, a compact Dickensian world of squares, gardens and barristers' chambers, whose records go back to 1422. The old Hall, and Inigo Jones' Chapel, can be viewed on application to the Gatehouse in Chancery Lane.

2 Staple Inn
High Holborn WC2. The nine Inns of Chancery were subordinate to the four Inns of Court and, unlike the latter, did not survive the 18thC. Some have left their names – Clifford's Inn, Furnival Inn – Staple Inn alone remains as a court with a restored 16thC hall, now used by the Institute of Actuaries.

3 Law Courts
Strand WC2. An elaborate fairy-tale castle, with spires, turrets and statues, built by Street in 1874–80 to house the Royal Courts of Justice. Scene of the Quit Rent Ceremony at the end of October, a wholly English piece of eccentricity involving payment to the Queen's Remembrancer of two faggots, six horseshoes and 61 nails for two pieces of land whose whereabouts are not certain. *Free. Closed weekends.*

4 St Clement Danes Church
Strand WC2. The church of the nursery rhyme whose carillon includes 'Oranges and Lemons' in its repertoire. Built for the Danes in the 9thC, rebuilt by Wren in 1680, with a steeple added by Gibbs in the 18thC and destroyed by enemy action in 1941. In the 1950s it was rebuilt to Wren's original plan and is now the central church of the RAF.

5 Twinings Tea Shop
216 Strand WC2. 01-353 3511. Beautifully packaged teas, both plain and fancy. Look above the door at the trade sign of 1787 with its two Chinese figures – a reminder that the first Indian Tea Company was not formed until 1832.

With the hams at Smithfield Market

6 St Dunstan in the West Church
Fleet St EC4. Rebuilt in 1832 by John Shaw, who copied All Saints Church in York. The clock with its two 'striking jacks' who club the bell on each hour is 17thC, from the former church, and the statue of Queen Elizabeth I over the side entrance is the only known contemporary portrait of her.

7 Fleet Street
EC4. London's 'street of ink' has been associated with printing since the days of Caxton. Most national and provincial newspapers have their offices on or near it still.

8 Dr Johnson's House
17 Gough Sq Fleet St EC4. 17thC house where he lived, and in whose huge attic he worked on his dictionary, from 1748–59. Relics, letters, early editions and portraits of Johnson and Boswell. *Closed Sun. Charge.*

9 Ely Court
EC1. Here stood the town house of the Bishops of Ely. The Olde Mitre Tavern was built in the 16thC, and the small and exquisite 13thC Ely Chapel, St Etheldreda's, is the last remnant of the bishops' rule. It is one of the few medieval churches in England to have reverted to its Catholic origin. The area is still a sanctuary, outside the jurisdiction of the Metropolitan Police.

10 St Andrew's Church
Holborn Circus EC1. Wren's largest parish church, built in 1686 but restored after bombing with a cool, simple, modern interior. The pulpit, font, organ and tomb of Thomas Coram come from the chapel of his 18thC Foundling Hospital – *see Map 15.*

Holborn Viaduct

11 Holborn Viaduct
EC4. William Heywood's 1400 foot long viaduct of 1863, its cast-iron work brightly painted, is decorated with massive bronze statues representing Commerce, Agriculture, Science and Fine Art. Very Victorian.

12 Cowcross Street
EC1. The route once taken by cattle on their way to a fatal appointment at Smithfield.

13 Smithfield Wholesale Meat Market
EC1. The world's largest wholesale meat market on a site originally called Smooth Field. The famous Bartholomew Fair was held here and so were tournaments and public executions. The Italianate-style buildings, designed by Horace Jones and erected between 1868–99, are interesting – but don't visit with a weak stomach.

14 St Sepulchre's Church
Holborn Viaduct EC1. Rebuilt in the 15thC, altered by Wren in 1667, and restored again in the 18thC and 19thC which makes for an intriguing if confused interior. Its history has a grisly side; the bells tolled for the condemned in nearby Newgate Prison and its graveyard was ransacked for bodies for St Bartholomew's Medical School.

15 St Bartholomew's Hospital
West Smithfield EC1. 01-600 9000. Founded in 1123, with an adjoining Augustinian priory,

and spared at the Dissolution – in memory of which London's only statue of Henry VIII stands over the doorway. William Harvey, who first understood the circulation of the blood, was its chief physician from 1609–43, and its Medical School is highly respected.

16 Old Bailey
EC4. 01-248 3277. On the site of old Newgate Prison, and with some of the prison's stones incorporated in the lower parts of their walls, stand the impressive buildings of the Central Criminal Court. The public may watch trials – as once they watched executions (outside until 1868, inside until 1901). *Closed weekends.*

17 National Postal Museum
King Edward St EC1. 01-432 3851. A philatelist's dream – more than 350,000 stamps are on display. First day covers are sold in the Post Office below and the museum has its own postmark. *Closed weekends. Free.*

St Paul's Cathedral

18 St Paul's Cathedral
EC4. 01-248 4619/2705. Sir Christopher Wren's greatest work, built from 1675–1710 to replace a church destroyed in the Fire of London. Superb dome and porches are dwarfed by modern building but the interior has lost nothing with its magnificent stalls by Grinling Gibbons, ironwork by Tijou, paintings by Thornhill, mosaics by Salviati and Stephens. The setting in 1981 for the marriage of Charles, Prince of Wales, and Lady Diana Spencer.

19 St Nicholas Cole Abbey
Queen Victoria St EC4. Originally by Wren, 1671–81, but extensively restored after war-damage. The modern stained glass is by Keith New, but much of the woodwork, clean and fresh though it may look, is original.

20 Royal College of Arms
Queen Victoria St EC4. Discreet brick building of 1671 behind splendid gates wherein the three Kings of Arms, six Heralds and four Pursuivants arrange matters ceremonial and heraldic and store the official records of English and Welsh genealogy. *No access.*

21 Mermaid Theatre
Puddle Dock, Blackfriars EC4. 01-236 5568. Launched by Sir Bernard Miles in 1945, and established here in the late 50s as an Elizabethan-style theatre across the river from the site of Shakespeare's Globe. Renovated in 1980 and reopened 1981. Classical and modern drama; a restaurant, and two bars overlooking the Thames.

22 St Martin Ludgate Church
Ludgate Hill EC4. Rebuilt by Wren in 1677–87, incorporating part of the medieval city wall on its west side. Restored since, though most of the woodwork is 17thC.

23 Blackfriars Bridges
EC4. The railway bridge opened in 1886; the road bridge by James Cubitt opened in 1889. Between them, at low water, the Fleet River can be seen running into the Thames.

24 St Bride's Church
Fleet St EC4. 01-353 1301. The printers' church, its crypt museum – itself part Roman part Saxon – warmed by the heat of Reuters next door. This is the Wren church whose tiered spire has been the model for a million wedding cakes. Restored after war damage. Christ almost dances in the stained glass window in the Wren-style altarpiece.

25 Temple
Inner Temple, Crown Office Row EC4. 01-353 8462; Middle Temple, Middle Temple La EC4. 01-353 4355. You may wander around the courtyards, alleys and manicured gardens (where pairs of darkly suited lawyers pace in deep debate) by privilege, not by right. The 12th–13thC early Gothic round church, built by the Knights Templar, has a chillingly romantic air with its stone effigies of knights lying in stately wait below grey marble pillars. *Closed 16.00 & all weekend, except church.*

26 Prince Henry's Rooms
17 Fleet St EC4. 01-353 7323. Above the arch-way to Inner Temple Lane is the oldest domestic building in London, dating from 1610. The room itself, named after James I's son, has a beautiful plaster ceiling. *Open weekday afternoons. Charge.*

EATING AND DRINKING

A Olde Mitre *Tavern*
Ely Court, Ely Place EC1. First find the gas lamp in Ely Place, turn the corner and you face this charming 16thC inn. But note, it closes at 20.00 and all weekend.

B Old Bailey Tandoori *Restaurant*
19–20 Old Bailey EC4. 01-248 1651. Friendly unlicensed Indian restaurant. The menu is long but the attractively presented tandoori dishes are the best bet. *Closed Sun.* ££.

C Magpie and Stump *Pub*
18 Old Bailey EC4. 01-248 3819. Partly rebuilt in 1931 but with a feeling of age. Long bar upstairs is called Court 24 (the Old Bailey has 23). Two bars downstairs often full of barristers, crime reporters and the celebrating acquitted. Plain bar snacks. *Closed weekends.* £.

D Sir Christopher Wren *Pub*
28 Paternoster Row EC4. 01-248 1708. Modern pub with 17thC fittings. Dining room serves English lunches. On Sat evenings in August it opens to watch the Scottish dancing in the square. Otherwise *closed weekends* £.

E Slenders *Restaurant*
41 Cathedral Pl EC4. 01-236 5974. Wholesome and vegetarian with the pine and hessian decor that seems to go with vegetarian food – wholemeal bread, fresh salads, choice flans. *Closed 18.15 & all weekend.* £.

F Oodles *Restaurant*
31 Cathedral Pl EC4. 01-248 2550. One of a chain of not strictly vegetarian restaurants. However, flans are savoury, salads are crunchy, and sweets are sticky. *Closed 19.00 & all weekend.* £.

G Balls Bros *Wine Bar*
2 Old Change Ct EC4. 01-248 8697. A branch of an old-established chain with a sound selection of wines and a superior snack counter. *Closed 19.30 & all weekend.* £.

H Blackfriar *Pub*
174 Queen Victoria St EC4. 01-236 5650. Like an Art Nouveau temple of marble and bronze, with bas reliefs of friars singing and working. Even more stunning 'side chapel' has an arched mosaic ceiling, red marble columns, friars, demons, fairies and alabaster animals. A drink seems superfluous but there is real ale, and lunchtime sandwiches. *Closed 22.00 & all weekend.* £.

J Old King Lud *Pub*
78 Ludgate Hill EC4. 01-236 6610. Named for the legendary British Chief whose carved face gazes woodenly out over the door. Gas lit, low ceilinged, respectable (though the cellars were once part of Newgate Prison) with hand-pumped beer and excellent snacks. £.

K Ludgate *Cellars*
Apothecary St EC4. 01-236 6808. Large linked bars, with sawdusty floors and candles on barrels, ramble underground to Blackfriars Lane. Beer, wine, hot and cold food, relaxing atmosphere. *Closed weekends.* £.

L White Swan *Pub*
28/30 Tudor St EC4. 01-353 5596. Here is a large and genuine local, packed with darts-playing printers and affectionately known as the Mucky Duck. *Closed Sat lunchtime.* £.

Ye Olde Cheshire Cheese

M Ye Olde Cheshire Cheese *Pub*
145 Fleet St EC4. 01-353 6170. Aged and famous (rebuilt after the Great Fire with the 14thC crypt of Whitefriars Monastery intact beneath). Beloved of Johnson, Goldsmith, Pope, and Dickens. Small low-ceilinged rooms, sawdusted floors, Marston's Bitter, massive portions of English food. Famous for winter game puddings. *Closed 21.00 & all weekend.* £.

N First Edition *Restaurant*
61 Fleet St EC4. 01-353 4772. International menu with a strongly Italian accent. Popular with printers in search of chicken Kiev, veal in wine and sage sauce, profiteroles. Small dance floor with discreet disco nightly (not Mon). *Closed Sun.* ££.

O Printer's Pie *Restaurant*
60 Fleet St EC4. 01-353 8861. Printers, it appears, are fond of simple, traditional English food – grills, steak and kidney pie, jam roll. Pleasant, vaguely Victorian setting. *Closed 21.45 & all weekend.* £.

Law Courts

P Old Bell *Pub*
95 Fleet St EC4. 01-353 3796. Small and unpretentious with draught bitter and a practical past – it was built by Wren in 1670 to take care of the workmen restoring nearby St Bride's. *Closed Sun.* £.

Q El Vino *Wine Bar*
47 Fleet St EC4. 01-353 6786. A bit of an institution. Like a musty journalists club with a strict code of conduct – gents must wear jacket and tie even in a heatwave and ladies were not allowed to buy drinks until 1982. Excellent wines, good cold food, restaurant below. *Closed Sat evening & Sun.* £.

R Printer's Devil *Pub*
98 Fetter La EC4. 01-242 2239. Despite its demonic sign, the pub is called by the nick-name for a printer's apprentice. Has two working models of presses, specimens of prints and a printing trade clientele. Restaurant serves lunches. *Closed Sun.* £.

S Ye Olde Cock *Tavern*
22 Fleet St EC4. 01-353 8570. Small but good tavern which used to stand in Apollo Court but crossed the road at the end of the 19thC to make way for new building. Nell Gwynne, Pepys, Goldsmith, Sheridan and Garrick drank at the sign of the Cock. Dining room specialises in puddings, pies and roasts, lunchtime only. *Closed 20.30 & all weekend.* ££.

T George *Pub*
Fleet St EC4. 01-353 9238. The timbered exterior looks good and old – in fact it was rebuilt in the 30s. Pleasantly beamed and cosy, handy for the Law Courts, with an à la carte lunchtime restaurant above. ££.

Morning Coffee and Afternoon Tea
Broomfields; 232 Strand WC2. 01-353 7933. Also good snacks all day.
Holborn Viaduct Station; Tea Bar.
Slenders; 41 Cathedral Pl EC4. 01-236 5974.

Map 24 THE CITY AND THE BARBICAN

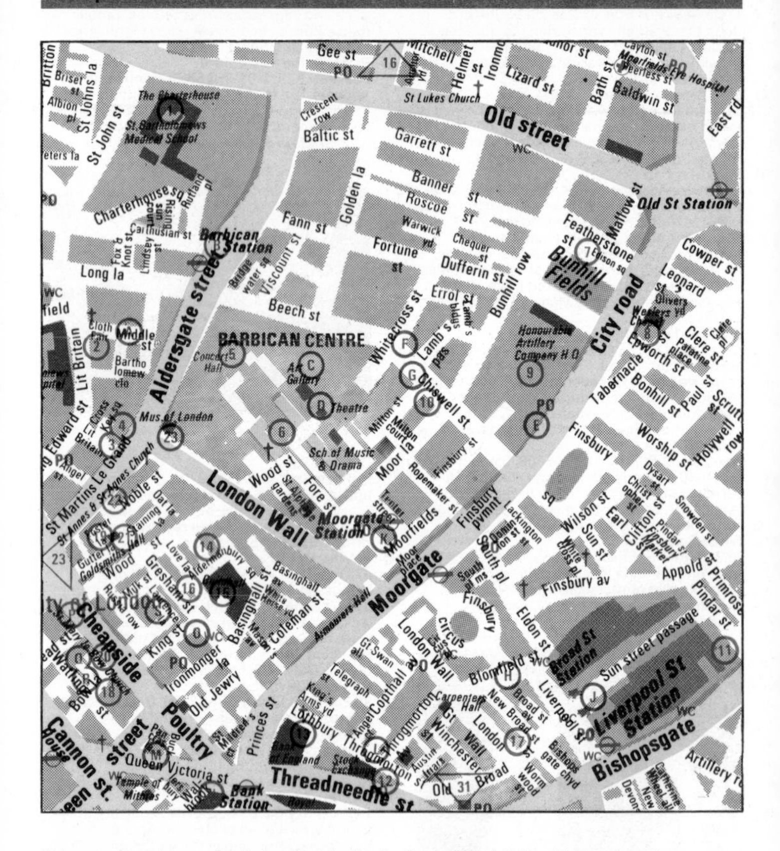

This part of London was badly bombed during the Second World War which explains the overpowering amount of post-1950 building, the largest single grouping of which is the Barbican, just north of London Wall. Designed by Chamberlin, Powell and Bon and constructed between 1957 and 1979, it houses 6,000 people, a girls school, the Guildhall School of Music and an important arts centre made up of theatres, art gallery, cinema and concert hall. The Barbican has changed the face of the City in two ways. Firstly it towers severely above the older buildings, as if watching indignantly for intruders. Secondly it rouses the City from the weekend sleep that used to envelop it until the start of business on Monday morning gave it the kiss of life.

To the north east, beyond the boundaries of the medieval City wall, is an area heavily settled by non-conformists in the 17th and 18thC. John Wesley's house and chapel still stand. So do the memorials in Bunhill Fields where those of controversial belief were buried until 1852. Next to it is the HQ of the Honourable Artillery Company, the British Army's oldest regiment with its traditional links with the City; it guards the Lord Mayor and visiting Royalty and is permitted to march through the City with bayonets fixed. Here too is a prestigious Territorial Force HQ, whose members may be glimpsed through the gates, drilling, some of them still in their City suits.

To the south of the map lies the hem of business London; the Guildhall from which the City is governed, the Bank of England which stores its gold and the Stock Exchange where fortunes are made, lost and manipulated daily.

PLACES OF INTEREST

London's Wall
Sections of Roman and medieval wall are still preserved around the City – the Roman sections are those with thin red tiles between the stones. Look near St Alphage on the north side of the wall, EC1; St Giles Cripplegate within the Barbican; Jewry Street EC3; off Trinity Square EC3 and in the Tower of London.

1 **Charterhouse**
St John St EC1. Historically important building which has served various purposes. It was established as a Carthusian Priory in 1371, suppressed by Henry VIII, used as a private mansion by the Earls of Norfolk and Suffolk, turned into an almshouse and school (later the famous public school), taken over by the Merchant Taylors School, severely bombed in World War II, and finally adapted as a medical school for St Bartholomew's Hospital.

2 **St Bartholomew the Great**
West Smithfield EC1. 01-606 5171. Great indeed. The oldest church in London (apart from the chapel in the Tower) is this Norman choir of the Augustinian priory founded in 1123, together with St Bartholomew's Hospital, by Rahere, a courtier of Henry I. Notice the 13thC entrance arch, the heavy rounded pillars, Rahere's tomb and the last Prior's special little bay window opposite.

3 **St Botolph Aldersgate Church**
Aldersgate EC1. Plain outside, apart from the little bell turret, with a lovely interior by Nathaniel Evans, 1788. Some of the furniture, including the pews, is Victorian.

4 **Postman's Park**
Churchyard of St Botolph, Aldersgate EC2. If you have the nerve to turn your back on Michael Ayrton's threatening bronze of The Minotaur, spare a glance for the series of Victorian tile tablets poignantly commemorating the courage of ordinary individuals.

5 **Barbican Arts Centre**
EC2. 01-628 8795. This great walled bastion of the arts, encircled by up-market high-rise flats, has been called the Bermuda Triangle of the City because its size and complexity make navigation a problem. However, if the Royal Shakespeare Company can get in and out, so can the rest of us. The main theatre is their new home while The Pit stages the work of new British playwrights; the cinema shows classic repeats; the concert hall is the base of the London Symphony Orchestra and also offers a full range of other musical experiences from guest performers; and the art gallery mounts changing exhibitions. There are also long bars, a restaurant and a café overlooking a wide artificial lake with fountains and ducks.

6 **St Giles Cripplegate Church**
Fore St EC2. 01-606 3630. The massive modernity of the Barbican scheme surrounds the church where Cromwell was married and Milton is buried, its interior almost wholly rebuilt after bombing. Behind it stands a corner bastion of the Roman City wall. (Cripplegate comes from 'crepel', Anglo-Saxon for a kind of underpass used for entry after curfew.)

7 **Bunhill Fields**
City Rd EC1. The Nonconformists' burial ground, possibly on the site of a Saxon cemetery called Bonehill Fields. You may pay your respects to the tree-shaded tombs and memorials of John Bunyan, Daniel Defoe, Dr Isaac Watts and William Blake. *Closed 16.00.*

John Wesley's Chapel and Statue

8 **John Wesley's Chapel and House**
47 City Rd EC1. 01-253 2262. The chapel of 1777 has a statue of Wesley before it, his pulpit within, and his grave behind. The house has simple relics – his bed, his umbrella, some letters. *Closed 16.00 & all Sun. Charge.*

9 **Honourable Artillery Company's HQ**
City Rd EC1. Victorian castellated fortress contains the Georgian (1735) HQ of the oldest regiment in the British Army, which supplies the Guard of Honour for the Lord Mayor's Show and for royalty visiting the City.

Honourable Artillery Company's HQ

10 **Whitbread Brewery**
Chiswell St EC2. 01-606 4455. Most famous as the repository of the Overlord Embroidery, the story of the D-Day landings in Normandy stitched by the Royal School of Needlework. There is also a pleasant coffee shop within the brewery precincts. *Closed Sun morn. Free.*

11 **Liverpool Street Station**
EC2. 01-283 7171. Cast-iron and brick Victorian-Gothic pile which dispatches trains to the east and north east London suburbs, Cambridge, Colchester, Norwich and Harwich Harbour.

12 **Stock Exchange**
Old Broad St EC2. 01-588 2355. Began in a coffee house but has been established here

since 1801. Watch the antics of the smartly dressed dealers in negotiable securities from a sound-proofed visitors gallery. Daily film shows explain all. *Closed 15.15 & all weekend. Free.*

13 Bank of England
Threadneedle St EC2. 01-601 4444. The guardian of the nation's gold. Security precludes visitors but the pink-coated, red-waistcoated, top-hatted messengers and doormen are colourfully visible.

14 Chartered Insurance Institute Museum
20 Aldermanbury EC2. 01-606 3835. In the days before the Fire Brigade the insurance companies did the job – but each company would only douse flames on a building bearing its own firemark. Here you may inspect these marks and the fire-fighting equipment that protected them. *Closed weekends & B. hols. Free.*

Guildhall

15 Guildhall
Off Gresham St EC2. 01-606 3030. The City is governed from this primarily 15thC building with a façade by George Dance, 1789, and later restoration by Sir Giles Gilbert Scott. You may view the medieval Great Hall unless a council meeting is in progress. The library is wonderfully rich in works on London and the art gallery has occasional exhibitions from visiting art societies. *Closed Sun. Free.*

16 St Lawrence Jewry Church
Gresham St EC2. 01-600 9478. The City Corporation church with a sense of pomp and ceremony aided by the Royal and City of London Arms. By Wren in 1670–86 but restored by Cecil Brown in the 1950s after severe war damage.

17 All Hallows by the Wall Church
83 London Wall EC2. 01-588 3388. 13thC church on and beside the medieval City wall, rebuilt in 1765–7 by the younger Dance. The huge pulpit is entered through the vestry, itself just over the wall and, strictly speaking, outside the City.

18 St Mary Aldermary Church
Watling St EC4. 01-248 4906. Rebuilt by Wren in 1682 and refurbished in 1867. The ceiling is Wren's personal expression of late perpendicular fan-vaulting. Outside, the tips of the tower pinnacles gleam with gold coloured fibreglass, added in 1962.

19 St Vedast Foster Lane Church
Cheapside EC2. By Wren on a medieval church site with facing seats, a striking black and white floor and 17thC organ case, and a ceiling glittering with silver, aluminium and gilt.

20 St Mary le Bow Church
Cheapside EC2. 01-248 5139. Bow Bells, within whose sphere of sound all true cockneys are born, still ring out. A Wren church gutted in the bombing of 1941 and rebuilt by Laurence King. The modern rood is a present from Germany. 11thC crypt, with quiet chapel, houses the Ecclesiastical Court of Arches, the Archbishop of Canterbury's appeal court.

21 Goldsmiths' Hall
Foster La EC2. Classical-style palazzo rebuilt in 1835 by Philip Hardwick for the Company whose duty it is to assay gold and silver plate and stamp it with its own leopard-head hallmark. Occasional exhibitions. (For information on tours of all Livery companies: the Information Centre, St Paul's Churchyard EC4. 01-606 3030.)

22 St Anne and St Agnes Church
Gresham St EC2. 01-606 4986. Simple red-brick Wren church once called 'by the willows', now surrounded by modern blocks. 17thC woodwork survived the bombing, the rest is restored.

23 Museum of London
London Wall EC2. 01-600 3699. It's worth setting aside a day to enjoy the relics and reconstructions of the City of London from its beginnings through all its phases, including the Elizabethan and Dickensian ones, to the present. *Closed Sun morn & Mon. Free.*

EATING AND DRINKING

A Hand and Shears *Pub*
1 Middle St EC1. 01-600 0257. The local for Barts Hospital, which is why scenes for the film of 'Doctor in the House' were shot here. The name comes from the nearby Cloth Fair. *Closed Sat & Sun.* £.

B San Carlo *Trattoria*
129 Aldersgate St EC1. 01-253 3240. Cheerful and reliable Italian restaurant with a smattering of French dishes on the menu and reasonably priced set lunch and dinner. *Closed Sat lunch & all Sun.* ££.

C Cut Above *Restaurant*
Level 7, Barbican Centre EC2. 01-588 3008. The carvery is self-service, the rest is brought by a waitress. Food is, so far, undistinguished, but it's handy for meals before or after a play, concert or film. ££.

D Waterside *Café*
Level 4, Barbican Centre EC2. 01-588 3008. Snacks, sandwiches and wine bar buffet in a glass fronted café with extensive outdoor seating around the artificial lakes and fountains at the centre's heart. £.

E L'Abat Jour *Restaurant*
14 City Rd EC1. 01-638 2630. Gentle French cum Italian place, more concerned with fresh, quality ingredients than sophisticated sauces; the salmon trout come from a farm not a market, vegetables are seasonal, pastries made by a local patisserie. *Closed evenings & weekends.* ££.

Barbican Arts Centre

F Chiswell Street Cellars *Wine Bar*
Chiswell St EC1. 01-588 5733. The cellars of the old Whitbread Brewery are the perfect setting in which to sample the extensive selection of wines, with or without a snack or a hot meal in the restaurant section. *Closed 20.30 & all weekend.* £.

G St Paul's *Tavern*
Milton St EC1. 01-606 3828. Ordinary but pleasant pub which prides itself on the fact that it can always offer food – usually in the sparsely furnished *Whispering Gallery Wine Bar* upstairs. *Closed weekends.* £.

H Le Marmiton *Restaurant*
4 Blomfield St EC2. 01-588 4643. Crowded City restaurant with rapid service for busy customers; quiches and terrines, sole and steaks, good cheese board. Booths upstairs for peace and privacy. *Closed weekends.* ££.

J Great Eastern Hotel *Restaurants*
Liverpool St EC2. 01-283 4363. The City's only hotel offers you the *City Gates Bar and Restaurant* with lavish self-service breakfast and a carvery-style lunch and dinner, open every day, all day. ££. *The Entrecote Restaurant* serves lunches only – green salad starter and steak followed by apple flan with orange cream or cheese. *Closed weekends.* ££. *The Abercorn Bar* has real ale and ploughman's lunches. *Closed weekends.* £.

K Penny Black *Pub*
Tentor House, Moorfields, Moorgate EC2. 01-628 3675. Good stamping ground for philately enthusiasts – the Postal Museum has supplied photostats of originals for the walls. Separate dining area goes in for gammon, steaks and seafood platter. *Closed 20.30 & all weekend.* £.

Throgmorton *Restaurant*
27 Throgmorton St EC2. 01-588 5165. Something of the atmosphere of a gentleman's club with its oak panelled dining room, its roasts and steak and kidney pies and its Stock Exchange clientele. The mirrored grill room serves slightly pricier steaks and chops. *Closed evenings & weekends.* £.

Sweetings *Restaurant*
39 Queen Victoria St EC4. 01-248 3062. Scrubbed and basic in that uniquely up-market masculine way that prepares you for oysters, lobster, baked salmon, strawberries, stilton and fine old port. *Closed evenings & weekends.* £.

N Aykoku-Kaku *Restaurant*
9 Walbrook EC4. 01-236 9020. Comfortable Japanese restaurant, popular with Japanese business men. Waitresses in kimonos serve in the luxurious dining room – for a cheaper meal try the sushi bar with its selection of delicately served raw fish with rice and sauces. *Closed weekends.* £££.

O Mr Garroway's *Wine Bar*
46 Gresham St EC2. 01-606 8209. Typical City bar – plain wood floor, wines fit for the discerning, friendly slightly clubby atmosphere. There's food downstairs at lunch time – home-made soup, crab quiche, moules, steak, sweets. *Closed 19.30 & all weekend.* £.

P Le Poulbot *Restaurant*
45 Cheapside EC2. 01-236 4379. The City partner of Le Gavroche, with all you would expect from one of London's top French restaurants – excellent food presented with panache and finesse and a fine wine list. Slightly less expensive upstairs. *Closed evenings & weekends.* £££.

Q Williamson's *Tavern*
1–3 Grovelands Ct, Bow La EC4. 01-248 6280. A most amiable place, reputedly the oldest tavern in the City and said to mark its exact centre. Serves 4 real ales, nice snacks, and has a basement games room with pool and darts. £.

St Bartholomew the Great

R Ye Olde Watling *Pub*
29 Watling St EC4. 01-248 6235. Pleasant oak-beamed tavern on one of London's oldest roads, used as digs by the builders of St Paul's. Pies and puddings are served upstairs at lunchtime. *Closed 19.30 & all weekend.* ££.

S Stag *Restaurant*
23 Laurence La EC2. 01-606 4610. Where the bankers and brokers congregate for excellent French cuisine. Start with escargots or fish pâté, go on to steak or escalope de veau Normande, finish with crêpe au citron or something choice from the cheese trolley. *Closed evenings & weekends.* ££.

Morning Coffee and Afternoon Tea
Liverpool Street Station; EC2. Snack Bar.
Great Eastern Hotel; Liverpool St EC2. Tea and biscuits.
Barbican Centre; Barbican EC2. Waterside Café.
Museum of London; London Wall EC2. Tiny snack bar.

Map 25 BATTERSEA

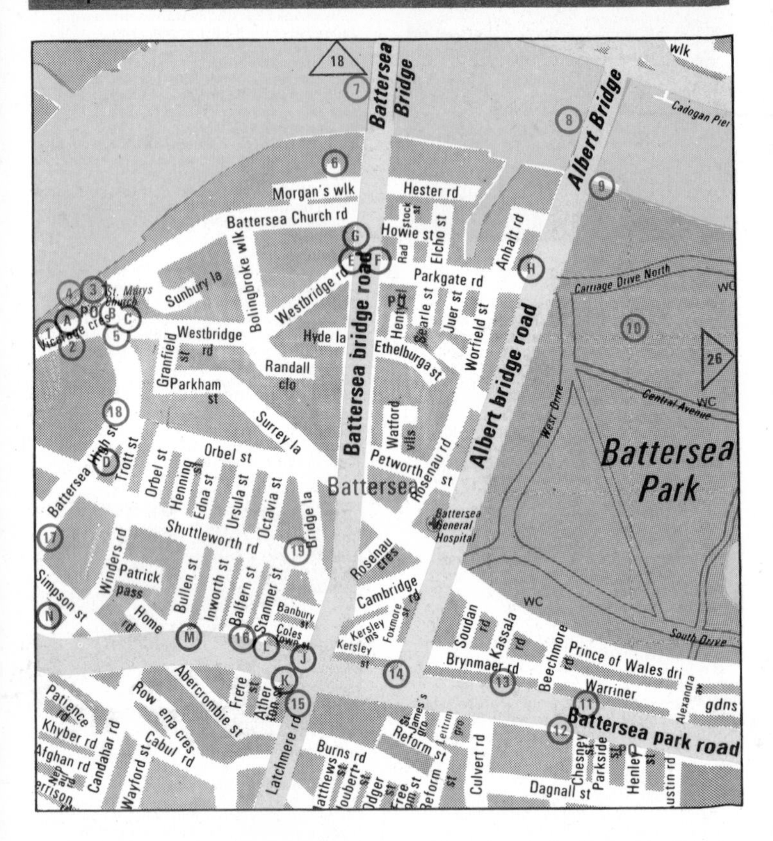

This part of Battersea is principally residential, although there is a certain amount of light industry. There has been a settlement of some kind on this site since the Iron Age. By the 17th and 18th centuries it was a flourishing village, earning its keep chiefly by market gardening. But it was in 1845, when the railway reached nearby Clapham Junction, that it really began to grow and dwellings began to rise on its fields.

Victorian Battersea is still in evidence, with a few notable earlier houses near Battersea Square where the village began, but there is also a great deal of modern building. Much of this consists of bland, functional, high-rise estates, put up in the 50s and 60s, but redevelopment continues and some of the recent building has been more sensitively designed.

There is disagreement about the origin of the name. A charter of 693 calls it 'Badric's Ege', meaning 'Badric's Island', but the Domesday Book has it down as 'Patricsey Isle', meaning 'Peter's Island', and it is true that the area was once owned by the monks of Westminster Abbey and that Peter was their patron Saint. Either way, the early settlement was clearly an island until the marshy area to the south and east, including what was Battersea Fields and what is now the park, was reclaimed from the river.

When the monks lost the land at the Dissolution of the Monasteries it passed to the St John family and the earls Spencer, lords of the manor whose memory lingers on in the names of streets and pubs and the memorials in the church of St Mary.

PLACES OF INTEREST

1 Vicarage Crescent
SW11. Here there are two attractive 18thC houses; the three-storey Devonshire House with its Doric porch, and the Old Vicarage, once the home of the Antarctic explorer and naturalist Edward Adrian Wilson who died with Scott on the tragic return journey from the South Pole.

2 Old Battersea House
Vicarage Crescent SW11. Late 17thC house which, in the 19thC, was the home of the potter William de Morgan and the pre-Raphaelite painter Evelyn de Morgan. A fine collection of their work is in store here and may one day be put on public show.

St Mary's Church

3 St Mary's Church
Church Rd SW11. Built in 1775 by Joseph Dixon, with a 17thC stained glass window and memorials to the St John-Bolingbroke family from the previous church on the site. Here William Blake married Katherine Boucheron and J. M. W. Turner painted sunsets over the river from the vestry window, seated on a chair which is still in its place. The parish registers go back to 1559 and are almost complete.

4 Church Dock
SW11. To the west of the churchyard is the landing place or dock, called a 'porta' in early documents, which was for centuries the main point of access to the settlement. Of historic rather than immediate interest.

5 Battersea Square
SW11. This is the ancient heart of the village, and although most of the buildings are Victorian, and nothing older than the 17thC Raven public house still stands, the small scale makes it possible to visualise the square as it once was, with its village pump and, before that, the parish watch-house which reported on approaching strangers.

Battersea Square

6 Morgan Crucible Company
Morgan's Walk SW11. The name of Morgan's Walk is out of date now that this huge company (founded in 1856 by two brothers who were inspired by the German crucibles on show at the Great Exhibition) has moved to Wales and Worcestershire. Like so much of Battersea, the site is about to be redeveloped.

7 Battersea Bridge
SW11. The picturesque wooden structure made familiar in the paintings of Turner and Whistler has long gone, replaced in 1890 by Sir Joseph Bazalgette's plain iron bridge.

8 Albert Bridge
SW11. A combined cantilever and suspension bridge and one of the prettiest spanning the Thames. It was built by R. W. Ordish in 1873 to carry light pedestrian and carriage traffic and still bears a sign at each end asking troops to break step when crossing to reduce the strain. In 1970 the central support was added, but heavy modern traffic may yet prove too much for its light structure.

9 Toll huts
Albert Bridge SW11. The huts incorporated in the design at either end served as shelters for the 19thC toll collectors.

10 Battersea Park
SW11. Laid out as a public park in 1853. This side of the park has the ornamental lake and fountains, designed in the 50s as part of the Festival Gardens, sculptures by Henry Moore and Barbara Hepworth and a tri-annual outdoor exhibition of modern sculpture. The far side of the park has a boating lake, tennis courts and other facilities (see Map 26).

Battersea Park

11 Marie Blanche Laundry
154 Battersea Park Rd SW11. There is a preservation order on the outside wall of this 100-year-old building to protect the appealing series of bas-reliefs which decorate it, each showing a laundress at work. The central logo of the lady in a balloon is more recent and is of Marie Blanche herself, the celebrated laundress to the first French balloonists.

12 St Saviour's Church
Battersea Park Rd SW11. Small church, designed in French Gothic style by E. C. Robins in 1870. (Records show that the deed of conveyance was presented to the bishop by one of the 'most generous friends of the undertaking', a Mr Evill.)

Toll huts

13 **Sporik Patisserie**
194–6 Battersea Park Rd SW11. 01-622 2774. A tiny shop, selling wonderful English and Continental cakes, its walls hung with naive paintings of landscapes and of a white-clad chef piping icing onto a magnificent gateau. Mr Sporik, who came from Budapest with his wife in the 30s, is responsible for both – a master baker with artistic leanings.

14 **Jungle Jim**
238a Battersea Park Rd SW11. 01-720 6076. A neat little corner site conservatory, purpose built at the end of the 70s to house a lush collection of tropical house plants. *Closed Sun.*

15 **The Gate Theatre at the Latchmere**
503 Battersea Park Rd SW11. 01-328 2620. Opened in 1982, lengthening the list of London's good fringe theatres. There is also a restaurant which, if possible, serves food appropriate to the play, and a 'real ale' pub below. Evening performances only.

The Gate Theatre at the Latchmere

16 **Battersea Pottery**
278 Battersea Park Rd SW11. 01-223 8574. A small studio with a resident potter who creates handthrown stoneware as you watch, some for sale in the shop and some to order, often from customers' own designs. Pots, models of pets and teasets are currently the most popular. *Closed Wed afternoon & Sun.*

17 **Battersea High St Market**
SW11. A shadow of its former self, yet still a real market, chiefly concerned with selling food to local people. A good place to buy fruit and cheese for a picnic in the park. *Closed Sun.*

18 **Sir Walter St John's School**
Battersea High St SW11. The school was founded in 1700 but rebuilt by sections in the 19thC and added to in the 20th, all in Tudor Gothic style. It includes a section designed in 1859 by Butterfield, one of the grand exponents of Victorian Gothic. Over the door, under the wisteria, is the stern motto of the St John family – 'Rather deathe than false of faythe'.

Sir Walter St John's School

19 **Bridge Lane Theatre**
Bridge La SW11. 01-228 5185. A new and welcome theatrical venture in a large lecture hall behind the church. Professional resident and visiting companies offer new plays, neglected foreign plays and special children's holiday matinees. Café and bar.

EATING AND DRINKING

A **Old Swan** *Pub*
Vicarage Cres SW11. 01-228 7152. The angular white wooden structure, with views of the Thames, does look rather like a swan settling its wings. The *Lighterman Bar* goes in for taped pop, while the *Barge and Cygnet Bar* has live music. The restaurant serves a steak and fried fish type of menu. Popular and jolly. *Restaurant closed Sat lunch and all Sun.* £.

Old Swan Pub

B **Riots** *Restaurant and Disco*
Vicarage Clo SW11. 01-223 2244. Hot spot oasis south of the river. If you feel like dancing, or watching the efforts of others, try this disco club with its two restaurants. In the conservatory exotic plants cluster and the

menu is à la carte and pricey. In *Face Feeders* one large plateful of hot food has a set price. The dance floor is dazzlingly lit from underneath. You may join at the door. *Closed lunchtime.* £££ or £.

Raven Pub

C **Raven** *Pub*
140 Westbridge Rd SW11. 01-228 1657. A 17thC Dutch-gabled coaching inn which has been gently modernised without disturbance to the original ships' timbers and crooked doors. Snacks at lunchtime and Director's Bitter on draught. £.

D **Castle** *Pub*
Battersea High St SW11. 01-228 1968. Pleasant family house where you can drink Young's ale, pumped from traditional wooden casks, and eat a lunchtime snack on a weekday. The building went up in 1965, on the site of the first 'Castle', whose foundations were laid in 1600. £.

E **Prodigal's Return** *Pub*
74 Battersea Bridge Rd SW11. 01-228 2060. In an area with few restaurants, it's good to know of a pub which serves full lunches daily and snacks every evening. The large bar in this hefty three-storey building is in 'old cottage-style', which means there are plates on the walls and tapestry upholstery. Separate room for pool and darts. £.

Battersea Bridge

F **Victoria** *Pub*
57 Battersea Bridge Rd SW11. 01-228 3856. One way to get the feel of an area is to drink in a genuine local. And here is just that – ordinary, unsmart, with elderly regulars, a popular dart board and the occasional sandwich. £.

G **Toad Hall** *Restaurant*
64 Battersea Bridge Rd SW11. 01-228 8380. Small, popular, whimsical restaurant with a nice little conservatory at the back. Much labour goes into attaching incomprehensible titles to the well-cooked dishes. You can start with Deb's Delight, and go on to Cock-in-a-Frock or Dirty-Weekend-in-a-VW. House wine is French and drinkable. *Closed lunchtimes & all Sun.* £.

Toad Hall Restaurant

H **Prince Albert** *Pub*
85 Albert Bridge Rd SW11. 01-228 5577. Large, pistachio-green house with a slightly up-market clientele and good weekday luncheons. £.

J **Pooh Corner** *Restaurant*
246 Battersea Park Rd SW11. 01-228 9609. Unassuming façade, decorated with a picture of Pooh and his friends, leads into a young, lively, reasonably priced restaurant. Menu uses its own language, but you can probably guess what Fowl Broth and Chauvinist Pig really are! *Closed lunchtime & Sun.* £.

K **Latchmere** *Pub and Restaurant*
503 Battersea Park Rd SW11. 01-228 4011. The good, new fringe pub theatre, The Gate, is upstairs (book on 01-228 2620). Next to it is a cocktail bar and enterprising à la carte restaurant. On street level, enjoy real ales and substantial snacks. ££ or £.

L **Frog's Legs** *Wine Bar*
264 Battersea Park Rd SW11. 01-228 3794. French owned and run, with predominantly French wines. Serves breadcrumbed frog's legs, soups, pâtés, steaks, French apple flan. An 8-track stereo provides the background music. Nice unhurried French ambiance. £.

M **Angela and Peter's** *Wine Bar*
300 Battersea Park Rd SW11. 01-228 6133. A very English wine bar where the dish of the day is quite likely to be bangers and mash. Good puddings. The proprietor used to run an antique shop in the same premises which accounts for the quantities of appealing Victorian junk around. *Closed Sun.* £.

N **Maggie Brown's** *Restaurant*
Battersea High St SW11. 01-228 0559. A genuine old eel and pie shop, popular in the area for more than 50 years. The high-backed settles support many faithful regulars, which gives it a homely air, but newcomers are welcomed too. Take away service as well. *Closed 21.00 & Sun.* £.

Map 26 BATTERSEA PARK

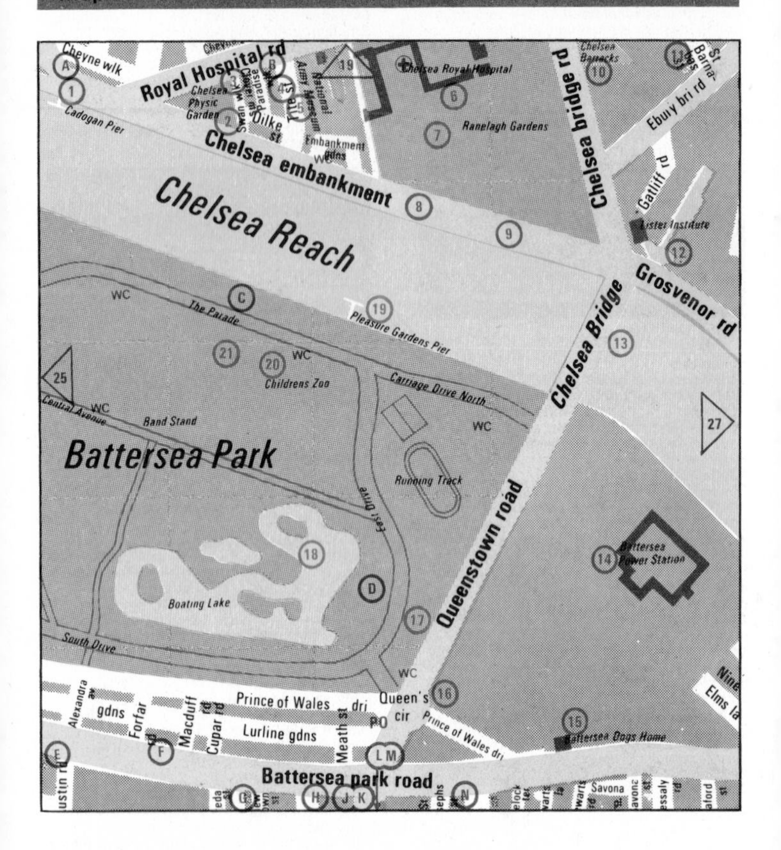

Although this area includes part of Chelsea it is chiefly filled by the green expanses of Battersea Park. The streets to south and east, apart from the imposing mansion blocks of Prince of Wales Drive, take their character from the railway, the workshops of light industry and the towering estates which in recent years have replaced the terraced houses. But the park is dominant.

The river side of the park has a long history as a pleasure ground. From the middle of the 18thC it was a fashionable place to stroll on a Sunday afternoon. Small private inns along the waterfront competed with each other to provide bands, rose arbours and flower gardens, and young blades who'd danced all night converged on them for 'Flounder breakfasts'. The land to the south was still open fields where market gardeners grew asparagus and simples (medicinal herbs) on the marshy ground.

But in the early 19thC the area grew disreputable. The inns attracted unsavoury characters and duels were fought. Cubitt (whose name lives on in one of London's largest firms of builders) persuaded Prince Albert to put an idea to the Queen, and in 1853 she commissioned Sir James Pennethorne to lay out the park as a public garden. Thus decorum returned.

In 1951 John Piper and Osbert Lancaster designed the fabulous 'Festival Gardens' for the Festival of Britain, creating a fantasy-land of attractions; illuminated walkways among the treetops, formal lakes, fountains, fortune tellers and a spectacular Fun Fair. Today, few vestiges remain, but the park still has plenty to delight the visitor.

PLACES OF INTEREST

1 Cadogan Pier
To begin with, an ending. This is the finishing point for the annual Doggett's Coat and Badge Race, in which Thames watermen have competed for the right to wear an orange uniform and silver arm badge since 1715 – when William Doggett launched the custom to celebrate the accession of George I. It is umpired by the liveried Bargemaster of the Fishmongers' Company, one of the four guilds historically connected with the river. (The other Bargemasters are the Vintners', the Watermen's, the Dyers' and, of course, the Queen's.) *Last Fri in July.*

2 Chelsea Physic Garden
Royal Hospital Rd SW3. 01-352 5646. Partly visible through its wrought iron gates lies the second oldest botanical garden in the UK. (Oxford is older.) It was founded by the Society of Apothecaries in 1673. The seeds which grew into the cotton fields of the southern US originated here. Plants are grown for research and teaching purposes. Entry by appointment only.

3 Sir Hans Sloane
Chelsea Physic Garden, Royal Hospital Rd SW3. The white marble statue that can be seen through the gate in Swan Walk is of the botanist and collector whose name is preserved in Sloane Street and Square, and whose personal museum and library is the basis of the British Museum. He presented this site to the Apothecaries in 1772 on condition that they supply 50 samples of dried plants annually to the Royal Society.

4 Tite Street
SW3. One of several in Chelsea famous for its elegant late-Victorian architecture and the aura of aesthetic endeavour left by past tenants. J. S. Sargent died at No 31, Oscar Wilde lived at 34, and Whistler, who painted so much of Chelsea and worked his way through 8 addresses, had the White House designed for him by Godwin (though he had to sell it due to bankruptcy and subsequently lived at Nos 13 and 46).

5 National Army Museum
Royal Hospital Rd SW3. 01-730 0717. March in and marvel at the story of the British Army from 1480 to 1914. Medals, weapons, personal effects and dioramas. Push buttons produce soldiers' songs, and the electronic rifle range is often in working order. *Closed Sun morn. Free.*

6 Chelsea Royal Hospital
Royal Hospital Rd SW3. 01-730 0161. Unique retirement home founded by Charles II for aged and infirm soldiers – the 'Chelsea Pensioners' – whose scarlet frock coats and black tricorns dazzle visitors. The building is by Wren and has a small museum, the grounds hold the famous massed blooms of the Chelsea Flower Show each May, and in the well-stocked cemetery lie two unexpected graves – of Christiana Davis and Hannah Snell who went to war disguised as men hoping to find their husbands. *Closed Sun morn. Free.*

7 Ranelagh Gardens
SW3. Once part of the Earl of Ranelagh's estate. Famous in the 18thC as a 'pleasure park' with a central rotunda in which masques were mounted and the 8-year-old Mozart once played the harpsichord. Now part of the Royal Hospital grounds. Open to the public, but no trace of the rotunda remains, and only a massive imagination could conjure up a ghostly masque. *Free.*

Cheyne House

8 Chelsea Embankment
SW3. Laid out by Sir Joseph Bazalgette in 1874, it changed the character of Chelsea riverside, especially when houses began to rise along it. Don't miss the beautiful Swan House at No 17, or Cheyne House at No 18, both famous as good examples of the work of Norman Shaw, one of the most influential of 19thC domestic architects.

9 Westbourne Outlet
Chelsea Embankment SW3. At low tide a round opening in the embankment can be seen disgorging a thin trickle of water. This is the Westbourne, one of London's lost rivers, which feeds the Serpentine and then creeps underground, by way of Sloane Square Station, to lose its identity here in the Thames.

10 Chelsea Barracks
Chelsea Bridge Rd SW3. Sleek, early 60s building which is one of the homes of the Grenadier, Welsh, Scots and Coldstream Guards. Some weekdays they parade at 10.20 and leave at 10.55 to relieve the Guard at Buckingham Palace. On other weekdays, and at weekends, they leave from Wellington Barracks, near Buckingham Palace, where details of their movements are posted outside.

11 St Barnabas Church
St Barnabas St SW1. Built by Sir Thomas Cundy Jr, together with the vicarage and school, in 1847–50. The St Paul's Ecclesiological Society remarked that it was 'the most sumptuous and correctly fitted church created in England since the Reformation'. And you can't say fairer than that.

12 Western Pumping Station
Grosvenor Rd SW1. The attractive tower-like chimney, with its round eyes and fencing crown, served the Chelsea Waterworks when the pumping station was coal-powered. It is still used, by the Thames Water Authority, but the chimney is redundant. And no, you can't go up it, the stairs are unsafe.

St Barnabas Church

13 **Chelsea Bridge**
SW3. 700 feet of handsome suspension bridge linking Battersea Park with Chelsea. It was rebuilt in the 1930s, 60 years after Albert Bridge, and recently repainted to enliven its distinctive structure.

14 **Battersea Power Station**
Central Electricity Generating Board (SE Region), Kirtling St SW8. 01-622 1051. This is the building that looks like a massive sideboard, upside down with its legs in the air. It generates 146 megawatts of power a day for the London Electricity Grid, and also supplies the heating, from its hot water waste, for Churchill Gardens Estate and Dolphin Square, on the north bank, by way of under-river pipes. Visits are possible, by appointment, but if intrigued, don't delay. Its days as a power station are numbered and its future under immediate discussion.

Battersea Power Station

15 **Battersea Dogs Home**
4 Battersea Pk Rd SW8. 01-622 4454. Gathering point for thousands of homeless dogs and cats, some lost, some callously evicted by their owners. Many do find good homes and the genuinely lost are usually reclaimed. Open weekdays if you want to buy.

16 **Balloon Factory**
Queens Circus SW8. Underneath the railway arches there used to be a hot air balloon factory, run by the Short Brothers, who chose the location because it was so easy to fill up at the gas works behind.

Battersea Park
SW11. 01-228 2798. The marshy area known as Battersea fields, where the Duke of Wellington and the Earl of Winchelsea once fought a duel, was stabilised with earth displaced by the building of Victoria Docks to make this 200 acre park. The trees and water attract large numbers of wild birds. There are playing fields, a running track, tennis courts, a sub-tropical garden and sculpture by Henry Moore. *Closes at dusk.* Special features are:

17 **Deer Enclosure**
Near Queen's Circus entrance. Here are Chinese Water deer, Axis deer who are European by birth, and a family of Black Bucks whose ancestors came from Africa.

Boating lake, Battersea Park

18 **Boating Lake**
A large, curvaceous and interesting lake, with thick vegetation, two islands, numerous ornamental ducks, geese, herons, and boats for hire from Easter to Sept. Free fishing, in season, for roach, tench, dace and gudgeon.

19 **Pleasure Gardens Pier**
The red and white striped pillars of the pier are two of the last remaining vestiges of the once-famous Festival Pleasure Gardens and Fun Fair.

Pleasure Gardens Pier

20 **Children's Zoo**
01-228 9957. A small zoo, now being redeveloped. There are monkeys, penguins, wallabies, mynah birds, parrots, pigmy goats, and pony rides. *Closed first week Oct to Easter. Charge.*

21 **Amphitheatre**
The old band-stand has gone and now the out door music happens here on Tue evening and Sun afternoon. Brass bands or jazz concerts. *No music end Sept to Easter.*

Events
There's usually something happening in the summer, but here are three main regulars.

Easter Parade
A grand march-past of lavishly decorated floats, clowns, and tumblers in animal suits, all in aid of charity, on Easter Sunday afternoon.
Historic Vehicles Rally
Veteran and vintage cars, still explosively operational, meet on the first weekend of May.
South London Carnival
Stalls for home-made jam, antiques, handcrafts, and numerous sideshows, all on a grand scale, for one week in mid-August.

EATING AND DRINKING

A **Cheyne Walk** *Wine Bar*
Pier House, 31 Cheyne Walk SW3. 01-352 4989. Owned by Balls Bros, whose chain of quality establishments stretches all the way to the City. This one looks across David Wynne's gravity-defying sculpture, Boy with a Dolphin, to the fairytale Albert Bridge. Good food, and good wine with an acceptable house version. *Closed Sun evening.* £.

David Wynne's Boy with a Dolphin

B **Tante Claire** *Restaurant*
68 Royal Hospital Rd SW3. 01-352 6045. High class French food at high class prices. This is a family concern, with colourful walls, Klimt prints and a varied menu. Specialities include andouillette de la mer au vinaigre de cassis, followed by pigeonneau aux choux verts and, for a triumphant finale, biscuit glacé aux noisettes avec son coulis. *Closed Sat & Sun.* £££+.

C **Riverside** *Bar*
Battersea Pk SW11. Ordinary modern bar in the centre of the riverside Parade. View of the river through the floor-to-ceiling windows. Wide terrace. *Closed end Sept–June.* £.

D **Battersea Park** *Café*
Battersea Pk SW11. The usual café food, inside or outside, in the company of greedy pigeons and geese. *Closed end Sept–Easter.* £.

E **Cricketers** *Pub*
317 Battersea Pk Rd SW11. 01-622 9060. Seedily eccentric, and lively at night with rock bands on Mon and Thur, a disco on Fri, a gay women's night on Tue, and a drag night on Sat with a 3-piece band, gay male regulars and impromptu acts from customers. No food.

Chelsea Bridge

F **Westminster College Teaching** *Restaurant*
Battersea Pk Rd SW11. 01-720 2121. A chance to 'eat in a classroom' inside a listed building decorated with statues of the muses just visible through the screen of plane trees. Only seats 30, so book. High-class food (student-cooked and served, under close supervision) at low prices. Good wines. *Mon–Fri only. Last orders 12.30.* £.
Doddington Estate *Pubs*
Battersea Pk Rd SW11. As estates are so much a part of the area, why not try this one, laid out by the GLC complete with pubs, restaurant, laundrette, a library and shops to serve its high-rise tenants.

G **Grove** *Pub*
Small and peaceful, with middle-aged regulars, no jukebox and lunchtime bar food. £.

H **Eagle** *Pub*
Sometimes has live folk or country-and-western music in the evenings. Much patronised by students of Westminster College, opposite. Hot food. £.

J **Battersea Tavern** *Pub*
Also popular with the young. Large tv shows the racing at lunchtime and in the evening from Wed through Sat a disco drowns discreet chat. Hot and cold food. £.

K **Rehana Tandoori Indian** *Restaurant*
01-720 9815. Bright shiny and new, with taped Indian music and friendly waiters. Eat here or take away. ££.

L **Alonso's** *Restaurant*
32 Queenstown Rd SW8. 01-720 5986. Just off the map to the south, but worth it for Alonso's cooking, especially his fruited rack of lamb and apple soufflé. Mostly French food with a touch of Spanish. Ring the bell to get in. *Closed lunch Sat & all Sun.* ££.

M **Atuchaclass** *Bistro*
24 Queenstown Rd SW8. 01-622 7800. Alonso's newest venture is just down the road, with its bistro-like atmosphere and international menu. Food less exciting, but nice, and cheaper. *Closed lunch & all Sun.*

N **Mason's Arms** *Pub*
169 Battersea Pk Rd SW11. 01-622 4738. High in a niche on this late Victorian building is (in both senses of the term) a stone mason. Pleasant, middle-aged atmosphere. Upstairs, a professional gym where you might see well-known fighters in training. Bar food.

Map 27 PIMLICO

A strange and intriguing part of London which visitors rarely examine closely. It seems to have little to offer them but cheap accommodation in endless small hotels, and access to Victoria station and to the more glamorous West End. So they sleep here, then leave the amiable conglomeration of shabby stucco and crisp modern estates behind them. And this surge in and out, together with the powerful traffic along Vauxhall Bridge Road and the plethora of bedsitters housing a young, working population, contributes to the restless energy of the place.

Architecturally it is fascinating. Between 1830 and 1850 Thomas Cubitt, the architect of Belgravia, began to develop what was then an area of market gardens and wasteland. His scheme was less grandiose than in the classier Belgravia but attractive squares and pleasant terraces remain. Neglect between the wars allowed the area to run down but after the Second War imaginative modern estates rose from the bomb damage – the famous prototype, Churchill Gardens, and the later and lovely Lillington Gardens among them. When Pimlico was linked to the London Underground system it became a practical place to live and work and the last of its torpor was shed.

Pimlico is believed to have been named after a drink, now long lost. Suitably enough it has some cheery pubs among its reasonably priced restaurants. Its view of this commercial stretch of the Thames is slightly wistful – on its own side the wharves are derelict or converted into restaurants; on the other, industry and commerce visibly flourish in modern buildings.

PLACES OF INTEREST

1 **St Gabriel's Church**
Warwick Sq SW1. Overlooking the large, pretty and private gardens of the square is this church of 1853, in the decorated style, by Cundy Jnr. Many of its more obvious charms were added in the 1890s – Bentley's high altar, Powell's chancel mosaics, Kempe's stained glass east window.

2 **Royal Horticultural Society Halls**
Vincent Sq SW1. 01-834 4333. The Society was founded in 1805 to promote the knowledge of horticulture and botany. Its offices and extensive library (by appointment only, please) are here, together with one show hall (the other is round the back). Sixty exhibitions of beautiful flowers and plants are held annually, clustered in spring, summer and autumn. The exhibitions are smaller than the massive Chelsea Flower Show, but also cheaper.

3 **Vincent Square**
SW1. This sudden, wide expanse of green, glimpsed first from the busy Vauxhall Bridge Road, was once a bear garden but is now the playing fields for Westminster Public School. *Plus ça change, plus c'est la même chose?*

Lillington Gardens Estate

4 **Lillington Gardens Estate**
Vauxhall Bridge Rd SW1. One of the few successful London estates of the 1960s. In warm red brick, low-rise yet high density, with inner courtyards and balconies planted with slight yet full-grown trees and cascading shrubs. By Darbourne and Darke, the deserving winners of architectural awards.

5 **St James the Less Church**
Vauxhall Bridge Rd SW1. The imaginative Lillington Gardens council estate curves protectively around this amiably eccentric church by G. E. Street, one of the best examples of Victorian Gothic in London. Atmospheric interior, richly patterned with red, black and cream bricks and tiles; massively canopied font and bible stories carved into the stocky pillars. Above the chancel arch, a fresco by Watts.

6 **Barry Guppy's Pimlico Pottery**
4–6 Moreton St SW1. 01-834 7904. Highly independent studio pottery where lessons are given and commissions undertaken. You are welcome to watch work in progress and buy from the reasonably priced range of individual and appealing stoneware and porcelain. *Closed Sat & Sun.*

7 **Tachbrook Street Market**
SW1. Busy general market, particularly strong on fruit and vegetables, backed up by a row of good small shops including a bakery wafting out the scent of new bread and a rattling good pot and pan shop.

8 **Apples Household Stores**
78 Tachbrook St SW1. 01-834 5932. Proper old fashioned hardware store, stacked to the ceiling with kettles, cheesegraters, skewers, washers, mops and plugs – and in amongst it all 'seconds' of old-fashioned china – willow patterned tea pots, shapely little jugs, plates with bucolic scenes under their glazes.

9 **St Saviour's Church**
St George's Sq SW1. Large, tree-protected church with a dainty spire, built by Thomas Cundy Jnr in the 1860s and restored by Romaine Walker in the 1880s. The vestry and the altar canopy are relatively modern, added by Nicholson and Corlette just before the First World War.

10 **St George's Square**
SW1. Not so much a square as a rectangle, laid out in the 1840s but with most of its buildings dating from the 1850s or 60s. Apart from its distinguished London plane trees, the central green looks more like a strip of enclosed commonland than a formal garden.

11 **Pimlico Gardens**
SW1. A rather bleak little strip of green separated from the Thames by a massive flood wall. To the east side stands the marble William Huskisson, who has the dubious distinction of being the first person to be killed in a railway accident. Carved by John Gibson, most unsuitably attired in a toga, and described by Osbert Sitwell as 'boredom rising from the bath'.

William Huskisson

St James the Less Church

12 Vauxhall Bridge
SW1. Important-looking iron and stone structure, designed by Maurice Fitzmaurice in 1900 to replace an older one. Above each supporting pier stands a larger-than-life-size allegorical figure representing Science, Engineering and so on. The lady with a miniature St Paul's in the palm of her hand is Architecture.

13 Covent Garden Market
1 Nine Elms La SW8. 01-720 2211. Early risers can join the greengrocers of London to buy fruit, vegetables, flowers and plants, at wholesale prices, in these modern premises of an ancient market which was held next to the Royal Opera House in WC2 until 1974. *Open Mon–Fri 04.00–11.00, & Sat morn in summer.*

14 Battersea Power Station
Central Electricity Generating Board (SE Region) Kirtling St SW8. 01-622 1051. This is the building that looks like a massive sideboard, upside down with its legs in the air. It generates 146 megawatts of power a day for the London Electricity Grid, and also supplies the heating for Churchill Gardens Estate and Dolphin Square, on the north bank, by way of under-river pipes. Visits are possible, by appointment, but if intrigued don't delay. Its days as a power station are numbered and its future under immediate discussion.

15 Dolphin Square
Grosvenor Rd SW1. Big and boring to look at but this is where the rich live, not to mention a few MPs. Said to be the largest block of flats in the world – more than 1200 of them, weighing down 7½ acres of land. By Gordon Jeeves, 1937.

Dolphin Square

16 Churchill Gardens Estate
Grosvenor Rd SW1. The first of the post-war council housing estates which became the prototype for some of the best of the rest. Designed in 1946 by Powell and Moya, who won the job in competition, its hot water and heating piped from across the river – the waste from Battersea Power Station opposite.

Pimlico Comprehensive School

17 Pimlico Comprehensive School
Lupus St SW1. This strange late 60s structure by the GLC's Architects Department gives the impression of being made entirely of sheets of glass, sloping inwards towards the roof, with a modicum of concrete to hold them in place. More like a hothouse than a school, its pupils presumably lightly braised in summer.

18 Peabody Estate
Peabody Av SW1. These oppressive-looking estates crop up throughout the traditionally poorer parts of London, to a design by Darbishire which suitably reflects the heavy hand of Victorian charity. The trust was founded by an American banker in the 1870s and still has charitable status. The interiors have been modernised and the new buildings are practical and cheery; the old exteriors are visually beyond redemption.

19 St Barnabas Church
St Barnabas St SW1. Charming Early English revival group of church, vicarage and school, by Thomas Cundy Jnr, with the help of Butterfield, erected in 1847–50. It was the pioneer Anglo-Catholic church in London. The St Paul's Ecclesiological Society called it 'a model of excellence . . . the most sumptuous and correctly fitted church erected in England since the Reformation . . .'.

EATING AND DRINKING

A Rising Sun *Pub*
44 Ebury Bridge Rd SW1. 01-730 4088. Cosmopolitan and congenial with real ale from a brewery just south of the Thames. Full lunches, some slick model boats, and the bands of the Guards among its patrons. £.

B Fountain *Pub*
16 Gillingham St SW1. 01-834 2777. Small, busy local, dishing out snacks and one real ale. £.

C Gran Paradiso *Restaurant*
52 Wilton Rd SW1. 01-828 5818. More

impressive outside than in, but friendly and busy with a staunch Italian menu and a patron who keeps a fatherly eye on his customers. *Closed Sat lunch & all Sun.* £££.

D **Le Steak Nicole** *Restaurant*
72–73 Wilton Rd SW1. 01-834 7301. Nothing but steaks, in ten different forms, presented with French finesse, and salads or fresh vegetables. Light puddings, ice cream or cheese to finish with. Eat outside if weather permits. *Closed Sat lunch & all Sun.* ££.

E **Mimmo and Pasquale** *Restaurant*
64 Wilton Rd SW1. 01-828 6908. Italian, with a shiny wooden outside and fresh white-washed inside, leading onto a covered terrace for summertime. Good hors d'oeuvres, freshly made pastas, sea bass in white wine, rich Italian puds. *Closed Sat lunch & all Sun.* ££.

F **Constitution** *Pub*
42 Churton St SW1. 01-834 3651. Named after the ship which featured in the Boston Tea Party controversy. Polished and pleasant with reliable snacks, keg beer and a draught lager. £.

G **Grumbles** *Restaurant*
35 Churton St SW1. 01-834 0149. Jolly and chummy – Britain's version of a French bistro. The food is freshly cooked to order and much of it comes from the nearby Tachbrook Street market. Many devoted regulars. *Closed Sat lunch & all Sun.* ££.

Tachbrook Street Market

H **Silhouettes** *Restaurant and Wine Bar*
48 Churton St SW1. 01-834 7311. Ground floor wine bar is small with lighting that turns its customers green and with a salad and sandwich menu. Downstairs restaurant is larger, with silhouettes of nudes on its white walls. Fast or continental food – from burgers to chicken chasseur. *Closed Sun lunch.* £ or ££.

J **Pimlico** *Bistro*
22 Charlwood St SW1. 01-828 3303. Small, with limited elbow space and a short but imaginative menu chalked on blackboards without and within. Much seafood, lamb, chicken and interesting sauces. *Closed Sun lunch.* ££.

K **Pimlico Tram** *Pub*
6 Charlwood St SW1. 01-828 0448. Pianist and drummer regale locals and tourists with music each night, mostly old-time. Modern, narrow house which evokes memories of trams with pictures and route maps. Nice snacks. £.

L **Lord High Admiral** *Pub*
43 Vauxhall Bridge Rd SW1. 01-828 3727. If you want to raise a glass to the highly admirable Lillington Estate, and you should, do it here in this genial and unassuming modern pub. Solid snacks daily, with chips or mash. £.

M **Surprise** *Pub*
110 Vauxhall Bridge Rd SW1. 01-828 5322. At the moment the surprise is that the nicely painted exterior gives on to such a tatty inside – but it's friendly and it's fun. Different groups play country and western and a bit of rock from Wed to Sun evenings and you can usually get a bite (not much more) to eat. £.

N **Westminster Hotel School** *Restaurant*
76 Vincent Sq SW1. 01-828 1222. The snags of this place (you have to book and it's only open for weekday lunches in termtime) are outweighed by the advantages. It is heavily subsidised so the invariably successful efforts of the student catering staff are ludicrously cheap and even wine is below usual prices. £.

O **Pomegranates** *Restaurant*
96 Grosvenor Rd SW1. 01-828 6560. Multi-national food and wine in a large and stately dining room, hung with paintings and lit by Tiffany lamps. Choose from a menu that wanders around Wales, Turkey, Greece, France, Italy, Malaysia and China, with every dish prepared on the premises from fresh (not frozen) ingredients. International finale of sorbet, gateaux or honey-cognac ice cream. *Closed Sat lunch & all Sun.* £££.

Villa dei Cesari Restaurant

P **Villa dei Cesari** *Restaurant*
135 Grosvenor Rd SW1. 01-828 7453. Large riverside warehouse sumptuously converted into a movie-buff's vision of classical Rome, with dancing nightly until the early hours. Waiters are in tunics, menu is in Latin, customers tend to be in oil. *Closed Mon.* £££.

Morning Coffee and Afternoon Tea

Tudor Tea Rooms; Regency St SW1. Despite the name, coffee only. Fresh sandwiches, lovely apple doughnuts.

Vauxhall Café; Tachbrook St SW1. Hot drinks except at mealtimes. Hearty snacks.

Map 28 VICTORIA AND LAMBETH

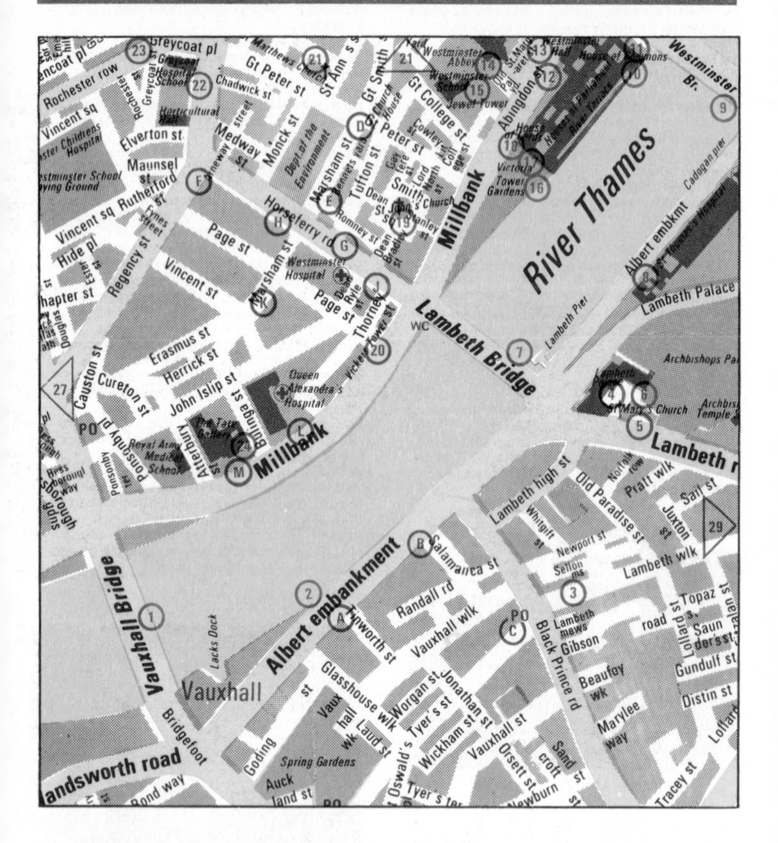

The river Thames, its once majestic Victorian skyline made dramatically agitated by tall modern blocks, cuts the map neatly into two parts, each with its important buildings.

On the north bank, are the Gothic turrets of the New Palace of Westminster, more familiarly known as the Houses of Parliament and, westwards along the embankment, the treasures of the inimitable Tate Gallery and the drama of the Vickers skyscraper. They stand like towering rocks in a sea of plain streets and offices with a strongly civil service flavour. Eat amongst these brief-case-carriers at lunchtime, drink beside them in the early evening, but at weekends when they withdraw, expect to find most of the restaurants and even pubs closed, peaceably awaiting the new activity that Monday will bring.

On the south bank the high walls and crenellated gateway of Lambeth Palace, London seat of the Archbishops of Canterbury, front the traditionally cockney Lambeth – a muddle of decaying, partially bombed Victoriana and modern housing and shopping developments. Its pubs reflect the cockney heritage, and one of its roads, the Lambeth Walk, became the subject of a music hall song and dance that is still a familiar number from the pub piano. Most of this part of Lambeth is residential with few places to eat out, though a pie and a pint at lunchtime is not hard to come by and the fish and chip shops flourish.

Up and down the river itself, among the barges and police launches, cruise the tour boats, with their spectacular views of historic edifices and bridges.

PLACES OF INTEREST

1 **Vauxhall Bridge**
SW1. Built of iron and stone to a design by Maurice Fitzmaurice in 1900, Lean cautiously over the parapet to admire the larger-than-life allegorical figures above each supporting pier. The lady holding a scaled-down St Paul's represents Architecture.

2 **Albert Embankment**
SE1. This one-mile stretch, with the plump, coy dolphins twined engagingly around its lamp-posts, was completed in 1869.

3 **Lambeth Walk**
SE1. Famous since the cockneys made a song and dance about it. Now a modern shopping precinct with a lively market in its centre.

4 **Lambeth Palace**
SE1. In red brick with castellated gate-house and high protective wall, the London residence of the Archbishops of Canterbury for 700 years. Begun in the early 13thC, most of the present structure is medieval. Part of the grounds is a public park but the library of fine illuminated manuscripts is no longer open to the public. The Lollards Tower is said to have held the followers of Wyclif in the 14thC. Certainly the palace has been used as a prison, and suffered two major attacks – by Wat Tyler and friends in 1381, who burnt books and drank the cellars dry, and by enemy bombs in 1940. Groups sometimes admitted on application to the Secretary.

Lambeth Palace

5 **St Mary at Lambeth**
SE1. Pale and pretty church in the shadow of Lambeth Palace, now administered by The Tradescant Trust (01-373 4030) as a museum of garden history in memory of the two John Tradescants, father and son, gardeners to Charles I and inveterate plant hunters who introduced 200 species to England, including phlox, stocks, lupins and of course Tradescantia. The garden is planted with their discoveries and with the family vault, carved with botanical rarities and oddities (their collection of which formed the nucleus of the Ashmolean Museum in Oxford). *Free.*

6 **Captain Bligh**
St Mary's Churchyard SE1. The Tradescant family, in their curiously carved tomb, have Bligh of the Bounty as a next-door neighbour under a massive Coade stone monument.

7 **Lambeth Bridge**
SE1. Smart scarlet and black steel, by G Topham, 1932, replacing an earlier bridge which in turned replaced the old horse ferry. Decorated with golden pineapples as a graceful tribute to John Tradescant who first brought them to Britain and who lies in St Mary's Churchyard nearby.

8 **St Thomas's Hospital**
Lambeth Pal Rd SE1. 01-928 9292. Large general hospital, originally founded at Southwark in 1213. It was at 'Tommy's' that Florence Nightingale founded the first English school of nursing in 1860 and it is still famous as a teaching hospital.

St Thomas's Hospital

9 **Westminster Bridge**
SE1. Here, in September 1803, Wordsworth observed of the view, in his sonnet *Upon Westminster Bridge*, 'Earth has not anything to show more fair'. The view is still fair, though both it and the bridge have changed considerably since his day – the present flat stone structure, by Thomas Page, was erected in 1862.

10 **Houses of Parliament**
St Margaret St SW1. 01-219 3000. Properly the New Palace of Westminster, by Barry and Pugin in 1840–68. A grand and glorious Gothic structure built around the late 11thC Westminster Hall whose 14thC timber roof rivals any in Europe. On the site of the sovereign's chief residence in London until the time of Henry VIII, and still with royal status. You may tour the building when the house is not sitting, or listen to debates from the Strangers Gallery when it is. Write to your MP for an invitation or join the queue outside. Duty policemen will advise on your chances of getting in. *Free. Closed Sun.*

11 **Big Ben**
Houses of Parliament SW1. The name is often applied to the clock and the tower which contains it – but it actually belongs to the bell, cast at Whitechapel in 1858, whose hourly chimes are broadcast to the nation.

12 **Houses of Parliament Statues**
Charles I. Magnificent equestrian statue, cast in 1663 by Hubert le Sueur.
Winston Churchill. An elderly overcoated Churchill by Ivor Roberts-Jones, his forward-leaning stance expressive of dominance.

Oliver Cromwell. Hamo Thornycroft's statue of 1899 shows the one-time Lord Protector 'warts and all', his back to the Houses of Parliament and his spurs, unfortunately, upside down.
Richard I. Romantic representation of the Lionheart, mounted and raising his sword with vigour, by Baron Carlo Marochetti, 1860.

Winston Churchill

13 St Margaret's Westminster
Parliament Sq SW1. 01-222 6382. Somewhat dwarfed by the massive bulk of the Abbey is this parish church of the House of Commons, rebuilt in the 16thC with a splendid east window and some wondrous modern stained glass by John Piper.

14 Westminster Abbey
(The Collegiate Church of St Peter in Westminster) Broad Sanctuary SW1. 01-222 5152. Magnificent repository of much of the royal history of Britain, wherein God and Mammon meet on a grand scale. Original church by Edward the Confessor, 1065, rebuilt by Henry III, completed in 1376–1506, with the towers finished by Hawksmoor in 1734. In fine perpendicular with a mighty and soaring Gothic nave, lavish and beautiful side chapels and displays of riches, elaborate tombs and prestigious monuments. Scene of the coronation, burial and sometimes marriage of England's sovereigns. *Free.* Museum of plate and effigies asks small entry *charge. Charge* to see Royal Chapels.

15 Jewel Tower
Old Palace Yd SW1. 01-937 9561. Discreet amidst the Gothic finery stands this 14thC fragment of the Old Palace of Westminster. Once Edward III's treasure house it now displays medieval carvings and 11thC capitals from Westminster Hall. *Free. Closed Sun.*

16 Victoria Tower Gardens
SW1. Green and pleasant resting place with shady trees and river views. The immensely ornate pink granite and mosaic drinking fountain which glitters in the centre was put up in 1865 by the MP Charles Buxton in joint memory of his father and the emancipation of slaves for which he laboured.

17 Rodin's Burghers of Calais
Victoria Tower Gdns SW1. The dark and grumbling group of tall bronze men are a replica of Rodin's original, honouring the men who surrendered to Edward III in 1340 to divert attack from their city.

Jewel Tower

18 Emmeline Pankhurst
Victoria Tower Gdns SW1. The 1930s bronze figure, by A. G. Walker, gestures towards her conquest, the nearby Mother of Parliaments. The medallion to her left commemorates her daughter Christabel, also a fighter for women's suffrage.

19 St John's, Smith Square
Smith Sq SW1. 01-222 1061. 18thC church by Thomas Archer, now one of London's most unusual concert halls. The exterior has been compared to a fancy footstool lying upside down. Inside there are solo recitals, chamber, orchestral and choral works, lunchtime and evening. Creep into the crypt for box office, licensed buffet and art exhibitions.

20 Vickers Tower
Millbank SW1. Statuesque 387 foot landmark erected in 1963 for Vickers Armstrong.

21 St Matthew's Church
Gt Peter St SW1. Sir George Gilbert Scott's once handsome mid 19thC church has been gutted by fire. Restoration is hoped for.

22 Greycoat Hospital School
Greycoat Pl SW1. The appealing early 18thC building with its neat cupola was restored by Laurence King after wartime bomb damage. Don't miss the wooden 'charity children' above the door, symbols of a free school in the days before state education.

23 St Stephen's Church
Rochester Row SW1. Respected Gothic Revival, built in 1847–9 to a design by Benjamin Ferrey. The passage of time has lopped off its spire and painted it a glowering sooty black.

24 Tate Gallery
Millbank SW1. 01-821 1313. The classical 19thC building by Sidney R. J. Smith has been enlarged 3 times to provide adequate housing for its representative collection of British painting from the 16thC to the present day, and its rich store of foreign paintings from 1880. Here you will find works by Blake, Turner, Hogarth, the Pre-Raphaelites, Francis Bacon, Picasso, Chagall, Mondrian and Degas and sculpture by Moore and Hepworth. Wander at will or enjoy film shows, lectures and guided tours. *Free. Closed Sun morn.*

EATING AND DRINKING

A Crown *Pub*
35 Albert Embankment SE1. 01-735 1054. Contemplate the Tate Gallery and the Houses

of Parliament across the river with a glass of real ale in your hand. Full weekday lunches and generous snacks at other times. £.

B Old Father Thames *Pub*
12 Albert Embankment SE1. 01-735 7004. Large and smart, separated from its namesake by the embankment and its busy road. You can get a set-price businessman's lunch in the restaurant on weekdays and a snack in the bar every lunchtime and most evenings. *Pub Closed Sun evening.* £.

C Jolly Cockney *Pub*
49 Black Prince Rd SE11. 01-735 1800. Handleless door makes it look always closed – go in and it's warm and friendly, if self-consciously cockney. Live music of the sing-along sort from Wed to Sun. Real ale and lunchtime snacks. £.

D Tevere *Restaurant*
47 Gt Peter St SW1. 01-222 4901. Large, simple and clean with reliable spaghetti, pizza, chops, egg and chips and a daily roast. (The building, not the restaurant, is owned by the Band of Hope who won't permit an alcohol license.) *Closed 17.30 & weekends.* £.

Houses of Parliament

E Wilkins Natural Foods *Restaurant*
61 Marsham St SW1. 01-222 4038. Most of the trade is take-away but there are a few chunky pine tables for eaters on the premises. Vegetarian, vegan and macrobiotic soups, savouries, salads and sweets, both cheap and good. Shop at No 53 sells health foods to cook at home. *Closed 17.30 & weekends.* £.

F Barley Mow *Pub*
104 Horseferry Rd SW1. 01-222 2330. Bright and pretty with red and white striped awnings, seats and tubs of shrubs outside and a cosy interior with an open fire for winter. Upstairs lunchtime restaurant has a full English à la carte menu. The local for Westminster Hospital. ££.

G Grosvenor *Restaurant*
60 Horseferry Rd SW1. 01-222 5488. A cross between an upmarket snack bar and a cheap and simple restaurant, with red formica, a chef in tall cap and jeans, counter service and civil servant customers. *Closed 17.30 & weekends.* £.

H PJ's *Wine Bar*
37 Horseferry Rd SW1. 01-834 2907. Two cavernous rooms, with photos of old movie stars and a poster advertising the original 'Casablanca' on the walls. One half is a pizza house, the other serves chilli, quiche, pâté, salads. Both have wines, neither is open at night. *Closed 15.30 & weekends.* £.

J Kundan *Restaurant*
3 Horseferry Rd SW1. 01-834 3434. Chandeliers and shades of brown in this elaborately decorated basement restaurant with its beautifully presented tandoori dishes – tikka kebab, karahi kebab, charcoal grilled king prawns and seekh kebab sefrani. *Closed Sun.* ££.

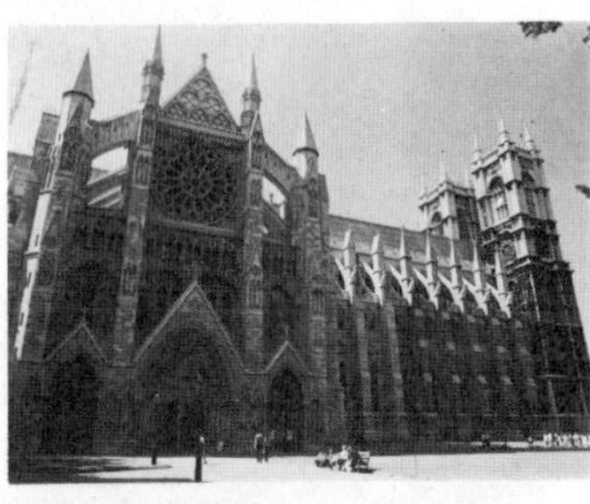

Westminster Abbey

K Lockets *Restaurant*
Marsham Court, Marsham St SW1. 01-834 9552. Olde Englishe dishes, doubtless suitable for the Lords and MPs who carry out their business so close by. 'Lamb in the manner of Shrewsbury' – with its port, juniper and redcurrant jelly sauce – zings with flavour. 'Raspberry Lockets' – its fruit, cream and liqueur coated with burnt sugar – is wholly delectable. *Closed weekends.* ££.

L Morpeth Arms *Pub*
58 Millbank SW1. 01-834 6442. Amiably raucous entertainment pub. Mon you get trad jazz, Tue a guest singer, Wed, Sat and Sun a sing-along (sometimes disrespectful towards Gilbert and Sullivan) and Thur and Fri a DJ plays numbers old and new. Lunchtime snacks. £.

M Tate Gallery *Restaurants*
Millbank SW1. 01-834 6754. The Gallery basement offers two contrasting lunchtime eating places: the slightly claustrophobic cafeteria with undisguised overhead pipes, freshly cut sandwiches and reasonably priced snacks, wine, milk, coffee or tea: or the pale and elegant Rex Whistler room where historical English dishes are beautifully presented. Try veal kidneys Florentine or Joan Cromwell's grand salad. *Closed Sun.* £ or ££.

Morning Coffee and Afternoon Tea
Wilkins Natural Foods Restaurant; 61 Marsham St SW1. 01-222 4038.
Grosvenor Restaurant; 60 Horseferry Rd SW1. 01-222 5488.
Tate Gallery; Millbank SW1. 01-834 6754.
Tevere Restaurant; 47 Gt Peter St SW1. 01-222 4901. Serves both, *but never on a Sunday.*

Map 29 WATERLOO AND ELEPHANT AND CASTLE

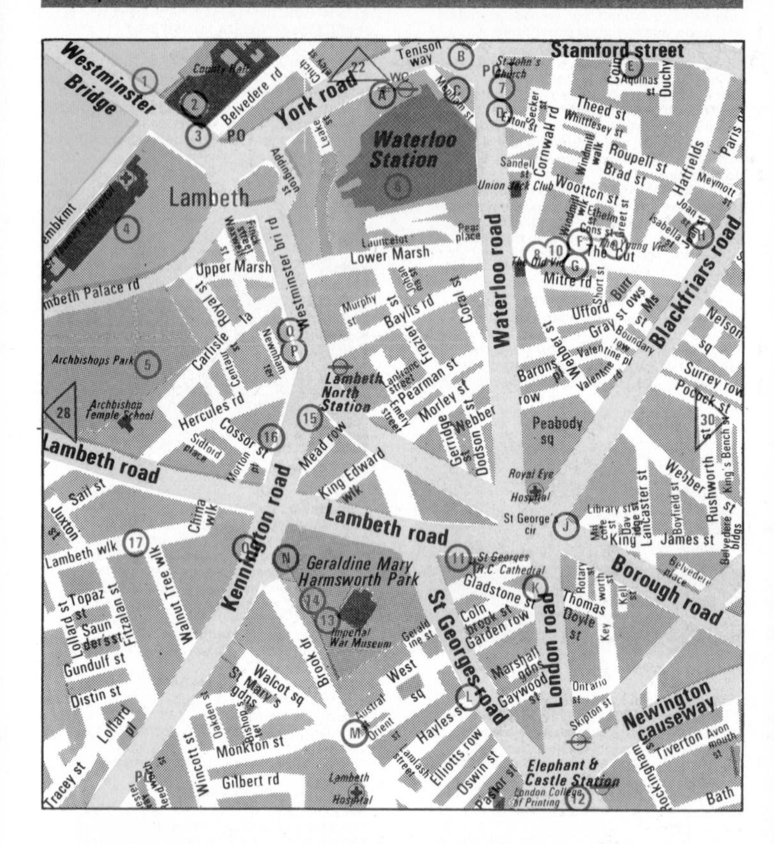

At first glance, sprawling and noisy, cut through at awkward angles by roads lined with oppressive buildings and filled with ferociously heavy traffic – but well worth the effort of a second glance.

Here is part of cockney London, with the Lambeth Walk itself coming in from the east, and the old workhouse where Charlie Chaplin's mother lived to the south – now Lambeth Hospital, an outpost of St Thomas's. Despite modern developments, like the gargantuan Elephant and Castle itself, the narrow streets of terraced houses still exist, the street markets still sell the necessities of life, and the older pubs are still the warm centres of small communities.

The whole area hums with activity from Monday to Saturday. By day it centres around the office blocks, the small businesses, the vast County Hall, Waterloo Station which links the Surrey commuter belt to London, the massive teaching hospital of St Thomas's, the Imperial War Museum, and the colleges to the south – Morley, The London College of Printing and the Polytechnic of the South Bank. By night the attention is on the two theatres, the Old and Young Vic. On a Sunday all lies quiet.

The once gently rural nature of this part of Lambeth – now administered from County Hall by the most notoriously 'red' of all London councils – began its gradual development into its present urban state in 1750 when the first Westminster Bridge crossed the Thames and joined it to London, and specifically to the Palace of Westminster, whose neo-Gothic towers are dramatically visible at its northern end.

PLACES OF INTEREST

1 Westminster Bridge
SE1. Here, in September 1803, Wordsworth observed of the view, 'Earth has not anything to show more fair', in his sonnet *Upon Westminster Bridge*. The view is still fair, though both it and the bridge have changed considerably since his day – the present flat stone structure, by Thomas Page, was erected in 1862.

2 County Hall
SE1. 01-633 5000. Impressive 20thC Renaissance-style construction by Ralph Knott and W. E. Riley. This is where the Greater London Council holds its fortnightly meetings, open to the fascinated gaze of the Greater London public. The Record Office cares for nearly 200 parish registers and the library's collection specialises in local government and London history. Both by appointment only.

3 The South Bank Lion
Westminster Br SE1. A large, white, anxious-looking lion, made from an artificial stone developed at the now defunct Coade factory which once stood nearby. The secret formula of Coade stone, which resists London's corrosive atmosphere so well, was lost when the Coade family died out.

The South Bank Lion

4 St Thomas's Hospital
Lambeth Pal Rd SE1. 01-928 9292. The hospital moved from Southwark to this large modern complex in the 60s. It was founded in 1213, and it was at 'Tommy's' that Florence Nightingale set up the first English school of nursing in 1860. Still famous as a teaching hospital.

5 Archbishop's Park
SE1. Pleasant public park formed from part of the grounds of Lambeth Palace, which stands at its western end and which is the London base of the Archbishop of Canterbury. *See Map 28.*

6 Waterloo Station
SE1. To approach the station in style try the grand Edwardian entrance opposite Mepham Street, with its sweeping steps, sunray clock and guardian statues, built in 1848 and modernised in the 20s and again in the 80s. From here Southern Region's rails stretch to the 'Stockbroker Belt' of Surrey. To observe City gents, en masse and in a hurry, attend its morning or evening rush hour.

St John's Church

7 St John's Church
Waterloo Rd SE1. Only the neo-classical shell of this early 19thC church survived the wartime bombs. Restored, by Ford, in time for the 1951 Festival of Britain, which was celebrated on the ground now occupied by the South Bank Complex. *See Map 22.*

8 Old Vic
Waterloo Rd SE1. 01-928 7616. Built 1818. For a long time the home of the National Theatre Company, then housed the Prospect Theatre Company. Bought for renovation and a renewed theatrical future in 1982.

Old Vic

9 Young Vic
66 The Cut SE1. 01-928 6363. Theatre in the round in which a professional repertory company presents exciting productions of established modern plays and classics to a primarily young audience. Informal and friendly with a good snack bar, open before performances and also for lunch Mon–Fri.

10 The Cut Market
The Cut SE1. A small-scale Petticoat Lane. The market flourishes on weekdays until about tea-time – food, clothes old and new, small household items, but no frivolities like antiques or bric-a-brac.

11 St George's Roman Catholic Cathedral
Lambeth Rd SE1. Barrack-like from without but gracious within, incongruously covering the site of the 1780 'No Popery' riots. It was designed by Pugin in the 1840s, never completed, destroyed by bombing in 1941 and rebuilt by Romily Croze, who adapted the original plans.

12 Elephant and Castle Development
SE1. A typical 1960s development, using concrete, glass and height for impact and allowing space for offices, high rise flats and a mammoth shopping centre. The area takes its name from a pub, now sadly gone. The London College of Printing is close by.

13 Imperial War Museum
Lambeth Rd SE1. 01-735 8922. The story of the British Army and the impact of war since 1914; uniforms and weapons, paintings and dioramas, ops maps, vehicles and other impedimenta of war. Housed in what was the notorious Bethleham Hospital, moved here in 1815. 'Bedlam' was the first lunatic asylum, its horrors graphically recorded in Hogarth's *The Rake's Progress.*

Imperial War Museum

14 Geraldine Mary Harmsworth Park
SE1. On the site of the wings of the old Bedlam Hospital, which were demolished in the 30s, leaving only the central block. Laid out by Harold Harmsworth, the newspaper proprietor, younger brother of Lord Northcliffe, in memory of his mother.

Waterloo Station

15 Christ Church and Upton Chapel
Kennington Rd SE1. The Lincoln Tower, built by American subscription as a memorial to the former President, is a survivor of the church of 1876. The rest was bombed in the Second World War and rebuilt as part of an office block. Notice the modern stained glass window across which people from all walks of life stride enthusiastically towards eternity.

16 John Tunstill's Soldiers' Shop
24 Kennington Rd SE1. Small shop to intrigue the military-minded – helmets, caps, gas-masks, books on campaigns, startled-looking shop dummies in uniform, badges, medals, models – mostly from within the last 100 years.

17 Lambeth Walk
SE1. Gave its name to that well known and jaunty costermonger's song and dance. A traditional market site with stalls stacked with fruit and vegetables, rails of cheap clothes, and entertaining sales chat from the modern merchants. *Closed Thur afternoon & Sun.*

County Hall

EATING AND DRINKING

A Il Papagallo *Restaurant*
35 York Rd SE1. 01-928 1003. Sit beneath rather rude murals, in which the gods joyously disport themselves, for a quick pasta or a more elaborate veal cordon bleu, chicken Kiev or tournedos Rossini – steak wrapped in pâté in a brandy sauce. Tempting fresh cream cakes. *Closed Sun.* ££.

B La Ronde *Café*
17 Tenison Way SE1. 01-928 3907. Light, cheerily noisy eating place, marooned on the large roundabout between the station and the National Theatre. Sandwiches, teas, snacks, a substantial daily special and wholesome home-made puddings. *Closed 20.00, 16.00 on Sun.* £.

C Hole in the Wall *Pub*
5 Mepham St SE1. 01-928 6196. Tucked away in a railway arch by the station and generally bursting at the seams with discerning drinkers downing the eight real ales which are always on tap. Snacks too. £.

D Wellington *Tavern*
81 Waterloo Rd SE1. 01-928 6083. Decorated with murals of the Battle of Waterloo, beneath which commuters preparing for the Battle of Waterloo Station gather to enjoy one of the 10 real ales. Good snacks. £.

E RSJ *Restaurant*
13A Coin St SE1. 01-928 4554. Friendly French-café ambiance in this converted warehouse, now smart in brown and cream. French-based menu – fish in classical sauces, game in season, lamb glazed in honey. The initials stand for Rolled Steel Joist, since two hefty ones support the structure. *Closed Sat lunch & Sun.* ££.

F Windmill *Pub*
86 The Cut SE1. 01-928 7276. Large, hearty and crowded with office workers at lunch time, commuters and theatre-goers at night. Plentiful food counter. £.

G Buster Brown *Restaurant*
The Cut SE1. 01-928 2157. Relaxed, Continental-café-style place, proud of its 'genuine doorstop sarnies' and zappy cocktails. Also barbecued meats, burgers, salads and rich puddings. *Closed Sun.* £.

H South of the Border *Restaurant*
8 Joan St SE1. 01-928 6374. Charming farmhouse atmosphere in this converted bed factory, its walls hung with embroidered rugs, its roof garden level with the elevated railway track. Try avocado with crab, lamb cutlets with coriander and yoghourt. Cheese or ice cream to follow. *Closed Sat lunch & Sun.* ££.

J Duke of Clarence *Pub*
St George's Circus SE1. 01-928 6291. 150-year-old pub with a lively disco every night but Mon. No dance floor, but that doesn't inhibit anyone.

K Brass Crosby *Wine Bar*
4 London Rd SE1. 01-928 8452. Named for the 16thC Lord Mayor of London who lived nearby and whose memorial obelisk now stands outside the War Museum. Short but well-chosen wine list, lovely pork casserole in wine, spicy chilli, baked potatoes with interesting fillings, salads. *Closed Sun.* £.

L Prince of Wales *Pub*
51 St George's Rd SE1. 01-735 1546. Warm friendly local where students from the nearby College of Printing congregate at lunchtime for toasted sandwiches. A pianist and singer entertain on Fri and Sat, and on Sun evening the Golden Oldies Disco wrenches many a heart. £.

M Two Eagles *Pub*
27 Austral St SE11. 01-735 2826. Big Victorian pub which has featured in several tv films and the American-made *Life Story of Charles Chaplin*, one of the area's most famous sons. Three real ales and substantial grills and snacks. £.

N Three Stags *Pub*
69 Kennington Rd SE1. 01-928 5974. Two doors from the old home of Captain Bligh of the Bounty stands this attractive 100-year-old pub with draught beer on hand pumps, cold food with salad, hot food with chips, and sing-along cockney music at weekends. £.

Westminster Bridge

O Perdoni's *Restaurant*
18 Kennington Rd SE1. 01-928 6846. Big, bustling Italian-run restaurant serving a solidly satisfying mixture of English and Italian food – spaghetti bolognese, veal escalopes, toad in the hole, jam roll. Home cooking, generous helpings and breakfasts 6 days a week. *Closed evenings, Sat lunch & Sun.* £.

P New Crown and Cushion *Pub*
133 Westminster Bridge Rd SE1. 01-928 4795. Aptly decorated with bits and pieces from old railways, though none from Waterloo – a gas lamp, a station clock, signal equipment. Nice home-made lunches and toasted sandwiches in the evenings. *Closed Sun evening.* £.

Q Cabin *Restaurant*
135 Westminster Bridge Rd SE1. 01-928 4268. Friendly, intimate little Turkish steak and kebab house with a charcoal grill. Light and honey-coated Turkish pastries. Take-away operation attached. *Closed Sun.* £.

Morning Coffee and Afternoon Tea
La Ronde Café; 17 Tenison Way SE1. 01-928 3907.
Perdoni's Restaurant; 18 Kennington Rd SE1. 01-928 6846. *Closed Sun.*
Waterloo Station buffets; any time but somewhat grimy.

Map 30 SOUTHWARK

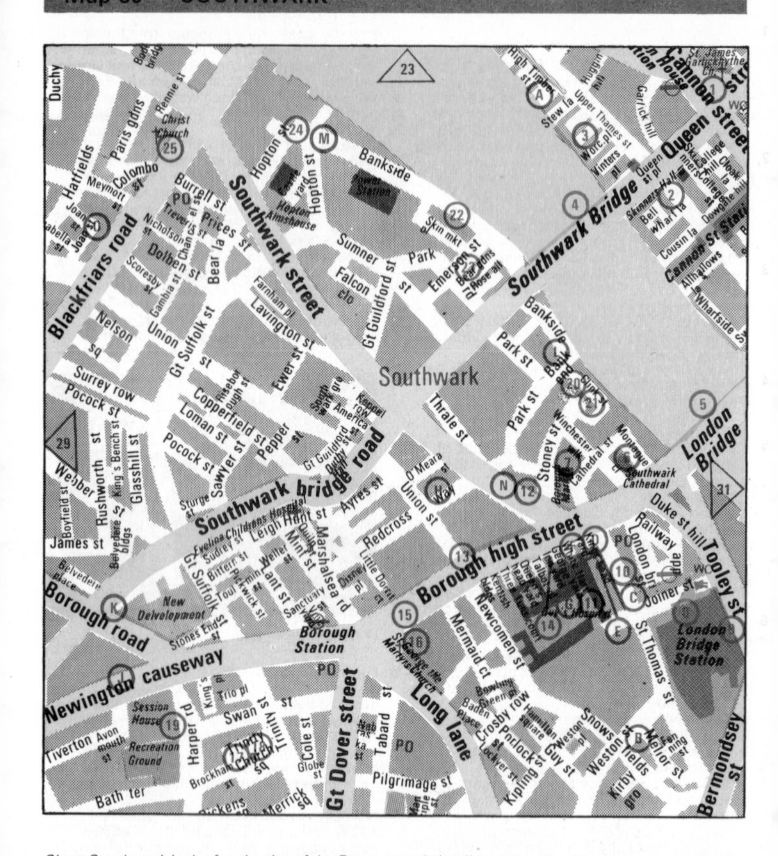

Since Southwark is the focal point of the Roman roads leading to London it has been populated for a very long time, with a steady surge of growth which began in the 16thC when the coaches used it as a major staging post. But the key to understanding its raucous and bawdy past is the fact that, even though a part of London, it was always outside the jurisdiction of the City, and the taming influence of the Mayor and his Aldermen. So the brothels flourished here, and the bear gardens, the alehouses, the theatres and the other places of ill repute. It is true that there was also the magnificent church of St Mary Overie, now Southwark Cathedral, and the Palace of the Bishop of Winchester – but the latter had so many whorehouses on his land that the ladies who entertained in them were known as 'Winchester Geese'. It also had seven prisons, including Marshalsea where Dickens' father served his time for debt and the famous Clink.

Southwark was severely bombed in the Second World War, and has been equally severely built up since, but its points of interest stand out like beacon lights in a wilderness. Even the smartly landscaped river walk along Bankside cannot lay the ghosts around the site of Shakespeare's Globe and the rival Rose Theatre. That ancient tavern the Anchor, now in its second manifestation and a mere 230 years old, still serves ale and the Bear Gardens Museum evokes the whole tawdry glamour of Elizabethan low life.

The two bridges lead the eye, if not the person, across the river to the menacing towers of Cannon Street Station and also to sweeping views of St Paul's and the City of London around it.

PLACES OF INTEREST

1 **St James Garlickhythe Church**
Garlic Hill EC4. One of Sir Christopher Wren's City churches. Its distinctive steeple of 3 stone temples, each one smaller than the one below, was restored in 1713, possibly by Hawksmoor. The altar painting of the Ascension by Andrew Geddes was given to the church in 1815.

2 **Dowgate Hill**
EC4. Here stand three surviving City Livery Company halls – at No 4 the 17thC Tallow Chandlers'; at No 8 the Skinners' with its 18thC façade by Jupp added to an early 17thC building; at No 10 the Dyers' by Charles Dyer in 1839–40.

3 **City Waterfront**
SE1. London's most important docking area – until the modern docks were built east down river. Queenhithe was the largest wharf and it was here that the considerate Queen Maud caused the first public lavatory to be built, in the 12thC.

4 **Southwark Bridge**
SE1. Early 20thC structure by Sir Ernest George replacing a 19thC one. The best that can be said of it is that it spans the river.

5 **London Bridge**
SE1. There has been some kind of bridge here since the 1stC. The present concrete structure by Harold Knox King, 1967–73, had two especially illustrious predecessors – the 12thC wooden one decorated with small houses and, sometimes, traitors heads, familiar from old woodcuts; and John Rennie's construction of 1825–31 which was sold to America and now spans an artificial lake in Arizona.

6 **Southwark Cathedral**
Borough High St SE1. Officially the cathedral and collegiate church of St Saviour and St Mary Overie (the last word meaning 'over the water'). Founded in the 12thC and restored and partially rebuilt over the centuries, it is a living example of the development of ecclesiastical architecture. It has a particularly beautiful altar screen and some impressive memorials – including one to Shakespeare and one to John Gower, died 1408, the first poet to write in English. Good choral recitals.

Southwark Cathedral

7 **Borough Market**
SE1. Busy wholesale fruit and vegetable market. At its peak around 06.00, its interlocking market buildings have an air of dereliction by mid-morning.

8 **London Bridge Station**
SE1. London's first rail terminus, built in 1836 but modernised since. This is where the bulk of London's millions of commuters arrive daily and depart nightly. The relentless human flood crosses London Bridge to the City from 08.30–09.30 at a spanking pace and reverses the procedure from 17.30–18.30. Idle commuter-spotters are likely to be swept along with the tide.

9 **London Dungeon**
34 Tooley St EC1. 01-403 0606. Gruesomely realistic exhibition of the dark side of British history in a dank vaulted cellar; sacrifices, tortures, plagues, murders, executions – everything you need for a really vivid nightmare or several. Unsuitable for adults or those of a sensitive disposition. *Charge.*

10 **Old St Thomas' Hospital Operating Theatre**
The Chapter House, St Thomas' St SE1. 01-407 7600. A spiral stair leads up the tower of the ex-parish church to a garret where the hospital apothecary dried his herbs. Pause for a nervous look at the surgical instruments, opium-poppy seed-heads and contemporary pictures of people being separated from their limbs. Then continue upstairs to the only surviving early 19thC operating theatre in Britain. *Open Mon, Tue & Fri, 12.30–16.00 or by appointment. Charge.*

Guy's Hospital

11 **Guy's Hospital**
St Thomas' St SE1. 01-407 7600. A large and growing general hospital founded in 1725 by a City bookseller called Thomas Guy whose brass statue has stood in the courtyard since 1733. Has one of England's largest medical schools – once attended by Keats.

12 **Central Buildings**
Southwark St SE1. This was the old Hop Exchange, by R. H. Moore in 1866, with its great iron gate of fancy filigree, topped with scenes of hopping activity and with a giant eagle perched overall.

13 **War Memorial**
Borough High St SE1. This First World War memorial by P. Lindsey Clark is surmounted by a bronze of a fairly ordinary tin-hatted

soldier – but look at the side panels; one has battleships and the other a kind of dogfight of early bi-planes.

14 George Inn
George Inn Yard, 77 Borough High St SE1. 01-407 2056. London's last remaining galleried coaching inn, first mentioned in John Stow's 'History of London' in 1590 and rebuilt after fire damage in 1676. There are two bars, a wine bar, grill room and restaurant.

15 Borough High Street
SE1. If strolling the length of this rather tatty jumble of ancient and modern spare a glance for the 'Yards' which open off it, a reminder that this was a busy coaching thoroughfare in the first half of the 18thC with at least six important inns to offer succour to horses and travellers.

16 St George the Martyr Church
Borough High St SE1. This, as the plaque outside proudly proclaims, is 'Little Dorrit's church', built in 1734–6 by John Price on a medieval church site. Look carefully at the 4 clock faces on the tower – 3 are white but one is black and can't be seen at night. It faces Bermondsey whose parishioners failed to contribute to the building fund.

17 Holy Trinity Church
Trinity Sq SE1. An early 19thC building with massively porticoed porch by Bedford, in a square of unspoilt early 19thC terraces, on land owned by Trinity House, the body responsible for lighthouses and pilotage in British waters. The church is now dedicated to music, serving as a concert rehearsal hall.

18 King Alfred the Great
Trinity Church Sq SE1. It is generally assumed that the weatherbeaten statue of the venerable kingly figure, now standing in a bed of lavender, is Alfred the Great. It may have come from Westminster Hall – if so it dates from 1395 and is the oldest in London.

King Alfred the Great

19 Session House
Newington Causeway SE1. A large classical building of the 1920s by W. E. Riley where minor offences are tried and young lawyers hurry in and out.

20 Clink Street
SE1. The narrow way, squeezing between towering warehouses, bears a plaque to mark the site of the Clink prison where the Bishops of Winchester incarcerated heretics. It was destroyed by the Gordon rioters in 1780.

Rose window, Winchester House

21 Winchester House
Clink St SE1. Some venerable stone foundations and a wall with the skeleton of a lovely rose window are all that is now left of the 12thC town palace of the Bishops of Winchester. It was burned down in 1814 and its carefully preserved remains lie trapped between two dark warehouse walls.

22 Bankside
SE1. Southwark's waterfront, notorious in the 16thC for its whorehouses, taverns, bear baiting rings and playhouses, has been largely rebuilt. There is now a genteel, landscaped riverside walkway, dominated by Sir Giles G. Scott's monumental electric power station, but signs of the past linger; Rose Alley where the Rose Theatre stood, Bear Gardens, and one extant tavern, the Anchor.

23 Bear Gardens Museum and Art Centre
Bear Gardens SE1. 01-928 6342. An essential port of call if you want to get the flavour of the area in its Elizabethan heyday – a small exhibition leads you through the brothels, bear-pits and theatres. Evocative model of the first Globe and of the ice fairs held when the Thames froze over. Small replica of 16thC playhouse frequently stages suitable productions. *Closed Mon–Thur. Charge.*

24 Bankside Gallery
48 Hopton St SE1. 01-928 7521. An attractive modern gallery on the newly refurbished riverside walk which mounts ever-changing exhibitions of the work of contemporary British painters. *Closed Sun morning & Mon. Charge.*

25 Christ Church
Blackfriars Rd SE1. A church first stood on the site in 1671. Its replacement of 1738 was badly bomb damaged and the present modest brick building went up in 1960.

EATING AND DRINKING

A Samuel Pepys *Pub and Restaurant*
Brooks Wharf, 48 Upper Thames St EC4. 01-248 3691. Converted riverside warehouse with a two-tiered river-view terrace bar, a spacious cellar bar with well-stocked food counter and a light, airy restaurant serving game pie and spotted dick. Old lamps, prints and transcriptions of the famous diaries compete for attention with a ticker-tape machine. *Closed Sat lunchtime.* £ or ££.

B **Doc's Diner** *Restaurant*
48–50 Weston St SE1. 01-403 6826. There's a bar at the front and café-style seating at the back. The food is ordinary – steak and chips, gammon and pineapple – but good and hot. Service is chaotic but affectionate. A bit like being served by your baby sister who's doing her best. £.

C **Guys and Dolls** *Restaurant*
25 St Thomas' St SE1. 01-407 2828. Italian-run café open all day for snacks, kebabs, chicken Maryland, lasagne, puddings, cheese. Or you may just have a drink or a cup of tea – except at lunchtime. *Closed 19.00 & all weekend.* £.

D **Loose Vine** *Wine Bar*
2 St Thomas' St SE1. 01-407 3673. The decor hasn't changed much since it was a pub called The Grapes and it still serves beer, lager and spirits. Snacks in the bar or on the terrace and lunches in the restaurant above. *Closed Sun.* £.

E **Old King's Head** *Pub*
King's Head Yard, Borough High St SE1. 01-407 1550. The Old King is Henry VIII and though the present building is late 19thC there has been an inn on this site since 1533. Real ale and lunches. *Closed Sat & Sun evening.* £.

F **Beadles** *Wine Bar*
47 Borough High St SE1. 01-407 6124. Cosy candlelit basement with natural brick walls, booths for privacy and bottles for decoration. Specially good steak pie, fresh salads, passion cake, nice house wine. *Closed weekends.* £.

George Inn

G **George** *Inn*
77 Borough High St SE1. 01-407 2056. London's last galleried coaching inn, with real ales, wines, set lunches and an à la carte grill room. Very busy, so booking for meals is wise. £.

H **Boot and Flogger** *Wine Bar*
10–20 Redcross Way SE1. 01-407 1184. One of Davy's bars, most of whose names relate to the wine trade of 100 years ago and all of which have a carefully created Victorian image of old barrels, sawdust and panelling. Good cold buffet. *Closed weekends.* £.

J **Briefs** *Wine Bar*
34 Newington Causeway SE1. 01-407 8470. Large and smart, in a rough-walled sort of way. Good range of wines and, to eat, stroganoff, steak, quiche, sweets. (In case of misunderstandings, the name refers to the courthouse opposite!) *Closed weekends.* £.

K **Goose and Firkin** *Pub*
47 Borough Rd SE1. 01-403 3590. Now for something really different – a pub that brews its own beer in the cellar. Best and Borough bitter are traditional, Dogbolter is strong and Earthstopper is just what it says it is. At lunchtime try fresh baps filled with salad and meat or cheese. At night, enjoy the excellent pianist. £.

City waterfront

L **Anchor** *Pub and Restaurant*
Bankside SE1. 01-407 1577. Charming 18thC pub with small bars, open fires, exposed beams, antique oddments and a first edition of Dr Johnson's Dictionary. On the site of a disreputable earlier house which catered to smugglers, press gangs and warders from the Clink. Restaurant serves staunch English food, including Mrs Thrale's Very Special Steak and Mushroom Pudding, said to have been served by the lady herself to the ubiquitous Dr J. *No food Sun.* ££.

M **Founders Arms** *Pub*
Bankside SE1. 01-928 1889. Smart and modern, with views across river to St Paul's, on the site of the foundry which cast her bells. Salad bar, à la carte restaurant, wonderful beer. ££.

N **Dive Bar** *Pub*
24 Southwark St SE1. 01-407 2335. Between the Old Hop Exchange and the dungeons of the now extinct debtors prison stands this mock-Tudor bar with its 5 real ales and its lunchtime bar snacks. On Thur, Fri and Sat evening, when the City gents have left for home, the disco starts up – no dancing, though. £.

O **South of the Border** *Restaurant*
8 Joan St SE1. 01-928 6374. Charming farmhouse atmosphere in this converted bed factory, its walls hung with embroidered rugs, its roof garden level with the elevated railway track. Try avocado with crab, lamb cutlets with coriander and yoghourt. Cheese or ice cream to follow. *Closed Sat lunch & Sun.* ££.

Morning Coffee and Afternoon Tea
London Bridge Station; Snack Bar.

Map 31 THE CITY

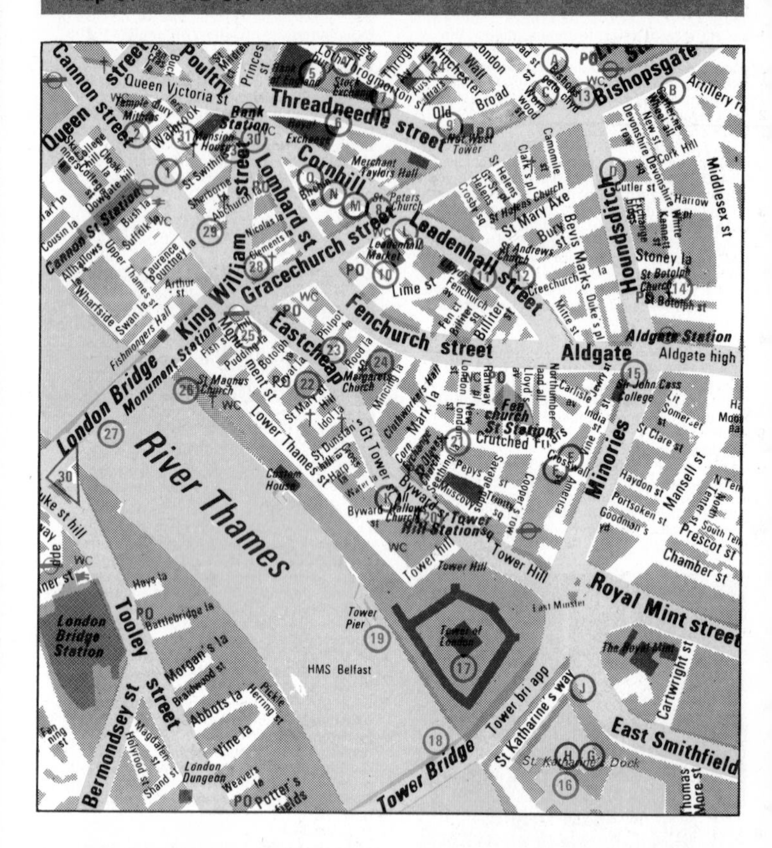

Once, the City was the whole of London and it is still London's heart, the centre of business and trade, pivoting around those great City institutions the Stock Exchange, the Bank of England and Lloyd's Insurance. Exceptionally busy during the working day it becomes still and silent in the evenings and at weekends. These are the best times to appreciate the curious effects created by the juxtaposition of glitteringly tall modern buildings and narrow medieval alleys – but bear in mind that the excellent and ancient taverns, pubs and chop houses, seething with business types on weekday lunchtimes, tend to close early in the evenings and rarely open at all at weekends.

Two major events helped to shape the City. The first was the devastation caused by the Great Fire of London in 1666 and the ensuing rebuilding which scattered the capital with the beautiful and amazingly varied Wren churches, among other buildings, and followed the earlier street plan. The second was the Blitz which resulted in another wave of rebuilding, much of it crude and disproportionately large, yet part of the City's face.

On the south eastern edge of the City stands the Tower of London, sombre setting of so much of British history. Begun by William the Conqueror and added to by Richard I, Henry III and Edward I it is better known as a prison than a fortress. Kings, Queens, statesmen and religious leaders have been incarcerated and beheaded here, and as recently as the Second World War spies were put to death within it. On a lighter note is its East End neighbour, St Katharine's Dock, now given over to tourism with its yacht marina, Maritime Museum and warehouses converted into jovial hostelries.

PLACES OF INTEREST

1 **London Stone**
Cannon St EC4. Set into the wall of the Bank of China and believed to be the original Roman millarium from which all road distances were measured.

2 **Temple of Mithras**
Queen Victoria St EC4. Mithraic temples were always underground. This was raised to its present site from 18 feet below Walbrook and has lost in the translation. The finds from the site are in the Museum of London.

3 **Mansion House**
EC2. 01-626 2500. Rather fine Palladian building of 1739–52 by George Dance, the official residence of the Lord Mayor of London and scene of his annual banquets. The grand hall – called Egyptian though it has no Egyptian architectural features – is well worth seeing. *View on application only.*

4 **St Margaret Lothbury Church**
Lothbury EC2. 01-606 8330. Built by Wren, 1686–1700, in white Portland stone. Some of its beautiful fittings were inherited from other Wren churches after their demolition. Lovely churchyard.

5 **Bank of England**
Threadneedle St EC2. 01-601 4444. The guardian of the nation's gold. Security precludes visitors but the pink-coated, red-waistcoated, top-hatted messengers and doormen are colourfully visible.

Bank of England

6 **Royal Exchange**
Threadneedle St and Cornhill EC3. 01-606 2433. Planned in 1564, as a meeting place for merchants, by Sir Thomas Gresham whose family grasshopper emblem crouches above. This third building by Tite, 1842–4, is now the premises of the Financial Futures Exchange.

7 **Stock Exchange**
Old Broad St EC2. 01-588 2355. Began in a coffee house but has been established here since 1801. Watch the antics of the smartly dressed dealers in negotiable securities from a sound-proofed visitors' gallery. Daily film shows explain all. *Closed 15.15 & all weekend. Free.*

8 **St Peter upon Cornhill Church**
Bishopsgate Corner EC3. 01-626 9483. By Wren on the City's oldest church site. Regular performances of Elizabethan music, and of medieval plays at Christmas. Don't miss the hideous devils on the adjoining building, put there by its architect who had just lost a dispute with the church authorities.

9 **Nat West Tower**
25 Old Broad St EC2. London's tallest building by that master of architectural overkill, Richard Seifert. The Nat West logo is on the roof, visible only from the air.

Nat West Tower

10 **Leadenhall Market**
Gracechurch St EC3. Horace Jones built the superb glass and iron hall in 1881, on the site of the old Roman basilica and forum, which still shelters a lively general market.

11 **Lloyd's of London**
Lime St EC3. 01-623 7100. Began as a coffee house where shipping deals were concluded. Now a world-famous international insurance market conducting business in 'The Room', said to be the largest room in the world. The Lutine Bell is rung once for bad news of a ship, twice for good. *Entry on application.*

12 **St Andrew Undershaft Church**
Leadenhall St EC3. Early 16thC East Anglian Gothic, once overshadowed by a maypole. The monument to John Stow, London's first historian, is annually furnished with a fresh quill pen by the Lord Mayor.

13 **St Botolph's Bishopsgate Church**
Bishopsgate EC2. 01-588 1053. Rebuilt in 1725–9 by James Gould and standing in a large churchyard with a 19thC charity school, complete with replicas of pupils, behind it.

14 **St Botolph's Aldgate Church**
Aldgate High St EC3. 01-283 1670. Rebuilt in 1741–4 by George Dance the elder. Restored in the 1890s and 1960s. Fine 17thC organ.

15 **Sir John Cass Foundation School**
Aldgate E1. Founded in 1710 as a charity school with the customary pair of stone 'charity children' in niches on the wall.

16 **St Katharine's Dock**
St Katharine's Way, Tower Bridge EC3. No longer a commercial dock, its three inter-linked basins form a yacht haven and an appropriate setting for the Thames Maritime Museum with its tug, lightship, sailing barges and Captain Scott's 'Discovery'. Some warehouses survive – converted into souvenir shops, the Dickens Tavern and the Warehouse Restaurant. *Charge to enter ships.*

St Katharine's Dock

17 Tower of London
Tower Hill EC3. 01-709 0765. This grim and famous fortress looks deceptively pale and innocent from outside. Red-clad Yeomen Warders and black ravens guard the Bloody Tower, the Traitor's Gate, the armoury, the executioner's block and axe and, of course, the Crown Jewels. The massively plain Norman chapel of St John is the oldest church in London. *Closed Sun morn. Charge.*

18 Tower Bridge
Splendid Victorian Gothic structure with hydraulicly operated drawbridge by Jones and Wolfe Barry, 1894. The vertiginous lattice-work footbridges, with their wonderful views, have recently been reopened. Don't look down.

19 Tower Pier
Tower Hill EC3. 01-709 9697. Daily river trips to Greenwich or Westminster and a ferry to HMS Belfast when she is open for view (01-407 6436). *Closed Sept to Easter.*

20 All Hallows by the Tower Church
Byward St EC3. 01-481 2928. A pre-Great Fire church, from whose tower Pepys watched the conflagration, gutted in 1941, restored by Lord Mottistone in the 50s. 14thC crypt has Roman paving and a small museum, *open at weekends or by arrangement.*

21 St Olave's Church
8 Hart St EC3. 01-488 4318. An appealing survival of the Great Fire, its churchyard protected by an arch with skulls – a sign that the plague-dead were buried here, as were Samuel Pepys and, so says the parish register, Mother Goose.

22 St Mary at Hill Church
Lovat La EC3. 01-626 4184. Wren church partly rebuilt in the 19thC by James Savage. Lovely, lavish interior with 17thC woodwork. Though Billingsgate wholesale fish market has departed its ancient site in Lower Thames Street, just down the hill, its traders still come here for the annual Harvest of the Sea Thanksgiving on the second Sun in Oct.

23 Plaster Mice
Off Eastcheap, in Philpot Lane EC3. The builders were forced to share their lunch with so many mice they made this tiny plaster effigy in their memory. Look at the side of the third pillar, about 12 feet up.

24 St Margaret Pattens Church
Rood La, Eastcheap EC3. 01-623 6630. The locally-made pattens or shoes are displayed in a cabinet in this Wren church of 1684–9 with its unusual canopied pews and punishment bench for naughty children.

25 Monument
Monument St EC3. Wren's monument to the devastating Fire of London. Built in the 1670s it is 202 feet high – the distance from its base to the fire's birthplace in Pudding Lane. 311 steps lead to a literally breathtaking view atop. *Closed Sun. Charge.*

26 St Magnus the Martyr Church
Lower Thames St EC3. 01-636 4481. Wren church with a fine steeple and Baroque interior. Note the plentiful sword rests.

27 London Bridge
There has been a bridge here since the 1stC. The present one, by Harold Knox King, 1967–73, had two illustrious predecessors – the 12thC wooden version familiar from old woodcuts; and John Rennie's construction of 1825–31, sold to America and now spanning an artificial lake in Arizona.

28 St Clement's Church
Clements La King William St EC4. 01-268 6121. A Wren church restored by Butterfield in the 19thC and by Comper in the 20th. Wonderful 17thC canopied pulpit. Competes with St Clement Danes to be the original 'Oranges and Lemons' church.

29 St Mary Abchurch
Abchurch Yd EC4. 01-626 0306. Plain brick and stone-dressed Wren church with an unexpectedly beautiful interior, especially William Snow's painted ceiling and Grinling Gibbons' altarpiece.

30 St Mary Woolnoth Church
Junction Lombard St & King William St EC3. 01-626 9701. Sumptuous Hawksmoor church of 1716–27 with regular relaxation classes as well as services. Bank underground station burrows disrespectfully underneath.

31 St Stephen Walbrook Church
Walbrook EC4. 01-626 2277. Parish church of the Lord Mayor of London and centre for the Samaritans, (01-283 3400) formed to help the suicidally desperate. By Wren, its dome possibly a prototype for St Paul's.

EATING AND DRINKING

Balls Brothers *Wine Bars*
3 Budge Row, Cannon St EC4. 01-248 7557.
42 Threadneedle St EC2. 01-283 6701.
St Mary at Hill EC3. 01-626 0321.
Chain of deservedly popular City wine bars, with more than 60 wines and reliable snacks and sandwiches. *Closed 19.30 & all weekend.* £.

A Gow's Oyster Bar *Restaurant*
81 Old Broad St EC2. 01-628 0530. Controlled by Balls Brothers, the wine merchants, so the wine list is extensive. Here you will find executive class simplicity with good fish, at good value, and chops to boot. *Closed evenings & weekends.* £.

B Dirty Dick's *Pub*
202 Bishopsgate EC2. 01-283 5888. Named after an 18thC miser who closed up his house on the death of his fiancée. On his own death it was found to be laced with cobwebs and sprinkled with mouse skeletons, all of which

were moved to the pub together with mouldering mummified cats and a certain amount of synthetic dirt. But no longer dirty since a big clean-up in 1982. Grill bar above. *Closed weekends.* £.

C Gallipolli *Restaurant*
8 Bishopsgate Churchyard EC2. 01-588 1922. A little jewelled folly of a Turkish restaurant which refused to make way for the modern buildings around it and sits defiantly under its crescent moon like a mini-mosque. Excellent international food and twice-nightly belly-dancing. *Closed Sun.* £££.

D Clanger *Pub*
Houndsditch EC2. 01-283 5858. A modern 'theme' pub, the theme being fire-fighting; genuine fire bell, insurance company firemarks, and the story of the Great Fire itself. Wine bar closes earlier than pub, according to demand. Restaurant offers English lunches only. *Closed 22.30 & all weekend.* £ or ££.

E City Volunteer *Restaurant*
Lloyds Chambers, Crosswall EC3. 01-481 8578. Large, red and rather flashily impressive place where businessmen treat each other to devilled whitebait, pike with lobster sauce, carved beef from the trolley, and stilton. *Closed evenings & weekends.* £££.

F Old Crutched Friars *Pub*
15a Crosswall EC3. 01-480 5282. Near the site of Crutched Friars Abbey stands this aged building, leaning on its neighbours. Friendly and busy, especially at lunchtime, with tables under the hanging baskets in Friar's Passage in good weather. *Closed Sun evening & all Sat.* £.

Tower of London

G Dickens Inn *Pub and Restaurants*
St Katharine's Way E1. 01-488 1226. Converted warehouse with incongruous window boxes, exposed beams, a brass-topped bar and sawdust on the floor. There is real ale and good food on three levels; pub grub in the *Tavern Room*; European food à la carte in the *Pickwick Room* (book on 01-488 2208); fish dishes in the *Dickens Room* (book on 01-488 9932). ££.

H Warehouse *Restaurant*
52 St Katharine's Way E1. 01-481 3356. Converted rum warehouse with great views of the Thames and Tower Bridge. English food with a French accent. Traditional Sunday lunches. Pianist plays some nights. *Closed Sat lunch, Sun dinner.* ££.

J Princes Room *Restaurant*
Tower Hotel, St Katharine's Way E1. 01-481 2575. Satisfying views of Tower Bridge and the river from the cocktail bar. The restaurant offers international cuisine – avocado with prawns in a spicy sauce, lamb cutlets en croute, escalope de veau Western Isles. Sweets from the trolley. £££. The *Carvery*, in the same hotel, has great views over St Katharine's Dock. ££.

Tower Bridge

K Wheeler's City *Restaurant*
19–21 Great Tower St EC3. 01-626 3685. One of a chain of friendly, reliable fish restaurants, all panelling and plush, with excellent fish and shellfish. Fruit or cheese to follow. *Closed evenings & weekends.* ££.

L Lamb *Tavern*
Leadenhall Mkt EC3. 01-626 2454. Plain old pub, built in 1780 and rebuilt in 1881, whose tiled walls give it a public lavatory ambiance, with a devoted following of businessmen who would defect were it smartened up. Well kept real ale, sandwiches, and a mention in Pickwick Papers. *Closed 19.15 & all weekend.* £.

M George and Vulture *Restaurant*
3 Castle Court EC3. 01-626 9710. Claims to be London's oldest hostelry and has certainly been around since the 14thC. Dickens set a scene from the Pickwick Papers here. Regulars get their pints in silver tankards – and all comers may partake of fine steaks, roasts, puddings and pies. *Closed evenings & weekends.* ££.

N Simpson's *Tavern*
38½ Cornhill EC3. 01-626 9985. 18thC pub and chop house lurking in Ball Court. Packed with businessmen – you'll have to share a table – enjoying excellent English, often olde-Englishe, food. The speciality of stewed cheese slips down a treat. *Closed evenings & weekends.* £.

O Jamaica *Wine Bar*
St Michael's Alley, Cornhill EC3. 01-626 9496. The first coffee house to be opened in London, was destroyed in the Great Fire, rebuilt by Wren in 1668, fire damaged again in 1748 and restored in 1858. Two large, packed bars, good snacks, wines, ports, lagers and draught beer. *Closed 20.00 & all weekend.* £.

Morning Coffee and Afternoon Tea
Tower Hotel; St Katharine's Way E1. 01-481 2575. In the lounge with its view of St Katharine's Dock. Also a restaurant and carvery.
City Buttery and Bakery; Aldgate High St EC2. Snacks, teas and luscious cakes to take away. *Closed weekends.*
London Bridge Station; Snack Bar.

Index

PLACES OF INTEREST

Academy 1, 2, 3, 51
8 Addison Road 4
Admiralty Arch 83
Albert Bridge 71, 99
Albert Embankment 111
Albert Memorial 43
All Hallows by the Tower Church 124
All Hallows by the Wall Church 96
All Saints Church 51
All Souls Church 51
Angel, The 62–65
Archbishop's Park 115
Baden-Powell House 39, 43
Bank of England 96, 123
Bankside 120
Bankside Gallery 120
Barbican Arts Centre 95
Barkers 8
Barnsbury Square 31
Barnsbury Station 31
Battersea 98–101
Battersea Bridge 72, 99
Battersea Dogs' Home 104
Battersea High Street Market 100
Battersea Park 99, 102–105, 104
Battersea Power Station 104, 108
Battersea Square 99
Bear Gardens Museum and Arts Centre 120
Beauchamp Place 44
Belgrave Square 79
Belgravia and Victoria 78–81
Berkeley Square 52
Berwick Street Market 51
Bharatiya Vidya Bhavan 35
Big Ben 84, 111
Billings, The 67
Blackfriar's Bridges 92
Bloomsbury and Clerkenwell 58–61
Bloomsbury Theatre 24
Bond Street, Old and New 52
Borough High Street 120
Borough Market 119
Bow Street Police Station 87
Bramham Gardens 40
Bridge Lane Theatre 100
British Museum and British Library 55
Broadcasting House 51
Brompton Cemetery 36, 67
Brompton Oratory 44
Brook Green 3
Buckingham Palace 79, 83
Bunhill Fields 95
Burlington Arcade 52
Bush Theatre 3
Bute Street 40
Cadogan Pier 103
Cadogan Square 75
Caledonian Road 31
Camden Passage 32, 63
Canal Walk 28
Canonbury Square 32
Captain Cook 83
Cardinal Newman's Statue 44
Carlton House Terrace 83
Carlyle's House 71
Cenotaph, The 84
Central Buildings 119
Centre Point 56
Chalton Street Market 27
Chapel Market 32, 63
Chartered Insurance Institute Museum 96
Charterhouse 64, 95
Chelsea 70–73
Chelsea and Brompton 74–77
Chelsea Barracks 76, 103
Chelsea Bridge 104
Chelsea Embankment 103
Chelsea Houseboats 72
Chelsea Old Church, All Saints 71
Chelsea Old Town Hall 76
Chelsea Physic Garden 76, 103
Chelsea Royal Hospital 76, 103
Cheyne Walk 71
Chiltern Street 19
Christ Church and Upton Chapel 116
Christ Church, SE1. 120
Christ Church, W8. 39
Christ Church, NW1. 23
Christ the King Church 24
Christies 40
Church Dock 99
Churchill Gardens Estate 108
Church of Our Lady of Victories 8
Church of the Annunciation 15
Church of the Holy Cross 27
Church of the Holy Redeemer 59
Church of the Holy Redeemer and St Thomas More 71
Church of the Immaculate Conception 52
Church Street Market 16
City, The 122–125
City and The Barbican 94–97
City Road Basin 64
City University 65
City Waterfront 119
Clarence House 83
Cleopatra's Needle 88
Clerkenwell Green 59
Clerks Well 59
Clink Street 120
College of Psychic Studies 40
Commonwealth Institute 8
Connaught Street 15
Coram's Fields 59
Coronet Cinema 7
County Hall 115
Courtauld Institute Galleries 55
Court Theatre 7
Covent Garden and The Strand 86–89
Covent Garden Complex 87
Covent Garden Market 108
Cowcross Street 91
Crawford Street Market 19
Crosby Hall 72
Curzon Cinema 52
Cut Market, The 116
Dance Centre 87
Dickens House Museum 59
Dog Lavatories 8
Dolphin Square 108
Dorset Square 19
Dowgate Hill 119
Downing Street 84
Dr Johnson's House 91
Duke of Wellington 47
Duncan Terrace 63
Earl's Court and South Kensington 38–41
Earl's Court Exhibition Hall 35
Earl's Court Market 36
Eaton Square 80
180 Ebury Street 80
Edgware Road 15
Eel Brook Common 68
Elephant and Castle Development 116
Ely Court 91
Emmeline Pankhurst 112
Empress State Building 36
Euston 22–25
Euston Station 24
Exmouth Market 59
Farringdon Road Market 59
Finsbury Leisure Centre 64
Finsbury Town Hall 63
First Church of Christ Scientist 75
Fitzroy Square 23
Fleet Street and the City 90–93
Fortnum and Mason 52
Fulham 66–69
Fulham Gas Works 68
Fulham Palace 68
Fulham Town Hall 67
Gate Cinema 7
Gate Theatre at the Latchmere 100
Gate Theatre Club 7
Gate Two 59
Geological Museum 43
George Inn 120
Geraldine Mary Harmsworth Park 116
Gibson Square 31
Goldsmiths' Hall 96
Gray's Inn 60
Green Park 79
Greycoat Hospital School 84, 112
Grosvenor Chapel 48
33 Grosvenor Place 79
Guards Chapel 84
Guards Memorial 83
Guildhall 96
Guy's Hospital 119
Halkin Arcade 47, 79
Hammersmith and Olympia 2–5
Hammersmith Palais 36
Harrods 44
Hatton Garden 59
Holborn Viaduct 91
Holland Park 4, 7
Holland Park, Notting Hill Gate and Kensington 6–9
Holy Trinity Church, SE1. 120
Holy Trinity Church, SW1. 75
Holy Trinity Church, WC2. 56
Holy Trinity Church NW1. 23
Holy Trinity Church, N1. 31
Holy Trinity Church, SW7. 44
Holy Trinity Church and St Joseph's Almshouses 3
Honourable Artillery Company's HQ 95
House of St Barnabas 56
Houses of Parliament 84, 111
Houses of Parliament Statues 111
Hyde Park 15, 43, 47, 48
Hyde Park and Park Lane 46–49
ICA 53
Imperial War Museum 116
Islington Town Hall 31
Islington Tunnel 32, 63
Jeanetta Cochrane Theatre 55
Jewel Tower 84, 112
Jewish Museum 24
John F. Kennedy Memorial 23
John Wesley's Chapel and House 95
Kensington Gardens 11, 12, 43
Kensington Gardens and Paddington 10–13
Kensington Palace 12
Kensington Palace Gardens 8
Kensington Town Hall and Library 8
King Alfred the Great 120
King's Cross and St Pancras 26–29
King's Cross Station 28
King's Head 31
King's Road, 68, 72, 75
Knightsbridge Barracks 44
Kynance Mews 39
Lambeth Bridge 111
Lambeth Palace 111
Lambeth Walk 111, 116
Lamp That Never Goes Out, The 88
Lancaster House 83
Law Courts 91
Leadenhall Market 123
Leather Lane Market 60
Leicester Square 87
Leighton House 4
23–24 Leinster Gardens 11
Liberty's 51
Lillington Gardens Estate 107
Lincoln's Inn 91
Lincoln's Inn Fields 60
Lindsey House 72
Linley Sambourne House 8
Little Angel Marionette Theatre 31
Little Venice 16
Liverpool Street Station 95
Lloyd's of London 123
London Bridge 119, 124
London Bridge Station 119
London Coliseum 87
London Dungeon 119
London Planetarium 19
London Stone 123
London Telecom Tower 23
London's Wall 95
London Zoo 23
Lonsdale Square 31
Lord Astor's House 87
Lots Road Power Station 67
Lyric Theatre 36
Madame Tussaud's 19
Mall, The 83
Mansion House 123
Marble Arch 15, 48
Margaret Roper Gardens 72
Marie Blanche Laundry 99
Marlborough House 83
Marylebone and Regent's Park 18–21
Marylebone High Street 20
Marylebone Station 19
Marylebone Town Hall and Library 19
May Fair Hotel 52
Mayfair and Soho 50–53
Melbury Road 4
Mermaid Theatre 92
Methodist Church, W1. 20
Michelin House 75
Minema 47
Monument 124
Motcomb Street 79
Museum of London 96
Museum of Mankind 52
Nat West Tower 123
National Army Museum 76, 103
National Gallery 87
National Portrait Gallery 87
National Postal Museum 92
Natural History Museum 39, 43
New River 32
New West End Synagogue 11
Normand Park 36
North End Road Market 36
Notre Dame de France Church 56
Oasis Baths 56
Octagon Library and Chapel 67
Odeon, Hammersmith 36
Old Bailey 92
Old Battersea House 99
Old Red Lion Pub 65
Old St Thomas' Hospital Operating Theatre 119
Old Vic 115
Olympia 3
Oxford Street 51
Paddington and Marylebone 14–17
Paddington Green 16
Paddington Station 11, 15
Paddington Street Park 19
Palace Gate 39
Palace Theatre 56
Paris Pullman 71
Park Lane 47
Peabody Estate 108
Pentonville and Islington 30–33
Percival David Foundation of Chinese Art 24, 55
Peter Jones 75
Peterborough Estate 68
Pheasantry, The 75
Piccadilly Circus 51
Pimlico 106–109
Pimlico Comprehensive School 108
Pimlico Gardens 107
Pindar of Wakefield 28, 59
Plaster Mice 124
PO Mount Pleasant 59
Pollocks Toy Museum 55
Porter's Rest 48
Portobello Road Market 7
Postman's Park 95
Prince Henry's Rooms 92
Queen Boadicea 84
Queen Victoria's Statue 12
Queen's Chapel 83
Queen's Club 35
Queen's Gallery 80
Queen's Ice Skating Club 11
Queensway 11
Ranelagh Gardens 76, 103
Red Lion Square 60
Regent Street 51
Regent's Canal 32, 63
Regent's Park 19, 23
RIBA Heinz Gallery 20
Richmond Avenue 31
Riverside Studios 36
Rodin's Burghers of Calais 112
Royal Academy of Arts 52

Royal Agricultural Hall 31
Royal Albert Hall 43
Royal Artillery Memorial 47, 79
Royal College of Arms 92
Royal College of Art 43
Royal College of Music 43
Royal College of Organists 43
Royal College of Surgeons 60
Royal Court Theatre 75
Royal Crescent 3
Royal Exchange 123
Royal Geographical Society 43
Royal Horticultural Society Halls 107
Royal Mews 79
Royal Opera House 87
Royal Society of Arts 88
Russian Orthodox Church 44
Sadler's Wells Theatre 63
Sandford Manor 67
Scala Cinema 28
Science Museum 43
Screen on the Green 31
Selfridge's 20, 51
Serpentine Gallery 43
Servite Church and Priory 71
Session House, EC1. 64
Session House, SE1. 120
Shaw Theatre 27
Shepherd Market 52
Sheraton Park Tower 47
Sir Hans Sloane 103
Sir John Cass Foundation School 123
Sir John Soane's Mausoleum 27
Sir John Soane's Museum 60
Sir Walter St John's School 100
Sloane Square 75
Sloane Street 75, 79
Smithfield Wholesale Meat Market 91
Society of Genealogists 40
Soho 51
Soho and Bloomsbury 54–57
Soho Square 56
Somerset House 87
Sothebys 52
South Bank Arts Centre 88
South Bank Lion, The 115
South Kensington and Knightsbridge 42–45
Southwark 118–121
Southwark Bridge 119
Southwark Cathedral 119
Speaker's Corner 15, 48
St Alban's Church 60
St Aloysius New Church 27
St Aloysius Old Church 27
St Andrew Undershaft Church 123
St Andrew's Church 91
St Andrew's National School 59
St Anne and St Agnes 96
St Anne's Church 56
St Augustine's Church 40
St Barnabas Church, W14. 4
St Barnabas Church, EC1. 64
St Barnabas Church, SW1. 103, 108
St Bartholomew the Great 95
St Bartholomew's Hospital 91
St Botolph' Aldersgate Church 95
St Botolph's Aldgate Church 123
St Botolph's Bishopgate Church 123
St Bride's Church 92
St Charles Church 23
St Christopher's Place 20
St Clement Danes Church 9
St Clement's Church 124
St Columba's Church of Scotland 75
St Cuthbert with St Matthias 35
St Cyprian's Church 19
St Dunstan in the West Church 91
St Gabriel's Church 107
St George the Martyr Church 120
St George's Church, WC1. 55
St George's Church, W1. 51
St George's Church, W8. 7
St George's Fields, 15
St George's Gardens 59
St George's Hospital 47
St George's Roman Catholic Cathedral 116
St George's Square 107
St Giles Cripplegate Church 95
St Giles in the Fields 56
St James's and Whitehall 82–85
St James' Church, W1. 20
St James' Church, W2. 11, 15
St James' Church, N1. 32
St James' Church, EC1. 64
St James' Church, W1. 51
St James Garlickhythe Church 119
St James's Palace 83
St James's Park 84
St James the Less Church 107
St John the Baptist Church 4
St John the Evangelist Church, W2. 15
St John the Evangelist Church, N1. 63
St John's Church, SW6. 67
St John's Church, SE1. 115
St John's Church, EC1. 64
St John's Gate 64
St John's, Smith Square 112
St Katharine's Dock 123
St Lawrence Jewry Church 96
St Luke's Church, SW3. 76
St Luke's Church, SW5. 40
St Luke's Church, EC1. 64
St Magnus the Martyr Church 124
St Margaret Lothbury Church 123
St Margaret Pattens Church 124
St Margaret's Church 84, 112
St Mark's Church 63
St Martin-in-the-Fields 87
St Martin Ludgate Church 92
St Mary Abbots Church 8
St Mary Abchurch 124
St Mary Aldermary Church 96
St Mary at Hill Church 124
St Mary at Lambeth 111
St Mary le Bow Church 96
St Mary-le-Strand 87
St Mary Magdalene Church 23
St Mary the Boltons 40, 71
St Mary the Virgin Church 80
St Mary Woolnoth Church 124
St Marylebone Parish Church 19
St Mary's Church, SW11. 99
St Mary's Church, N1. 31
St Mary's Church, W1. 15
St Mary's Church, W2. 16
St Mary's Hospital 15
St Matthew's Church, W2. 11
St Matthew's Church, SW1. 112
St Nicholas Cole Abbey 92
St Olave's Church 124
St Pancras Lock 29
St Pancras New Church 24, 27
St Pancras Old Church 27
St Pancras Old Churchyard 27
St Pancras Station 28
St Paul's Cathedral 92
St Paul's Church, WC2. 87
St Paul's Church, SW1. 47
St Paul's School for Girls 3
St Peter upon Cornhill Church 123
St Peter's Church, EC1. 59
St Peter's Church, SW1. 80
St Philip's Church 39
St Saviour's Church, SW11. 99
St Saviour's Church, SW3. 75
St Saviour's Church, SW1. 107
St Sepulchre's Church 91
St Sophia's Cathedral 11
St Stephen Walbrook 124
St Stephen's Church, SW1. 112
St Stephen's Church, SW7. 39
St Thomas of Canterbury 36
St Thomas's Hospital 111, 115
St Vedast Foster Lane Church 96
Stag, The 80
Stamford Bridge Football Ground 67
Staple Inn 91
Stock Exchange 95, 123
Strand 88
Swedish Church 16
Tachbrook Street Market 107
Tate Gallery 112
Television Gallery 44
Temple 92
Temple of Mithras 123
Thames Water Authority 63
Theatre Royal, Drury Lane 87
Thomas Coram Foundation for Children 59
Thornhill Square 31
Tite Street 76, 103
Toll huts 99
Tottenham Court Road 24, 55
Tower Bridge 124
Tower of London 124
Tower Pier 124
Tower Theatre 32
Trafalgar Square 87
Tyburn Convent 15
Tyburn Tree 15, 48
Union Chapel 32
United States Embassy 51
University College 24
University College Hospital 24
University of London 24, 55
Vanbrugh Theatre Club 55
Vauxhall Bridge 108, 111
Vicarage Crescent 99
Vickers Tower 112
Victoria 74
Victoria and Albert Museum 43
Victoria and Lambeth 110–113
Victoria Embankment Gardens 88
Victoria Memorial 83
Victoria Station 80
Victoria Tower Gardens 112
Vincent Square 107
Wallace Collection 20
Wallgrave Road 39
Walton Street 75
War Memorial 119
Water Gardens 15
Waterloo and Elephant and Castle 114–117
Waterloo Station 115
Wellcome Library 24
Wellington Arch 47, 79
Wellington Museum 47
West Cromwell Road 35
West Kensington and Earl's Court 34–37
Westbourne Outlet 103
Westbourne River 75
Western Pumping Station 103
Westminster Abbey 84, 112
Westminster Bridge 111, 115
Westminster Cathedral 80
Westminster Pier 84, 88
Whitbread Brewery 95
Whitehall 83
Wigmore Hall 20
Wilton Crescent 79
Winchester House 120
York Watergate 88
Young Vic 115
Zoo Waterbus 16

EATING

A La Pizza 69
Abat Jour, L' 96
Adams Barbecue 37, 40
Agra 25
Al Amir 17
Alcove 9
Alonso's 105
American, The 73
Anemos 56
Ark 9
Artiste Affamé, L' 37
Atuchaclass 105
Au Jardin des Gourmets 57
Aunties 25
Averof 25
Aykoku-Kaku 97
Bali 17
Bangkok 41
Battersea Park Café 105
Belvedere 9
Bentley's 53
Bertorelli Bros 56
Bill Bentley's 45
Bistingo, Le 13
Bistro Bistingo 73
Bitter Lemons 37
BJs 73
Blues Trattoria 69
Borshtch N'Cheers 73
Borshtch N'Tears 45
Brasserie, La, SW3. 77
Brasserie, La, W2. 13
Bumbles 81
Busabong 73
Buster Brown 117
Cabin 117
Café Royal 53
Café St Pierre 61
Carafe 49
Carlos'n'Johnny's 72
Carlo's Place 69
Carrier's 33, 65
Charing Cross Hotel 88
Chelsea Rendezvous 76
Chez Franco 13
Chez Moi 5
City Volunteer 125
Claridges Hotel 52
Click, The 69
Coconut Grove 21
Commonwealth Institute 9
Company Piano Bar and Restaurant 41
Costas Grill 9
Cranks 52
Crystal Palace 40
Cuisine Sri Lanka 25
Cut Above 96
Daphne's 77
Daquise 45
Dell 48
Deodar 17
Dickens Inn 125
Diwan-I-Am 25
Doc's Diner 121
Dorchester Hotel 49
Dragon Palace 40
Drones 81
Due Franco 33
Duke's Hotel 85
Dumpling Inn 57
Eatons 81
English Garden 77
Famiglia, La 73
Fawlty Towers 68
Fingal's 69
First Edition 93
Flanagan's Fish Parlour 21
Four Lanterns 25
Franco Ovest 5
Frederick's 33, 65
Gallipoli 125
Ganges 57
Gay Hussar 57
Geales 9
Genevieve 21
George 121
George and Vulture 125
Goan 29
Good Food 61
Gore Hotel 44
Gow's Oyster Bar 124
Gran Paradiso 108
Grandma Lee's Bakery 80
Grapes 33
Great Eastern Hotel 97
Great Mughal 17
Grosvenor 113
Grosvenor House Hotel 49
Grumbles 109
Guys and Dolls 121
Hard Rock Café 49
Harrods 45
Hellenic 21
Hungry Horse 73
Hunting Lodge 85
Hyde Park Hotel 48
Hyde Park Tea Bar 49
Ikaros 21
Il Girasole 73
Il Papagallo 117
Incognito 45
Indira 17
Ivy 57
Jimmy's 57
Joe Allen 89
Jonathan's 5
Joy King Lau 57
Julius 33

Justin de Blank at the ICA 85
Kennedy's 73
Kensington Hilton 5
King's Road Jam 73
Kleftiko 5
Knights 29
Kundan 113
Langan's Brasserie 53
Lee Ho Fook 57
Lockets 113
Loggia, La 17
London Hilton 49
Loose Box 45
Lotus House 17
Lowndes Hotel 49
Luba's 45
Lyons Corner House 89
Ma Barker 41
Maggie Brown's 101
Maharajah 13
Malaysian Kitchen 41
Mama San 5
Mandarin Kitchen 13
Mandeer 56
Mange Tout, Le 17
Manzes 33
Manzi's 57
Mardi Gras 41
Marmiton, Le 97
Martinez 53
Masako 21
Meridiana 76
Mignon, Le 13
Mijanou 81
Mikado 21
Mimmo and Pasquale 109
Mimmo d'Ischia 81
Mogador 29
Monte Grappa 29
Mr Bumble 33
Mr Chow 44
My Old Dutch 57
Netta's 37
New Lee Ho Fook 13
Nikita's 69
Nineteen 77
Old Bailey Tandoori 92
Oliver's 5
Oodles 93
Overton's, Terminus Pl 80
Overton's, St James's St 85
Panzer 44
Park Lane Hotel 49
Parsons 73
Peppermint Park 88
Perdoni's 117
Père Michel 16
Philbeach Hotel 37
Pimlico Bistro 109
Pizza Express, SW10. 72
Pizza Express, WC1. 56
Pizza Hut 13
Pizza on the Park 49
Plexi's 21
Poissonerie de l'Avenue 76
Pomegranates 109
Pooh Corner 101
Portofino 33, 65
Poulbot, Le 97
Poule au Pot, La 81
Primula, La 40
Prince Regent 21
Princes Room 125
Printer's Pie 93
Quality Chop House 61
Queenies 73
Raw Deal 17
Red Onion Bistro 69
Regency 88
Rehana Tandoori 105
Renato's 5
Reubens 21
Richoux 49
Riots 100
Ritz Hotel 53
Ronde, La 117
Ronnie Scott's 57
Roxy Diner 33
Royal Garden Hotel 9
Royal Kensington Hotel 5
Royal Scot Hotel 61
RSJ 117
Rules 89
Sailing Junk 41
Salamis 72
Salloos 49
San Carlo 96
San Frediano 76
San Martino 77
Saraceno 61
Savoy 89
Seashell Fish Bar 17
September 69
Serpentine Complex
Restaurants 44
Shah 25
Shepherd's Tavern 53
Sheraton Park Tower 48
Silhouettes 109
Slenders 92
Sloane's 44
South of the Border 117, 121
Sri Lanka 41
Stag 97
Steak Nicole, Le 109
Stockpot, SW3. 45
Stockpot, SW1. 85
Strikes 37
Sultan's Delight 33
Suntory 85
Suquet, Le 77
Sweetings 97
Swiss Coffee House 61
Tante Claire 105
Taormina 13
Tate Gallery 113
Tevere 113
Texas Lone Star 41
Throgmorton 97
Tiddy Dol's 53
Tiger Lee Chinese Seafood 37
Toad Hall 101
Toddies African Restaurant 37
Tootsies 9
Trattoria Aqualino 33, 65
Trattoria La Torre 25
Up All Night 73
Upper Crust 48
Uppers 33
Upstairs and Downstairs 45
Valencia 37
Viceroy of India 21
Villa dei Cesari 109
Walton's 77
Warehouse 125
Waterside 96
Westminster College Teaching
Restaurant 105
Westminster Hotel School
Restaurant 109
Wheeler's 85
Wheeler's City Restaurant 125
Wheeler's George and Dragon
77
White House Hotel 25
Widow Applebaum's Deli &
Bagel Academy 52
Wilkins Natural Foods 113
Wilton's 85
Windmill Wholefood 69
Witchity's 9
Wolfe's 49
Yangtze 9
Yasmine 81

DRINKING

Admiral Codrington 77
Albany 25
Anchor 121
Angel 21
Angela and Peter's 101
Antelope 81
Archduke 89
Archery 16
Audley 49
Bag o'Nails 80
Baker and Oven 21
Balls Bros, WC2. 89, EC4. 93,
City 124
Barley Mow 113
Battersea 105
Beadles 121
Bill Bentley's 45
Blackfriar 93
Blushes 77
Boltons, The 40
Boos 20
Boot and Flogger 121
Brass Crosby 117
Briefs 121
Britannia, SW6. 69
Britannia, W8. 9
Bunch of Grapes, SW3. 45
Bunch of Grapes, W1. 53
Captain's Cabin 85
Cardinal 81
Castle 101
Charco's 77
Chelsea Potter 77
Cheyne Walk Wine Bar 105
Chiswell Street Cellars 97
Clanger 125
Clarence 84
Clem Attlee 37
Cock and Lion 21
Coleherne 37
Constitution 109
Cork and Bottle 57
Courtfield 40
Cricketers 105
Crown, N1. 32
Crown, SE1. 112
Crown and Sceptre 25
Davico's 73
Dickens Inn 125
Dirty Dick's 124
Dive Bar 121
Drummonds 25
Duke of Buckingham 89
Duke of Clarence, W11. 5
Duke of Clarence, SE1. 117
Duke of Wellington 57
Eagle, SW11. 105
Eagle, N1. 65
Ebury 81
El Vino 93
Eliza Doolittle 29
Exmouth Arms 25
Finch's (King's Arms) 73
Founder's Arms 121
Fountain 108
Freemason's Arms 57
Frog's Legs 101
Fulham Volunteer 37
Gates Wine Bar 80
George, SE1. 121
George, EC4. 93
Goat in Boots 73
Goose and Firkin 121
Gordon's 89
Grafton Arms 25
Grapes 33
Grove, SW3. 45
Grove, SW11. 105
Gyngleboy 13
Hand and Flower 5
Hand and Shears 96
Hansom Cab 9, 41
Holborn Bars 61
Hole in the Wall 117
Hollywood Arms 72
Hoop (Finch's) 9
Hope and Anchor 33
I am the only running footman
53
Imperial Arms 69
Intrepid Fox 57
Island Queen 65
Jamaica 125
Jolly Cockney 113
Jörgens 17
King's Head, W2. 13
King's Head, SW6. 69
King's Head and Eight Bells 73
Klompen 29
Lamb, EC3. 125
Lamb, WC1. 61
Lamb and Flag 88
Latchmere 101
Lemon Tree 89
Loose Box 45
Loose Vine 121
Lord High Admiral 109
Lowndes Arms 81
Ludgate Cellars 93
Magpie and Stump 92
Marlborough Head 49
Mason's Arms 105
Mitre 13
Morpeth Arms 113
Mr Garroway's 97
Museum Tavern 57
Nag's Head 49
Narrow Boat 65
Nevada Bar 65
New Crown and Cushion 117
New Golden Lion 69
Normand Arms 37
Old Bell 93
Old Crutched Friars 125
Old Father Thames 113
Old King Lud 93
Old King's Head 121
Old Parr's Head 5
Old Swan 100
Olde Mitre 61, 92
Opera Tavern 89
Penny Black 97
Peterborough Arms 69
Phrogg's Music 5
Pied Bull 33
Pillar Box 61
Pimlico Tram 109
Pindar of Wakefield 29
PJ's 113
Polly's 61
Pontefract Castle 21
Prince Albert 101
Prince Alfred 13
Prince of Wales, SW1. 81
Prince of Wales, N1. 32
Prince of Wales, SW6. 37
Prince of Wales, SE1. 117
Prince Regent 21
Printer's Devil 93
Prodigal's Return 101
Queen's Elm 73
Queen's Head, W6. 4
Queen's Head, SW3. 77
Queen's Larder 61
Radnor Arms 5
Ram and Teazel 65
Raven 101
Red Lion 85
Rising Sun, N1. 33
Rising Sun, NW1. 29
Rising Sun, SW1. 108
Riverside 105
Ruby's 17
Salisbury 88
Samuel Pepys 120
Scamps 69
Scandies 41
Scarsdale 9
Shakespeare's Head 53
Shampers 53
Sherlock Holmes 89
Ship 61
Shires 29
Shirreffs 17
Silver Cross 85
Simpson's 125
Sir Alexander Fleming 16
Sir Christopher Wren 92
Slatter's 85
Sloane's 77
Smuggler's Tavern 25
St Paul's 97
St Stephen's 84
Stag 81
Stanhope 41
Sun 61
Sun in Splendour 9
Surprise 109
Swan, W2. 13
Swan, SW6. 69
Tattersall's 44
Thackeray's 9
Three Kings 37
Three Stags 117
Tournament 37
Tracks 57
Tutton's 89
Two Eagles 117
Uxbridge Arms 9
Victoria, W2. 17
Victoria, NW1. 29
Victoria, SW1. 81
Victoria, SW11. 101
Warwick Castle 17
Wellington 117
Westminster Arms 84
White Hart 57, 89
White Swan 93
Williamson's 97
Wilton Arms 49
Windmill 117
Windsor Castle 9
Worcester Arms 21
World's End 73
Ye Olde Cheshire Cheese 93
Ye Olde Cock 93
Ye Olde Watling 97
Yorkshire Grey 61